EARLY
AVIATION
DISASTERS

EARLY AVIATION DISASTERS

THE WORLD'S MAJOR AIRLINER CRASHES BEFORE 1950

DAVID GERO

The
History
Press

First published 2011

The History Press
The Mill, Brimscombe Port
Stroud, Gloucestershire, GL5 2QG
www.thehistorypress.co.uk

© David Gero, 2011

The right of David Gero to be identified as the Author
of this work has been asserted in accordance with the
Copyrights, Designs and Patents Act 1988.

British Library Cataloguing in Publication Data.
A catalogue record for this book is available from the British Library.

ISBN 978 0 7524 5987 5

Typesetting and origination by The History Press
Printed in Great Britain

CONTENTS

ACKNOWLEDGEMENTS

The author would like to thank the following organisations and individuals for their help in the preparation of *Early Aviation Disasters*:

Accident Investigation Board (Norway) – Contact: Tor Norstegard
Air Canada Flight Safety Division – Contact: J.A. Mitchell
Aircraft Accident Investigation Board (Iceland) – Contact: Thormodur Thormodsson
Airdisaster.russia
Air France Office of Public Affairs – Contact: Gail Muntner
Argentine Air Force – Contacts: Guillermo Raul Barreira and Mario Santamaria
Australian Transport Safety Bureau – Contacts: W.G. Duffy; F.St.G. Hornblower, D.J. Nicholas, Daniel J.T. O'Malley and R.J. Sibbison
Aviation Safety Network – Contact: Harro Ranter
Belgian World Airlines (SABENA) – Contact: J. Deschutter
British Airways Air Safety Branch – Contacts: Roy Lomas and C.N. Hall
Canada Aviation and Space Museum – Contact: Ian Leslie
Canadian Airlines International Ltd – Contact: P.G. Howe
Canadian Aviation Safety Board – Contacts: Nicole Brind'Amour, Manon Ouimet van Riel and Joyce Pedley
The Cutting Air Crash, by Nick Komons
Department of Aircraft Accident Investigation (Denmark) – Contact: Niels Jaksobsen
Departamento Administrativo de Aeronautica Civil (Colombia) – Contacts: Carlos German Barrero Fandino and William Mejia Restrepo
Direction des Officiels (France) – Contacts: Jeannine Valin and Monique Masson
Federal Aircraft Accident Investigation Bureau (Switzerland) – Contact: Erich Keller
Federal Aviation Administration (US) – Contact: Nick Komons
Inspection Generale de l'Aviation Civile et de la Meteorologie (France) – Contacts: Robert Davidson, M. Dulac
KLM Royal Dutch Airlines – Contact: Peter Offerman; Daniel Kusrow
Ministry of Defence (UK) – Contacts: Les Howard and Eric Munday
National Archives of Australia – Contact: Andrew Cairns
National Archives (US) – Contacts: Janet Kelly, Jane Lange, A'Donna Thomas and Jessie White
National Transportation Safety Board (US) – Contact: Susan Stevenson

Office of Air Accidents Investigation (New Zealand) – Contacts: L.J. Banfield, L.F. Blewett
   and Ron Chippindale
Poole Flying Boats Celebration Charity – Contacts: Aimee and Harry Alexander
Public Archives of Canada – Contact: Glenn Wright
Scandinavian Airlines System (SAS) – Contact: Gunnel Thorne
Smithsonian Institution (US) – Contact: Kate Igoe
Swissair – Contact: E. Lanz

Special thanks to: Monique Bouscarle, Inspection Generale de l'Aviation Civile et de la
Meteorologie (France); Loyita Worley, Civil Aviation Authority (UK); and the entire staff at the
Los Angeles Regional Office of the National Transportation Safety Board (US).

Research services provided by Herman Dekker (the Netherlands); Terry Denham (UK); Philip
Jarrett (UK), Graham K. Salt (UK), Hilary Thomas (UK) and Ronan Hubert (Switzerland).

Translation services provided by Else Bokkers, Flightline Language Services; Guillaume Gavillet,
Patrick Germain, Boris Hasselblatt; Inge Hochner; The Language Institute; Poly-Languages
Institute; and Lisolette Runde.

INTRODUCTION

In the motion picture field, it is known as a 'prequel'; a succeeding production in which the events taking place therein occurred before those depicted in the initial film. *Early Aviation Disasters* is my version of a 'prequel' to my original *Aviation Disasters*, which discussed major airline crashes occurring since the beginning of 1950.

First published in 1993, *Aviation Disasters* left a void for those interested in aircraft catastrophes occurring during the first half of the twentieth century, about which information, even with today's Internet, is relatively sparse. This new volume is designed to fill that void. As with the original, it might help generate considerable interest in the subject, and perhaps additional books and sources of information, as did the first.

The format of both books is generally the same. Both are done in chronological order, and utilise a summarised heading listing date and local time, if known; operator and type of aircraft; and serial number, if known; the body of the account contains the most important facts of an aviation disaster, including the number of casualties, nature of the flight and cause, again, if known. The crashes are not discussed in great detail, as they often are in books that refer to only a small number of incidents. But this also makes for more space in order to include far more disasters. As with the original volume, entry into *Early Aviation Disasters* is based primarily on the number of fatalities. I have included every known incident involving a commercial-type aircraft flown by a large civilian operator or manufacturer and resulting in at least ten fatalities. But I have also included incidents with fewer fatalities if they were considered historic, or if they were significant in some other way, such as a crash involving an aircraft that was new at the time. In other words, entry is also somewhat subjective, as is the case with *Aviation Disasters*. Not included are incidents involving aircraft operated by private individuals, which could be considered general aviation, or by military forces or government entities.

Unlike the original volume, *Early Aviation Disasters* recounts tragedies occurring in operations other than passenger flights, such as those occurring during test or training missions. As with the original, this volume describes every type of catastrophe, whether it resulted from faulty design, mechanical failure, pilot error, bad weather or sabotage. Even incidents resulting from wartime action are included. I have included photographs of some crash scenes, and in many other cases have pictures of the types of aircraft involved in these accidents, which should be useful when considering that many may not be easily recognised by modern aviation enthusiasts.

As with *Aviation Disasters*, I have endeavoured to obtain the most reliable information from as many sources as possible, this to guarantee accuracy. Unlike today, reports on aircraft accidents were generally not widely published, so in my research the general media proved to be a source of considerable information. Readers will also notice a slight bias on the nations represented, with a particular slant towards operators based in the UK and the US. This to a certain degree reflects the home nations of the publisher and the author, but also the information available from these countries. It should also not be forgotten that many of the nations represented here were, at the time, controlled by authoritarian governments, which often placed strict restraints on information. This might even be true in democratic nations during wartime, when censorship might not only be related to national pride but also public safety.

And as always, I'm interested in hearing from my readers throughout the world, some of whom, I have found, possess those extra few facts that, if offered, would help to make *Early Aviation Disasters* even more complete.

David Gero
San Gabriel, California

BETWEEN THE WORLD WARS (1920–1939)

Although human flight had existed for more than 100 years, commercial aviation really came into existence in the early twentieth century. The first regular passenger air service was launched in 1910 by the German company DELAG, using dirigibles, an operation that would experience accidents but no fatalities. (Large dirigibles would make another appearance in the 1930s, but service with these aircraft would end abruptly with a particularly high-profile disaster.) The first regular service using heavier-than-air craft began in 1914, with flying boats making, by today's standards, an almost ridiculously short trip over Tampa Bay between St Petersburg and the city of Tampa, in the American state of Florida.

Airline travel began in earnest after the First World War. One of the companies that first appeared during this time is easily recognised even today by travellers around the world: KLM Royal Dutch Airlines. The first British airline service was also launched around this time by Handley Page Transport, and this company would also experience the first fatal crash occurring during a regular passenger service. Flying in a commercial airliner was particularly adventurous at the time, and also quite hazardous. In the mid-1930s, the passenger fatality rate was approximately eight times greater for airliners than for automobiles. And due to their small size and lack of reliability, airliners could hardly compete with the railroads in carrying passengers over land or with steamships across the sea.

Government played a major role in the development of commercial aviation, particularly in the US, with the implementation of the Kelly Air Mail Act of 1925, which subsidised private operators to carry mail. Passengers would soon join the mailbags in the cabins of aircraft. This was also the time that official inquiries and reporting of aircraft accidents began, with Great Britain taking the lead in this area. After crashes involving high-profile individuals, the US Bureau of Air Commerce would begin doing the same. These reports would not only provide reliable details on the specific cause of an accident, if one could be ascertained, but the dissemination of such information would help spur changes and advances in aviation, helping to make flying safer. For this and other reasons, air travel would become a much safer and more reliable form of public transportation by the late 1930s.

Information from many of these reports has been used as sources of information in a number of disasters described in this chapter.

A Handley Page H.P.12, one of which was involved in the first commercial airline accident to result in passenger fatalities. (Philip Jarrett)

Date: 14 December 1920 (*c.*12:15)
Location: London, England
Operator: Handley Page Transport (UK)
Aircraft type: Handley Page H.P.12 (G-EAMA)

In the first commercial aviation disaster to result in passenger fatalities during a regularly scheduled service, four persons lost their lives when the twin-engine airliner crashed and burned immediately after its departure from Cricklewood Aerodrome, located within the city. The victims included the aeroplane's pilot and mechanic, while four other passengers survived, two of whom escaped injury.

Bound for Paris, France, G-EAMA reportedly failed to attain sufficient height after becoming airborne, then struck a tree and slammed into a house, the accident occurring in misty weather conditions, with a cloud base of around 1,500ft (500m).

The crash was caused by an error of judgement on the part of the pilot, who 'needlessly' proceeded to take off towards a hill, the presence of which created a 'source of danger' when considering the prevailing wind and weather, and the aircraft's low climb rate.

Date: 22–23 March 1922
Location: North Atlantic Ocean
Operator: Aero Limited (US)
Aircraft type: Aeromarine Model 85

Five passengers lost their lives in an accident involving the flying boat *Miss Miami*, occurring during a charter service to the Bimini Islands from Miami, Florida. Only the pilot survived.

The aeroplane was forced to set down in the water some 40 miles (65km) east of the Florida mainland, around 11:40 local time the first day and probably less than five minutes from its destination, when a propeller blade broke. Despite a successful landing, the *Miss Miami* began to sink the following day when its hull was punctured, and most of its occupants subsequently drowned or were lost at sea. The pilot, who had clung to floating wreckage, was finally picked up by a ship some 55 hours after the ditching.

Date: 7 April 1922 (*c.* 14:00)
Location: Near Grandvilliers, Picardie, France
First aircraft:
Operator: Grands Express Aeriens (France)
Type: Farman F.60 Goliath (F-GEAD)
Second aircraft:
Operator: Daimler Airway (UK)
Type: de Havilland 18 (G-EAWO)

Commercial aviation experienced its first mid-air collision resulting in fatalities in this accident, which involved aircraft flying in opposite directions between the two respective nations of registry. The collision took place some 60 miles (100km) north-north-west of Paris, the departure point of F-GEAD during a scheduled flight to London, and the destination of G-EAWO at the end of a mail service from the British capital. Killed in the accident were all five persons aboard the twin-engine Farman (three passengers and two crew members), and both occupants of the single-engine de Havilland.

The two aeroplanes had collided head-on, or nearly so, at an approximate altitude of 400ft (120m), after which both crashed and burned. Both of their pilots were apparently trying to maintain visual contact with the ground while flying under a low overcast, and must have simply failed to see each other's aircraft in time to prevent the accident. It was also reported that G-EAWO had been slightly to the left of the proper course.

Subsequently, new procedures were adopted for aircraft flying both ways along the Paris–London route, which involved the use of certain landmarks to guarantee the separation of opposing traffic and also made compulsory the use of wireless communications by flight crews.

Date: 16 July 1922 (*c.* 16:45)
Location: Near Saverne, Lorraine, France
Operator: Compagnie Franco-Roumaine de Navigation Aérienne (Free Romanian Company for Aerial Navigation)
Aircraft type: Potez 29

A Farman Goliath, of the type flown by Grands Express Aeriens that was involved in the collision with a British aeroplane over France. (Philip Jarrett)

The wreckage of G-EBBS, the Daimler Airway de Havilland 34 that crashed north-west of London during a domestic UK service. (Philip Jarrett)

The single-engine aeroplane crashed some 30 miles (50km) west of Strasbourg, from where it had taken off shortly before, on a regular domestic flight to Paris, and all five occupants (four passengers and the pilot) were killed.

It was believed that power plant trouble had necessitated a forced landing, but before this could be accomplished, the Potez probably got caught in strong, gusty winds, and stalled while making a turn.

Date: 14 May 1923 (*c.*13:40)
Location: Near Amiens, Picardie, France
Operator: Air Union (France)
Aircraft type: Farman F.60 Goliath (F-AEBY)

The twin-engine airliner crashed and burned some 70 miles (110km) north of Paris, from where it had taken off earlier, on a scheduled international service to London. All six persons aboard (four passengers and two crew members) were killed.

Reportedly, F-AEBY had suffered structural failure at an approximate height of 3,000ft (1,000m), and there was speculation that the break-up had been precipitated by a fire that itself resulted from a passenger carelessly discarding a match after lighting a cigarette.

Date: 14 September 1923 (*c.*18:00)
Location: Near Ivinghoe, Buckinghamshire, England
Operator: Daimler Airway (UK)
Aircraft type: de Havilland 34 (G-EBBS)

The single-engine biplane crashed around 30 miles (50km) north-west of London, from where it had taken off earlier, on a regular service to Manchester. All five persons aboard (three passengers and two crew members) were killed.

While apparently attempting a forced landing after encountering heavy rain, G-EBBS must have lost flying speed due to pilot error, then fell to the ground.

Date: 8 June 1924 (*c.*15:00)
Location: Near Barranquilla, Atlantico, Colombia
Operator: Sociedad Colombo-Alemana de Transportes Aéreos (SCADTA) (Colombia)
Aircraft type: Junkers F.13 (A-16)

All five persons aboard (three passengers and a crew of two) were killed when the single-engine aeroplane crashed and burned while taking off from the Barranquilla airfield, on a non-scheduled domestic service to Bogotá.

Reportedly, the F.13 had stalled immediately after becoming airborne, then struck a tree and slammed into a house.

Date: 24 December 1924 (*c.*12:00)
Location: Near London, England
Operator: Imperial Airways (UK)
Aircraft type: de Havilland 34 (G-EBBX)

Operating on a scheduled international service to Paris, the single-engine airliner crashed and burned in the vicinity of Croydon Aerodrome, serving London and from where it had taken off shortly before. All eight persons aboard (seven passengers and the pilot) lost their lives in the accident.

The biplane had apparently been attempting a forced landing when it went into a nose-down spin while stalled and plummeted to earth from an approximate height of 100ft (30m). It was determined that G-EBBX had experienced some type of mechanical malfunction prior to the accident, but the nature of the problem could not be determined. The fact that Croydon had been listed as an 'unsatisfactory' airport, because of its wind conditions, could have been a contributing factor, according to the investigative report.

Date: 22 March 1925
Location: Near Tiflis (Tbilisi), Georgian SSR, USSR
Operator: Zakavia (USSR)
Aircraft type: Junkers F.13 (R-RECA)

The single-engine aeroplane crashed and burned shortly after its departure from Tiflis, on a domestic service to Suchumi, and all five persons aboard lost their lives, including the two pilots. Its passengers were Soviet government officials bound for a Soviet Congress.

Date: 2 July 1926
Location: Near Streble, Bohemia, Czechoslovakia
Operator: Compagnie Internationale de Navigation Aérienne (CIDNA) (France)
Aircraft type: Caudron C.61 (F-AFBT)

The three-engine airliner crashed during a scheduled international flight from Paris to Budapest, Hungary, via Prague, Czechoslovakia. All six persons aboard (four passengers and two crew members) were killed.

Reportedly, F-AFBT struck a mountain while proceeding in adverse weather conditions below a safe altitude.

An Imperial Airways de Havilland 34, identical to the Paris-bound aircraft that crashed after take-off from Croydon Aerodrome, serving London. (Philip Jarrett)

A trimotored Fokker F.VII-3m of the type flown by the US carrier Reynolds Airways that crashed during a sight-seeing flight. (Smithsonian Institution)

Date: 27 July 1927
Location: Near Amöneburg, Hesse, Germany
Operator: Deutsche Luft Hansa AG (Germany)
Aircraft type: Junkers F.13 (D-206)

Operating on a regular service from Kassel to Frankfurt-am-Main, the single-engine aeroplane crashed and burned some 40 miles (65km) north of its destination, apparently while attempting an off-airport forced landing after experiencing some kind of power plant malfunction. All five persons aboard (three passengers and two crew members) were killed in the afternoon accident.

Date: 17 September 1927 (*c.*15:30)
Location: Near Dunellen, New Jersey, US
Operator: Reynolds Airways (US)
Aircraft type: Fokker F.VIIb-3m (NC-776)

Seven persons aboard lost their lives, including both crew members, when the trimotored transport crashed in an apple orchard on a farm some 20 miles (30km) south-west of Newark, while on a sightseeing flight. The five

surviving passengers suffered various injuries. The accident was attributed by a local official to the 'defective operation' of at least one engine.

Date: 23 September 1927 (*c.*10:00)
Location: Near Schleiz, Thuringia, Germany
Operator: Deutsche Luft Hansa AG (Germany)
Aircraft type: Dornier Merkur (D-585)

All six occupants (four passengers and two crew members) lost their lives when the single-engine aircraft crashed some 90 miles (145km) north-north-east of Nuremberg, during a scheduled domestic service from Berlin to Munich.

Reportedly, D-585 plunged to earth from a height of around 500ft (150m) after its left wing failed when the corresponding strut broke.

Date: 16 November 1927 (*c.*14:30)
Location: Gulf of Finland
Operator: Aero O/Y (Finland)
Aircraft type: Junkers F.13 (K-SALB)

The single-engine aeroplane crashed during a scheduled international service from Tallinn, Estonia, to Helsinki, Finland. All six persons aboard (four passengers and two crew members) were killed.

Date: 31 December 1927
Location: Near Marseille, Provence, France
Operator: Latécoère (France)
Aircraft type: Latécoère 23 (F-AIHP)

The twin-engine flying boat crashed shortly after taking off from the Marseille seaplane base, on a test flight. All five members of the aircraft's crew were killed in the accident. According to press reports, F-AIHP had suffered structural failure at an approximate height of 1,000ft (300m).

Date: 25 August 1928 (c.11:00)
Location: Near Port Townsend, Washington, US
Operator: British Columbia Airways (Canada)
Aircraft type: Ford 4-AT-B Tri-Motor (G-CATX)

Operating on a scheduled international service that had originated at Vancouver and last stopped at Victoria, also in British Columbia, Canada, with an ultimate destination of Seattle, Washington, the airliner crashed in Puget Sound approximately 30 miles (50km) north-west of its destination. Some wreckage and the bodies of three victims were later found, but there were no survivors among the seven persons who had been aboard the Tri-Motor (five passengers and two pilots). The accident had occurred during a heavy fog, which was probably a primary or contributing causative factor.

Date: 2 September 1928 (c.09:15)
Location: Near Toul, Lorraine, France
Operator: Compagnie Internationale de Navigation Aérienne (CIDNA) (France)
Aircraft type: Bleriot-Spad S.33

The single-engine aeroplane crashed and burned some 130 miles (210km) east of Paris shortly after it had taken off from the local airport, on a special flight to the capital city. All five occupants lost their lives in the accident, including the three crew members; the passengers were the French Minister of Commerce and Aviation, and the Technical Director of the airline.

Date: 4 September 1928 (c.12:00)
Location: Near Pocatello, Idaho, US
Operator: National Parks Airways (US)
Aircraft type: Fokker Super Universal (NC-7242)

The single-engine aeroplane crashed and burned while preparing to land at the local airfield, which was an en route stop during a scheduled US domestic service originating at Great Falls, Montana, with an ultimate destination of Salt Lake City, Utah. All seven persons aboard (six passengers and the pilot) were killed.

It was believed that NC-7242 had stalled during a steep left bank during its landing approach. However, approximately half an hour before the accident, and before it proceeded on towards Pocatello, the aeroplane was seen circling in what may have been an emergency situation, raising the possibility of a mechanical malfunction.

Date: 1 December 1928 (c.17:00)
Location: Near Spur, Texas, US
Operator: Sunbeam Air Transport Co (US)
Aircraft type: Ford 4-AT-C Tri-Motor (NC-7862)

All five occupants lost their lives when the trimotored airliner, which was on a delivery flight within the US, from San Antonio, Texas, to Denver, Colorado, crashed and burned in a field some 50 miles (80km) east of Lubbock, the accident occurring shortly before sunset.

Date: 3 December 1928 (c.08:00)
Location: Near Rio de Janeiro, Brazil
Operator: Kondor Syndikat Ltda (Brazil)
Aircraft type: Dornier Do.J Wal (P-BACA)

The twin-engine flying boat crashed in Guanabara Bay off the island of Cobras, and all fourteen persons aboard (ten passengers and a crew of four) were killed. Subsequently, the wreckage of the aircraft and the bodies of the victims were removed from the water, but a diver lost his life during recovery operations.

At the time of the accident, P-BACA had been participating in an 'aerial' exhibition celebrating famed Brazilian aviator Alberto Santos-Dumont. It was believed that the flying boat had been overstressed by an evasive manoeuvre to avoid another aircraft, resulting in the structural failure of one wing at a height of around 300ft (100m).

Date: 17 March 1929 (*c.*17:00)
Location: Jersey Meadows, New Jersey, US
Operator: Colonial Western Airways (US)
Aircraft type: Ford 4-AT-B Tri-Motor (NC-7683)

The trimotored aircraft crashed in a suburb of Newark, killing fourteen persons aboard. Only the pilot, who was seriously injured, survived the accident. Shortly after NC-7683 had taken off from Newark Municipal Airport, on a sightseeing flight, its left power plant failed at an approximate height of 500ft (150m) above the ground. There was also a 'remote' possibility that the centre engine had lost power. The pilot apparently tried to glide to a forced landing, but the Tri-Motor must have stalled after a loss of flying speed, then slammed into a railroad car loaded with sand. There was no fire after impact. Other factors identified in the investigation were the failure of the pilot to pay attention to the wind, his incorrect assessment as to the distance from the airport and his lack of familiarity with the surrounding area.

Date: 21 April 1929 (*c.*11:45)
Location: San Diego, California, US
First aircraft:
Operator: Maddux Air Lines (US)
Type: Ford 5-AT-B Tri-Motor (NC-9636)

Second aircraft:
Operator: US Army Air Corps
Aircraft type: Boeing PW-9D (28-37)

The trimotored airliner and the single-engine pursuit aeroplane collided at an approximate height of 2,000ft (600m), and both then crashed. All five persons aboard NC-9636 (three passengers and two pilots) and the pilot (and sole occupant) of 28-37, the latter of whom had attempted unsuccessfully to parachute from his aircraft, were killed in the accident.

At the time of the collision, the military biplane was reportedly 'buzzing' the commercial transport, which had itself taken off around 10 minutes earlier from the city's airport, on a scheduled US domestic service to Phoenix, Arizona. As a result of his actions, the Army pilot was deemed as 'criminally negligent' in causing the accident.

Date: 17 June 1929 (*c.*11:30)
Location: English Channel
Operator: Imperial Airways
Aircraft type: Handley Page W.10 (G-EBMT)

The twin-engine transport was ditched in the English Channel approximately 3 miles (5km) off shore from Dungeness, England, and south of Folkestone, and seven of its passengers lost their lives. Four other passengers and the aeroplane's pilot and mechanic were rescued from the water by a Belgian trawler. The bodies of four of the victims were recovered, and the main wreckage was subsequently brought ashore.

During a scheduled service from London to Paris, the starboard power plant of G-EBMT malfunctioned due to the failure of a connecting rod in one of its cylinders, which itself resulted from the rapid development of 'creeping' cracks in the roots of its port studs. After the malfunction, the pilot turned back towards land, but he apparently misjudged his height over the glassy, calm water, and was finally obliged to set it down in the sea. In the ensuing impact, the aircraft's empennage broke off.

Surface vessels participate in the recovery of the wreckage of the Imperial Airways Handley Page W.10 after its crash in the English Channel. (Topfoto)

Date: 29 June 1929 (*c.*21:00)
Location: Near Lindau, Bavaria, Germany
Operator: Bodensee Aerolloyd (Germany)
Aircraft type: Dornier Delphin III (D-1620)

Five persons aboard were killed, including the pilot, when the single-engine flying boat crashed in Lake Constance (Bodensee) as it was attempting to land during a tour flight. Two passengers, both of whom suffered injuries, were rescued by a boat, and except for the pilot's, the bodies of the victims were recovered.

The pilot may have been affected by the glare from the sun that was low on the horizon, shortly before dusk, and misjudged the height above the lake, resulting in a hard impact with the water, after which the aeroplane broke apart and sank.

Date: 3 September 1929 (*c.*12:00)
Location: Near Grants, New Mexico, US
Operator: Transcontinental Air Transport (TAT) (US)
Aircraft type: Ford 5-AT-B Tri-Motor (NC-9649)

Operating on a scheduled US domestic transcontinental service with an ultimate destination of Los Angeles, California, the airliner crashed and burned on Mount Taylor some 60 miles (100km) west-north-west of Albuquerque, from where it had taken off earlier. All eight persons aboard (five passengers and three crew members) were killed in the accident.

The Tri-Motor was believed to have encountered an area of thunderstorm activity that was localised and had not been indicated

A Short S.8 Calcutta flying boat, the type flown by Imperial Airways that was wrecked after a successful forced landing in the Gulf of Genoa. (Philip Jarrett)

in weather reports before it slammed into the mountain, which rises to above 11,000ft (3,300m).

Date: 14 September 1929 (*c.*18:00)
Location: Near Merriton, Ontario, Canada
Operator: Skyways, Ltd (Canada)
Aircraft type: Travel Air 6000B

The single-engine aeroplane crashed and burned around 40 miles (65km) south of Toronto while on a sightseeing flight, the accident occurring late in the afternoon, and all six persons aboard (five passengers and the pilot) were killed. Examination of the wreckage revealed nothing that could lead to a determination of the cause of the accident.

Date: 17 September 1929
Location: North Atlantic Ocean
Operator: Aéropostale (France)
Aircraft type: Latécoère 25 (F-AIUJ)

The single-engine aeroplane crashed in the evening during a scheduled international service originating at Toulouse, France, with an ultimate destination of Casablanca, Morocco. Subsequently, wreckage was located at sea some 30 miles (50km) from Larache, Morocco, which was its last en route stop, but no survivors or bodies were found among the five persons who had been aboard the Latécoère (four passengers and the pilot).

Date: 26 October 1929 (*c.*18:00)
Location: Gulf of Genoa
Operator: Imperial Airways (UK)
Aircraft type: Short S.8 Calcutta (G-AADN)

The three-engine flying boat was forced down at sea by a gale around 10 miles (15km) off La Spezia, Italy, landing safely and remaining afloat for several hours. However, after it had been taken under tow by a ship, the Calcutta broke away and then sank in the darkness. The bodies of three victims were recovered from the water, but there were no survivors among the seven persons who had been aboard the aircraft (four passengers and a crew of three).

Prior to the forced landing, G-AADN had been flying between two Italian cities, from Naples to Genoa, one segment of a scheduled international service that had originated in India.

Date: 6 November 1929 (*c.*10:10)
Location: Near Godstone, Surrey, England
Operator: Deutsche Luft Hansa AG (Germany)
Aircraft type: Junkers G.24 (D-903)

The trimotored airliner crashed and burned in hilly terrain some 7 miles (11km) south of Croydon Aerodrome, serving London, from where it had taken off about 15 minutes earlier, on a scheduled international flight to Amsterdam, the Netherlands. Seven persons aboard lost their lives in the accident, including the four members of its crew, while the sole surviving passenger escaped with only minor injuries.

After the aircraft's antenna wire had struck the ground and been partially torn off, D-903 turned back in an attempt to return to the airfield. But while flying in adverse meteoro-logical conditions, the Junkers slammed into a wooded area at an approximate elevation of 750ft (230m) and near the summit of a cloud-obscured hill, its pilot apparently unable to see the terrain while flying by visual reference.

Questioned in the investigative report by the UK Accidents Investigation Branch was the 'advisability' of allowing aircraft engaged in regular service to continue to fly outbound from Croydon Aerodrome at low altitudes when operating in bad weather.

Date: 30 December 1929 (*c.*17:00)
Location: Near Amarillo, Texas, US
Operator: Texas Air Transport (US)
Aircraft type: Travel Air 6000B

All five persons aboard were killed when the single-engine aeroplane, which had been conducting a demonstration flight, crashed on a golf course while 'preparing' to land.

Date: 19 January 1930 (*c.*18:30)
Location: Near Oceanside, California, US
Operator: Transcontinental Air Transport–Maddux Air Lines (US)
Aircraft type: Ford 5-AT-C Tri-Motor (NC-9689)

A Deutsche Luft Hansa Junkers G-24, one of which crashed in adverse weather conditions near London. (Philip Jarrett)

The transport crashed and burned some 70 miles (110km) south-south-east of Los Angeles, killing all sixteen persons aboard (fourteen passengers and two pilots). Designated as a 'race special', NC-9689 had been en route to Grand Central Air Terminal, serving Los Angeles, from the Agua Caliente track near Tijuana, Mexico, and the accident occurred in darkness and during a rain and low overcast, with the weather considered as a primary causative factor by an official inquiry board. Specifically, it was concluded that the Tri-Motor had encountered a local meteorological condition with 'unpredicted and unforeseen characteristics' that the flight crew apparently tried to avoid, but which must have caused them to become disoriented. After turning to the left towards an area devoid of lights, the aircraft's port wing struck the ground.

Date: 27 January 1930 (*c.*17:30)
Location: Near Kansas City, Missouri, US
Operator: Universal Aviation Corporation (US)
Aircraft type: Travel Air 6000A

All five occupants (four passengers and the pilot) were killed when the single-engine aeroplane crashed and burned in the vicinity of Fairfax Airport, serving Kansas City, where it was to have landed.

Having nearly completed a regular US domestic interstate service from Wichita, Kansas, the Travel Air was circling to land when it suddenly plummeted to the ground, the accident occurring around sunset. The cause of the crash could not be determined.

Date: 7 July 1930 (*c.*19:00)
Location: Baltic Sea
Operator: Deutsche Luft Hansa AG (Germany)
Aircraft type: Dornier Do.J Wal (D-864)

Five persons lost their lives after the twin-engine flying boat was forced down off the Danish island of Bornholm. Those killed included one of its three crew members; the

other two and one passenger were rescued.

The aircraft had been on a scheduled international flight to Stockholm, Sweden, from Stettin (Szczecin), Germany (Poland), when the crankshaft in one power plant apparently broke, causing the corresponding propeller to splinter. Although it successfully alighted in the sea around 16:30 local time and remained afloat, the Dornier capsized about 2½ hours later while under tow by a Danish ship, with high seas having prevented the transfer of its occupants to the vessel. Two of the victims' bodies were later found, one of which was wearing a life belt.

Date: 21 July 1930 (*c.*15:00)
Location: Near Meopham, Kent, England
Operator: Walcot Air Line (UK)
Aircraft type: Junkers F.13ge (G-AAZK)

Leased from its private owner and bound for London from Le Touquet, France, the single-engine aeroplane crashed around 10 miles (15km) east-south-east of its destination. All six persons aboard (four passengers and two pilots) lost their lives in the accident.

An aeronautical research committee attributed the crash to buffeting, or irregular oscillation, of the horizontal stabiliser of G-AAZK. This condition itself apparently resulted from wake 'eddies' produced by air flowing over the relatively thick main wing of the Junkers. Ultimately, the oscillation led to the separation of the port stabiliser/elevator assembly, then the entire empennage, after which the port wing broke off and the nose/power plant section separated.

Date: 22 August 1930 (*c.*15:45)
Location: Near Jihlava, Moravia, Czechoslovakia
Operator: Ceskolovenske Statni Aerolinie (CSA) (Czechoslovakia)
Aircraft type: Ford 5-AT-C Tri-Motor (OK-FOR)

Operating on a scheduled domestic service to Bratislava, the trimotored transport crashed

A Junkers F.13 monoplane, of the type operated by Walcot Air Line that crashed after in-flight structural failure. (Philip Jarrett)

some 70 miles (110km) south-east of Prague, from where it had taken off earlier. All but one passenger among the thirteen persons aboard were killed in the accident, including both of its crew members.

The airliner had reportedly attempted to avoid an area of heavy thunderstorm activity, but then had to initiate a sharp turn due to the presence in its flight of a chimney that was more than 100ft (30m) tall, and during this evasive manoeuvre it slammed to the ground and caught fire.

Date: 6 October 1930 (c.09:00)
Location: Near Dresden, Saxony, Germany
Operator: Deutsche Luft Hansa AG (Germany)
Aircraft type: Messerschmitt M.20b (D-1930)

All eight persons aboard (six passengers and two pilots) were killed when the single-engine aeroplane crashed in a wooded area while preparing to land at the Dresden airport, which was an en route stop during a scheduled international service originating at Berlin, Germany, with an ultimate destination of Prague, Czechoslovakia.

Witnesses observed D-1930 enter a steep nose-down spin and plunge to earth from an approximate height of 600ft (180m). The apparent loss of control may have resulted from an encounter with a gust of wind in the otherwise good weather conditions.

Date: 21 March 1931 (c.13:00)
Location: Near Cabramurra, New South Wales, Australia
Operator: Australian National Airways
Aircraft type: Avro Ten (VH-UMF)

The saga of the 'Southern Cloud' would remain for more than a quarter of a century one of Australia's great aviation mysteries, and for that reason probably remains to this day as one of the most famous airline crashes in the history of the island continent. Operating on a scheduled domestic service from Sydney, New South Wales, to Melbourne, Victoria, the British-built version of the Fokker F.VII-3m trimotored transport had met with disaster some four hours into its flight. Its wreckage was found accidentally in October 1958 by an individual explorer, in a forest-covered mountain region some 50 miles (80km) south-west

This American Airways Ford Tri-Motor is identical to the aircraft that crashed during a scheduled US domestic flight. (American Airlines)

of Canberra. It could not be determined with certainty whether the eight occupants of the aircraft (six passengers and two pilots) had been killed in the crash and/or ensuing fire, or whether some of them had initially survived and succumbed later.

The accident was believed to have occurred in an area of heavy rain and low clouds after VH-UMF had deviated from the direct course, a normal practice at the time, and apparently at a location where the weather had still been favourable. As indicated by the fact that the Avro was at the time of impact proceeding in the opposite direction of its destination, the pilot may have turned back after descending out of the overcast and finding himself over the mountainous terrain. Evidence showed that the pilot had no warning that the meteorological conditions existed along the route when he left Sydney, and it was of the opinion of the board of inquiry that had the aircraft

been equipped with two-way radio, the crash might have been averted.

Date: 31 March 1931 (*c.* 10:50)
Location: Near Cottonwood Falls, Kansas, US
Operator: Transcontinental and Western Air, Inc. (TWA) (US)
Aircraft type: Fokker F.X (NC-999E)

Designated as Flight 599 and on a US domestic service originating at Kansas City, Missouri, with an ultimate destination of Los Angeles, California, the trimotored airliner crashed about 75 miles (120km) north-east of Wichita, Kansas, which was an en route stop. All eight persons aboard were killed, including its two pilots; among the passengers was the one of the most famous sports figures in American history, Knute Rockne, who coached the University of Notre Dame gridiron team.

It was theorised that ice had formed on one propeller as NC-999E was proceeding through an area of rain, causing one blade to break, and that the resulting vibration led to the separation of the starboard wing. This in turn sent the Fokker plunging from a height of around 500ft (150m) into a pasture. Rot was found where the wooden members of the wing joined the fuselage, and the resulting fatigue would have contributed to the structural failure.

Date: 9 August 1931 (*c*.08:40)
Location: Near Cincinnati, Ohio, US
Operator: American Airways (US)
Aircraft type: Ford 5-AT-B Tri-Motor (NC-9662)

The airliner crashed approximately one minute after taking off from Lunken Field, serving Cincinnati, on a scheduled US domestic flight to Atlanta, Georgia. All six occupants (four passengers and two pilots) lost their lives in the accident. It was determined that prior to the crash, the aircraft's starboard power plant had torn loose in the air, apparently after the corresponding propeller broke.

Date: 15 September 1931
Location: Near Craiova, Oltenia, Romania
Operator: Compagnie Internationale de Navigation Aérienne (CIDNA) (France)
Aircraft type: Fokker F.VIIb-3m (F-AIGT)

The trimotored airliner, which was on a scheduled international service to Bucharest from Paris, France, crashed and burned in evening darkness and during a low overcast some 120 miles (190km) west of its destination. All six persons aboard (four passengers and two crew members) were killed.

Date: 5 November 1931 (*c*.18:20)
Location: Near Camden, New Jersey, US
Operator: New York, Philadelphia and Washington Airways (US)
Aircraft type: Lockheed 9D Orion (NC-12221)

Operating on a scheduled US domestic service from Newark, New Jersey, to Washington, DC, the single-engine aeroplane crashed and burst into flames on a golf course while approaching to land at Central Airport, serving Camden, which was an en route stop.

All five persons aboard (four passengers and the pilot) were killed in the accident, which occurred in darkness after an apparent loss of control.

Date: 6 December 1931 (*c*.06:00)
Location: Bangkok, Siam (Thailand)
Operator: Koninklijke Luchtvaart Maatschappij voor Nederland en Kolonien, NV (KLM) (the Netherlands)
Aircraft type: Fokker F.VIIb-3m (PH-AFO)

Five persons aboard were killed, including three members of its crew of four, when the trimotored airliner crashed while taking off around dawn from Don Muang Airport, serving Bangkok. The radio operator and the sole surviving passenger suffered injuries in the accident, although the latter succumbed more than a year later.

Operating on a scheduled international service to Rangoon, India (Myanmar), with an ultimate destination of the Netherlands, PH-AFO had become airborne only after an unusually long ground run, and after its undercarriage snagged a wall, the Fokker nosed over. There was no post-impact fire.

It was determined that the aircraft's cockpit hatch had not been closed prior to initiating the flight, which would have produced considerable aerodynamic resistance, and additionally, PH-AFO had not been properly trimmed to compensate for its weight. Combined with the attempt by the pilot to take off downwind, these factors apparently led to the inability of the Fokker to gain sufficient altitude.

Date: 29 January 1932 (*c*.16:00)
Location: Near Lebec, California, US
Operator: Century Pacific Lines (US)
Aircraft type: Stinson SM-6000B (NC-10813)

All eight persons aboard (seven passengers and the pilot) were killed when the trimotored aircraft crashed and burned during a scheduled US domestic intra-state service from Bakersfield to Grand Central Air Terminal, serving Los Angeles.

The Stinson had disappeared in 'blizzard' weather conditions, and its wreckage was located about a week later in mountainous terrain, the aeroplane not quite having reached the halfway point of the flight.

Date: 19 March 1932 (*c.*19:30)
Location: Near Calimesa, California, US
Operator: American Airways (US)
Aircraft type: Fokker F.X (NC-652E)

The transport crashed some 70 miles (110km) east of Los Angeles during a scheduled US domestic service to the airport in nearby Glendale, and which had originated at Phoenix, Arizona. Including one passenger who succumbed to his injuries the following day and the aircraft's two pilots, all seven persons aboard NC-652E were killed.

It was believed that its crew had become disoriented while flying in darkness under a low overcast. After it had struck power lines, the Fokker was apparently attempting a forced landing when it slammed into an apple orchard and caught fire.

Date: 16 July 1932 (*c.*08:00)
Location: Near Puente del Inca, Mendoza, Argentina
Operator: Pan American–Grace Airways (Panagra) (US)
Aircraft type: Ford 5-AT-C Tri-Motor (NC-403H)

Operating on a scheduled international service originating at Santiago, Chile, with an ultimate destination of Buenos Aires, Argentina, the airliner crashed in the Andes some 50 miles (80km) west of the city of Mendoza, which was an en route stop. All nine persons aboard (six passengers and a crew of three) were killed in the accident, which occurred in blizzard conditions. The wreckage of the Tri-Motor and the remains of the victims were finally located 20 months later.

Date: 2 November 1932
Location: Near Rohrbrunn, Bavaria, Germany
Operator: Deutsche Luft Hansa AG (Germany)
Aircraft type: Junkers F.13 (D-724)

The single-engine aeroplane crashed in a wooded area approximately 40 miles (65km) south-east of Frankfurt-am-Main, where it was to have landed at the end of a scheduled domestic service from Nuremburg. All five persons aboard (three passengers and two crew members) were killed in the afternoon accident.

It was determined that one wing of Junkers had broken in flight, possibly due to over-stressing when the pilot initiated a pull-up manoeuvre to avoid the terrain after descending out of a low overcast.

Date: 25 March 1933 (*c.*20:00)
Location: Hayward, California, US
Operator: Varney Air Service (US)
Aircraft type: Lockheed 9 Orion (NC-12226)

The single-engine aeroplane struck three houses and burst into flames while attempting to land at San Francisco Bay Airport, at the end of a US domestic intra-state service from Los Angeles. All three occupants of the Lockheed (two passengers and the pilot) and ten persons on the ground were killed in the accident. Another person on the ground was injured and three houses were destroyed.

Reportedly, NC-12226 had descended below a safe height during its approach being conducted in darkness and during a rain, and the crash occurred after its extended under-carriage had struck a rooftop. The underlying cause of the accident was considered to have been an 'unusual and unforeseen' meteorological condition that developed in intensity and affected the immediate area of the crash. It was not known if the pilot had received a

An Imperial Airways Armstrong Whitworth Argosy, the type that crashed in Belgium after a suspected act of sabotage. (BAe Systems)

special weather report broadcast only about 15 minutes earlier, which warned of rain and a low ceiling.

Date: 28 March 1933 (*c*.14:30)
Location: Near Veurne, West Flanders, Belgium
Operator: Imperial Airways (UK)
Aircraft type: Armstrong Whitworth Argosy II (G-AACI)

The first fatal airline disaster believed to have resulted from an act of sabotage involved the 'City of Liverpool,' which had been on a scheduled international service originating at Cologne, Germany, with an ultimate destination of London. All fifteen persons aboard (twelve passengers and a crew of three) were killed when the three-engine transport crashed and burned around 60 miles (100km) west-north-west of Brussels, where it had last stopped. Fire was initially observed near its tail assembly as the Argosy was cruising at an altitude of about 4,000ft (1,200m) and a speed of around 100mph (150kmh). As it descended,

its pilot apparently attempting an emergency landing in an open field, the aircraft experienced catastrophic structural failure, its fuselage splitting in two at an approximate height of 250ft (75m) above the ground.

There was no evidence of failure in the aircraft's power plants or fuel system, and the investigation traced the origin of the fire to somewhere in the fuselage forward of the aft cargo hold, and probably in either the lavatory or the cabin baggage rack. Although the underlying cause was listed as undetermined in a joint Belgian/British report of inquiry, two possible explanations for the blaze were the detonation of a timed incendiary device in a suitcase, or that it had been deliberately started in the lavatory. Significantly, the body of one passenger, a British dentist, was found about 1 mile (1.5km) from the main wreckage. With burns only on his hands and face, it appeared that he had either jumped or fallen from the Argosy before the fire had intensified. Other facts gathered pointed to him as perpetrating the tragedy.

Seated alone towards the rear of the cabin, the suspect would have had the opportunity to start the blaze without being noticed. There was also a strong motive: not only was he deeply in debt, but in his work he had access to anaesthetics, which can be highly inflammable. Also, his background was tainted with rumours of drug trafficking and addiction, and he had reportedly spoken of suicide. But despite what appeared to be overwhelming evidence, whether the passenger had actually brought down the 'City of Liverpool' was never proven with certainty.

Date: 23 April 1933 (c.07:40)
Location: Near Castrovillari, Calabria, Italy
Operator: Air Orient (France)
Aircraft type: Chantiers Aéro-Maritime de la Seine (CAMS) 53-1 (F-ALCE)

Five persons aboard were killed, including two crew members, when the twin-engine flying boat crashed and burned some 35 miles (55km) north of Cosenza. Two passengers and the third member of its crew survived the accident, none of whom were seriously injured.

The aircraft had been en route to Naples, Italy, from Corfu, in the (Greek) Ionian Islands, one segment of a scheduled international service originating at Saigon, Indochina (Vietnam), with an ultimate destination of Marseille, France, when it entered an area of adverse meteorological conditions consisting of snow flurries. After reportedly encountering an 'air pocket', it slammed into a mountain at an approximate elevation of 7,000ft (2,000m).

Date: 9 May 1933 (c.15:00)
Location: Near Viladrau, Catalunya, Spain
Operator: Aéropostale (France)
Aircraft type: Latécoère 28-1 (F-AGIT)

The single-engine aeroplane crashed and burned some 30 miles (50km) north-north-west of Barcelona, from where it had taken off earlier, bound for Perpignan, France, one

segment of a scheduled international service originating at Casablanca, Morocco, with an ultimate destination of Toulouse, France. All six persons aboard (three passengers and a crew of three) were killed.

It was believed that F-AGIT had been forced down into a ravine by a whirlwind while flying through a storm, and as it was attempting to manoeuvre out of the area, one wing broke off, after which the Latécoère slammed into a house. There were no casualties on the ground.

Date: 11 June 1933 (c.17:00)
Location: Glenview, Illinois, US
Operator: Palwaukee Airport (US)
Aircraft type: Sikorsky S-38B (NC-141M)

Nine persons lost their lives when the privately owned twin-engine amphibian, which the airport authority had been using to provide sightseeing flights over the World's Fair at Chicago, crashed and burned in a suburb of the city. The victims included both of the aircraft's crewmen; there were no survivors.

Having completed a tour, NC-141M experienced difficulty while alighting on Lake Michigan in windy weather conditions, and instead of completing the landing, the pilot took off and headed for an airport on the mainland. It was during this diversion that the aircraft's starboard wing failed, apparently due to structural damage suffered in the aforementioned landing, after which the Sikorsky plummeted to earth from an approximate height of 600ft (180m).

Date: 18 July 1933
Location: Aegean Sea
Operator: Societa Anonima Aero Expresso Italiana (Italy)
Aircraft type: CMASA Wal (I-AZEE)

The flying boat crashed during a scheduled service to the Italian island of Rhodes from Athens, Greece, with six persons aboard (two passengers and a crew of four). Only one body was recovered from the water; there were no survivors. Contact with I-AZEE was lost shortly after its departure at 15:30 local time, and it was believed that the aircraft had been forced down by a gale.

Date: 29 August 1933 (*c.*01:00)
Location: Near Tucumcari, New Mexico, US
Operator: Transcontinental and Western Air, Inc. (TWA) (US)
Aircraft type: Ford 5-AT-B Tri-Motor (NC-9607)

All five occupants (three passengers and two crew members) were killed when the tri-motored airliner crashed and burned on a mountain approximately 100 miles (150km) west of Amarillo, Texas, from where it had taken off late the previous evening, on a scheduled US domestic service to Albuquerque, New Mexico. The accident occurred in darkness and during a severe rainstorm.

Date: 12 September 1933
Location: Near Ljubljana, Slovenia, Yugoslavia
Operator: Société de Navigation Aérienne Yougoslave (Aeroput) (Yugoslavia)
Aircraft type: Farman F.306 (YU-SAH)

The trimotored airliner crashed and burned shortly after its departure from the airport serving Ljubljana, on a scheduled domestic service to Susak, Croatia. All eight persons aboard (six passengers and two crew members) were killed in the morning accident, which apparently resulted from engine failure.

Date: 10 October 1933 (*c.*21:00)
Location: Near Chesterton, Indiana, US
Operator: United Air Lines (US)
Aircraft type: Boeing 247 (NC-13304)

The first known case of sabotage in the history of commercial aviation involved Trip 23, which was en route from Cleveland, Ohio, to

A United Air Lines Boeing 247, identical to the aircraft destroyed in the first proven case of sabotage in commercial aviation history. (Smithsonian Institution)

Chicago, Illinois, one segment of a transcontinental US domestic service originating at Newark, New Jersey, with an ultimate destination of Oakland, California. All seven persons aboard (four passengers and three crew members) were killed when the twin-engine transport crashed and burned about 10 miles (15km) east of Gary.

It was concluded that the detonation of a bomb containing nitroglycerine, and probably attached to a timing device, had severed the empennage from the fuselage as the aircraft was proceeding in darkness at an estimated height of 1,000ft (300m). An investigation by federal and state authorities revealed no motive or potential victim, and no one was ever prosecuted in connection with the case.

Date: 21 November 1933 (*c.*15:00)
Location: Near Kharkov, Ukraine, USSR
Operator: Kalinin (USSR)
Aircraft type: Kalinin K-7

The six-engine airliner crashed during a test flight, and all fourteen persons aboard were killed in the accident, the victims including technicians and observers in addition to the crew.

Date: 11 December 1933 (*c.*16:00)
Location: Near Hamburg, Germany
Operator: Deutsche Luft Hansa AG (Germany)
Aircraft type: Focke Wulf A-17 (D-1403)

The single-engine aeroplane crashed in the vicinity of Fuhlsbuttel Aerodrome, serving Hamburg and where it was to have landed, killing six persons aboard, including both members of its crew. Four passengers survived the accident with various injuries.

Having nearly completed a regular service from Berlin, D-1403 had been on its landing approach to land when it struck an unspecified obstacle, the crash occurring in conditions of reduced visibility, with fog and snow flurries.

Date: 30 December 1933 (*c.*13:00)
Location: Near Ruysselede, West Flanders, Belgium
Operator: Imperial Airways (UK)
Aircraft type: Avro Ten (G-ABLU)

Ten persons aboard (eight passengers and two crew members) were killed when the trimotored transport crashed some 40 miles (65km) north-west of Brussels, from where it had taken off earlier. There were no survivors, and in addition to the fatalities, five others suffered injuries extinguishing the burning wreckage.

Bound for London, the final segment of a scheduled international service that had originated at Cologne, Germany, G-ABLU was flying approximately 10 miles (15km) off the normal course and at an abnormally low altitude in an area of heavy fog when it wandered into the vicinity of a long-range radio station. Although the pilot apparently turned to avoid one set of mast struts, the Avro struck another set, the impact tearing off parts of its wings and propellers.

Date: 15 January 1934 (*c.*19:00)
Location: Near Corbigny, Burgundy, France
Operator: Compagnie Nationale Air-France
Aircraft type: Dewoitine D.332 (F-AMMY)

Initiating a new service to Paris from Saigon, Indochina (Vietnam), the trimotored airliner crashed and burned some 120 miles (190km) south-east of the French capital. Including the four members of its crew, all ten persons aboard lost their lives in the accident; most of the passengers were officials of the French government or the airline.

Having taken off from Lyon, France, to where it had been diverted from its regular route, F-AMMY had been flying at a height of around 5,000ft (1,500m) in darkness and falling snow when it reportedly stalled and plummeted into a wooded area. The underlying cause of the crash was believed to have been an excessive accumulation of ice and/ or snow on the aircraft's wings, fuselage and horizontal stabiliser, with weight and balance factors a suspected contributing factor.

Date: 23 February 1934 (*c.*14:15)
Location: Near Coalville, Utah, US
Operator: United Air Lines (US)
Aircraft type: Boeing 247 (NC-13357)

Bound for Cheyenne, Wyoming, one segment of a scheduled US domestic service originating at Los Angeles, California, with an ultimate destination of Chicago, Illinois, the twin-engine transport crashed in the Wasatch Mountains some 20 miles (30km) east of Salt Lake City, from where it had taken off about 15 minutes earlier. All eight persons aboard (five passengers and three crew members) were killed.

The aircraft had slammed into a slope at an approximate elevation of 8,000ft (2,500m), the accident occurring in blizzard conditions. There was no fire after impact. The pilots had failed to gain sufficient altitude while proceeding eastward over the rapidly rising terrain.

Date: 9 May 1934
Location: English Channel
Operator: Compagnie Nationale Air-France
Aircraft type: Wibault 282T.12 (F-AMPH)

The trimotored airliner crashed in foggy weather conditions during a scheduled international service from Paris to London with six persons aboard (three passengers and a crew of three). A mailbag was later recovered from the water approximately 10 miles (15km) off the French mainland, and subsequently the body of one victim washed ashore, but there were no survivors. Before the cessation of communications with F-AMPH, at around 12:20 local time, the pilot requested a 'fix' and was informed of its position as approximately 20 miles (30km) south-west of Boulogne, Artois, France.

Date: 9 June 1934 (*c.*17:00)
Location: Near Debruce, New York, US
Operator: American Airways (US)
Aircraft type: Curtiss-Wright T.32 Condor (NC-12354)

This American Airways Curtiss Condor, serial number NC-12354, was the transport that crashed in the Catskill Mountains of New York state. (Smithsonian Institution)

All seven occupants (four passengers and three crew members) were killed when the twin-engine transport crashed in the Catskill Mountains while en route from Newark, New Jersey, to Syracuse, New York, the first segment of a scheduled US domestic service with an ultimate destination of Chicago, Illinois. The burned wreckage of NC-12354 was found on a peak some 80 miles (130km) north-west of New York City two days after it went missing while flying through a low overcast.

A local official attributed the accident to error by the pilot, who had deviated from the prescribed route and apparently tried to fly over the hazardous terrain at too low an altitude in the adverse meteorological conditions.

Date: 11 June 1934 (*c.*11:00)
Location: Near Junin, Buenos Aires, Argentina
Operator: Pan American-Grace Airways (Panagra) (US)
Aircraft type: Ford 5-AT-C Tri-Motor (NC-8417)

Five persons aboard were killed, including three members of its crew, when the airliner crashed some 100 miles (150km) west of the city of Buenos Aires, from where it had taken off earlier, on a scheduled international service to Santiago, Chile. The steward and five passengers survived the accident with various injuries. The Tri-Motor had plunged into a shallow lagoon while flying in weather conditions consisting of clouds and rain.

Date: 27 July 1934 (*c.*09:50)
Location: Near Tuttlingen, Wurttemberg, Germany
Operator: Swissair AG
Aircraft type: Curtiss-Wright AT.32C Condor (CH-170)

Operating on a scheduled international service to Stuttgart and Berlin, Germany, which had originated at Zurich, Switzerland, the twin-engine airliner crashed in a forest area some 20 miles (30km) north of the Swiss border. All twelve persons aboard (nine passengers and three crew members) were killed.

Flying at an approximate altitude of 8,000ft (2,500m), the Condor was seen to enter a cloud shortly before it plummeted to earth in pieces. The break-up was attributed to the failure of the aircraft's starboard wing due to fractures in the power plant/wing structure. Oscillations were blamed for causing the original fractures in the structure, with stress from unfavourable winds encountered in the cloud through which CH-170 had flown factoring in the ultimate failure.

The German investigative commission ruled that one of the original fractures was facilitated by defects with respect to construction and welding technology. A second fracture, occurring later, apparently resulted from what was described as 'brute' force.

Date: 31 August 1934 (*c.*22:45)
Location: Near Oregon, Missouri, US
Operator: Rapid Air Transport (US)
Aircraft type: Stinson SM-6000B (NC-1118)

All five occupants (four passengers and the pilot) were killed when the trimotored airliner crashed and burned in darkness and during heavy rain about 25 miles (40km) north-west of St Joseph, where it had last stopped during a US domestic service from Kansas City, Missouri, to Omaha, Nebraska.

Date: 2 October 1934 (*c.*10:50)
Location: English Channel
Operator: Hillman Airways (UK)
Aircraft type: de Havilland 89 Dragon Rapide (G-ACPM)

The twin-engine aeroplane crashed approximately 3 miles (5km) off shore from Folkestone, England, during a regular service from London to Paris, France. All seven persons aboard (six passengers and the pilot) lost their lives in the accident; a small amount of debris was subsequently recovered, as were the bodies of six victims, one of which washed ashore about two weeks later.

Occurring in adverse weather conditions consisting of a low overcast accompanied by mist or fine rain, the accident was attributed by the UK Air Ministry to a 'lack of skill and knowledge in matters of navigation' on the part of the pilot. Significantly, it was noted in the investigative report that he lacked both a navigator's license and previous experience in instrument flying.

Evidence indicated that the pilot had followed the coastline, remaining below the clouds, rather than proceeding on a direct compass course to his destination. Apparently losing sight of land while over the Channel, he may have turned back towards the west in order to once again make visual contact with the coast of England. It was theorised that while in a gradual descent through the mist he failed to distinguish the glassy surface of the water in time to avoid the accident. The crash was believed to have occurred fewer than 10 minutes after a second request from the pilot to Croydon Aerodrome for a 'posi-tion'. However, the delay and ultimate failure to provide bearing information was not considered a contributing factor.

Date: 19 October 1934
Location: Off Victoria Province, Australia
Operator: Holyman's Airways (Australia)
Aircraft type: de Havilland 86 (VH-URN)

Operating on a scheduled service from Launceston, Tasmania, to Melbourne, Victoria, the four-engine airliner vanished over Bass Strait with twelve persons aboard (ten passengers and two pilots).

In the last communications from the flight, received at 10:20 local time, VH-URN was reported to have been nearing Rodondo Island. No survivors, bodies or wreckage were found, and the cause of the crash could not be determined. However, one of the recommendations made by the accident investigative commission was to prohibit the changing of pilots in an aircraft while in flight, since one

A de Havilland 86 of the type flown by Holyman's Airways that was lost under unknown circumstances off south-eastern Australia. (Philip Jarrett)

theory into the disappearance of VH–URN pointed to a loss of control resulting from such action by the crew.

Date: 20 December 1934 (*c*.03:30)
Location: Near Rutbah Wells, Iraq
Operator: Koninklijke Luchtvaart Maatschappij voor Nederland en Kolonian, NV (KLM) (the Netherlands)
Aircraft type: Douglas DC-2 (PH–AJU)

The twin-engine airliner crashed and burned in the desert some 200 miles (320km) south-west of Baghdad during a special international service originating at Amsterdam, the Netherlands, with an ultimate destination of Batavia (Jakarta), Indonesia. All seven persons aboard (four passengers and three crew members) were killed.

Having last stopped at Cairo, Egypt, PH–AJU had been flying in darkness and through an area of thunderstorm activity. At the time of impact, it was proceeding in a westerly direction, possibly back towards Rutbah Wells. No evidence was found of either a lightning strike or structural failure as precipitating the accident.

Although the cause could not be determined, it was concluded by Dutch officials that the crash probably resulted from the extremely bad weather conditions coupled with what their report described as the 'unsatisfactory flying qualities' of the aircraft. The latter pertained specifically to difficulty in maintaining level flight due to inadequate rudder/elevator control. Tests were later performed on the type with a modified tail plane, and a larger unit would be incorporated into its successor, the DC-3, which would be known for its fine handling characteristics.

Date: 1934 (date unknown)
Location: Soviet Union
Operator: Aeroflot (USSR)
Aircraft type: Tupolev A.N.T.9

Ten persons lost their lives in the crash of the trimotored airliner, which presumably occurred during a scheduled passenger service within the USSR. The victims included the two members of its crew; there were no survivors. According to an unofficial Soviet report, the pilot of the A.N.T.9 did not have sufficient experience in the type and in fact did not even possess a valid airman's certificate.

Date: 31 January 1935 (*c*.19:00)
Location: Near Stettin (Szczecin), Germany (Poland)
Operator: Deutsch-Russische Luftverkehrs AG (Deruluft) (German-Russian Airlines)
Aircraft type: Junkers Ju.52/3m (D–AREN)

The trimotored airliner crashed in darkness and adverse weather conditions while en route to Berlin from Danzig (Gdansk), one segment of a scheduled international service that had originated at Konigsberg (Kaliningrad), in the USSR. Killed in the accident were all eleven persons aboard the Ju.52 (eight passengers and a crew of three).

After initially requesting navigational assistance from the ground, the flight crew reported that the aircraft was in an overcast, and that ice had begun to form on its aerial. Subsequently, D–AREN slammed into a hill named Podejuch, which rose to nearly 500ft (150m).

Date: 6 April 1935 (*c*.15:20)
Location: Near Brilon, Westphalia, Germany
Operator: Koninklijke Luchtvaart Maatschappij voor Nederland en Kolonien, NV (KLM) (the Netherlands)
Aircraft type: Fokker F.XII (PH–AFL)

All seven persons aboard (five passengers and two crew members) were killed when the trimotored airliner crashed approximately midway between Dortmund and Kassel during a scheduled international service originating at Prague, Czechoslovakia, with an ultimate destination of Amsterdam, the Netherlands. The accident occurred while the pilot was apparently trying to maintain visual contact with the ground while proceeding through an area of heavy fog.

A US Senator and four others lost their lives in the crash of a Transcontinental and Western Air Douglas DC-2, the type shown here. (Boeing)

Date: 6 May 1935 (*c.*03:30)
Location: Near La Plata, Missouri, US
Operator: Transcontinental and Western Air, Inc. (TWA) (US)
Aircraft type: Douglas DC-2 (NC-13785)

Though far from being the worst airline disaster in history in terms of fatalities, this could be described as a milestone accident because of one of its victims and the changes it brought about.

Designated as Trip 6, the 'Sky Chief' had been en route from Albuquerque, New Mexico, to Kansas City, Missouri, one segment of a transcontinental US domestic service originating at Los Angeles, California, with an ultimate destination of Newark, New Jersey. Diverted by bad weather, NC-13785 was unable to reach its alternate stop, Kirksville, Kansas. Critically low on fuel, the DC-2 was flying at tree-top level with its undercarriage retracted when it entered a draw, whereupon the pilot initiated a left turn. Its port wing then scraped the ground and the aircraft slammed into an embankment, the crash occurring some 15 miles (25km) south of Kirksville in

pre-dawn darkness and during a low overcast, with possible 'zero-zero' visibility. Despite the absence of a post-impact fire, NC-13785 was demolished. Five persons lost their lives in the accident, including both pilots; one of the passengers killed was Bronson Cutting, an American Senator from the state of New Mexico. The eight surviving passengers suffered various injuries.

Factors identified as contributing to the crash were the failure of the US Weather Bureau to predict the hazardous meteorological conditions that had developed during the latter part of the flight; the granting of clearance by the operator's personnel, specifically, their dispatch of an aircraft despite knowing that its radio was not functioning on the correct frequency and, later, for failing to instruct the crew to return to Albuquerque or to redirect them to where the weather was better when it became apparent that the ceiling at Kansas City was dropping to and below the authorised minimum for landing, and while the DC-2 still had sufficient fuel to reach an alternate airport; and an error in judgement on the part of the pilot in continuing the flight despite the fact that the radio malfunction prevented him from effectively communicating with the ground.

Though not directly causal to the accident, TWA was cited for several violations generally related to safety, most notably its failure to require the aircraft to carry a sufficient reserve of fuel that would have allowed for 45 minutes of flying, and for assigning a pilot to a route for which he was not officially qualified and a co-pilot who had been granted a waiver of the flight-time limitation rule. The airline at first refused to pay the penalties levied against it and blamed the crash on the incorrect information regarding the weather at Kirksville that had been given to the pilot.

An indirect outcome of this and several other US air carrier accidents was the enactment of the Civil Aeronautics Act of 1938, which assigned all regulatory functions to a single government agency. More directly related to safety was a significant increase in spending by the US government for improvements in the nation's airway system, including its radio-navigational facilities.

Date: 18 May 1935 (*c.*12:45)
Location: Moscow, Russian Soviet Federative Socialist Republic, USSR
First aircraft:
Operator: Gor'ky Eskadril'ya (USSR)
Type: Tupolev A.N.T. 20 'Maxim Gorki' (SSSR-120)
Second aircraft:
Operator: Soviet Air Force
Type: Polikarpov I-15

The eight-engine 'Maxim Gorki,' the largest land-based aeroplane at the time and a Soviet 'propaganda' tool, had been on a sightseeing flight, its passengers members of the Central Aerodynamic Institute, when it collided with the smaller biplane, and both crashed, the former in the Sokol district of the city. Killed in the accident were all forty-seven occupants of the A.N.T. 20, including eleven crew members, the pilot (and sole occupant) of the I-15, and either two or three persons on the ground.

It was believed that the single-engine fighter, which was performing aerobatics, had been blown into SSSR-120 by a gust of wind, the collision occurring at an approximate height of 2,300ft (700m). The 'Maxim Gorki' then suffered structural failure and fell in pieces.

Date: 24 June 1935 (*c.*15:00)
Location: Near Medellin, Antioquia, Colombia
First aircraft:
Operator: Sociedad Colombo-Alemana de Transportes Aéreos (SCADTA) (Colombia)
Type: Ford 5-AT-C Tri-Motor (C-31)
Second aircraft:
Operator: Servicio Aéreo Colombiano (SACO) (Colombia)
Type: Ford 5-AT-B Tri-Motor (F-31)

The two trimotored transports collided at Olaya Herrera Airport, serving Medellin, killing a total of seventeen persons aboard both of them. There were no survivors among the seven occupants of C-31, while three of the thirteen aboard F-31 survived with injuries.

Taking off on a scheduled domestic service to Cali, F-31 had during its ground run swerved off the runway and struck C-31, which was either standing or taxiing preparatory to its scheduled departure on a domestic service to Bogotá. Both aeroplanes were destroyed by impact forces and fire. It was considered possible that the SACO aircraft had encountered a gust of wind, resulting in a loss of control, but there was long-standing speculation that the swerve had been an intentional act by the pilot, possibly to antagonise the SCADTA pilot.

Date: 14 July 1935 (*c.*09:40)
Location: Near Amsterdam, the Netherlands
Operator: Koninklijke Luchtvaart Maatschappij voor Nederland en Kolonien NV (KLM) (the Netherlands)
Aircraft type: Fokker F.XXII (PH-AJQ)

Six persons aboard lost their lives, including all four members of its crew, when the four-engine transport crashed and burned shortly after taking off from Schiphol Airport, serving Amsterdam, on a scheduled international service to Hamburg, Germany. Among the fourteen surviving passengers, five suffered injuries.

The aircraft had just become airborne when both port power plants reportedly malfunctioned at an approximate height of 80ft (25m), and during an attempted off-airport emergency landing, its port wing struck a dyke. Factoring in the loss of power was fuel starvation, attributed to the inadequate flow of gasoline.

Date: 20 July 1935 (*c.*12:15)
Location: Near Pian San Giacomo, Graubunden, Switzerland
Operator: Koninklijke Luchtvaart Maatschappij voor Nederland en Kolonien NV (KLM) (the Netherlands)
Aircraft type: Douglas DC-2 (PH-AKG)

Operating on a scheduled international service to Frankfurt, Germany, with an ultimate destination of Amsterdam, the Netherlands, the twin-engine transport crashed about 50 miles (80km) north of Milan, Italy, from where it had taken off earlier. All thirteen persons aboard (nine passengers and four crew members) were killed.

The crew of the DC-2 had flown through the wrong passage when crossing the Alps, and after circling they entered a lower valley that had a dead end. Continuing to circle in an area of thunderstorm activity, which was accompanied by heavy rain and high winds, the captain finally decided to set down, but during the attempted forced landing a pull-up manoeuvre was initiated in order to avoid a cable, leading to a stall and an uncontrolled descent into the ground. Swiss authorities noted that pilots with mountain experience would never have tried to traverse the Alps in the first place during the inclement weather that had been forecast.

Date: 13 September 1935 (*c.*09:00)
Location: Near Tambo, Panama
Operator: Panama Airways
Aircraft type: Ford Tri-Motor

All eight persons aboard (seven passengers and the pilot) were killed when the airliner crashed and burned in mountainous terrain some 60 miles (100km) west of the capital city of Panama, from where it had taken off earlier, on a scheduled domestic service to David. The cause of the accident was believed to have been related to the adverse weather conditions encountered by the Tri-Motor.

Date: 2 October 1935 (*c.*10:00)
Location: North of Tasmania, Australia
Operator: Holyman's Airways (Australia)
Aircraft type: de Havilland 86 (VH-URT)

Inaugurating a new domestic service from Melbourne, Victoria, to Sydney, New South Wales, the four-engine airliner crashed in Bass Strait approximately 5 miles (10km) off Flinders Island, where it was scheduled to land. Among its five occupants (three passengers and two crewmen), no survivors or bodies were found. Some of the aircraft's wreckage was recovered, and examination of the debris indicated an impact with the water at great speed.

It was determined that VH-URT had gone into an uncontrollable spin, and three possible precipitating factors were: a loss of control after a power plant failure; the fouling of the tail surfaces while the trailing aerial was being reeled in; or structural failure. There was also evidence of a small fire in the rear of its cabin, which may have occurred before the crash, but this probably did not factor in the accident. And in view of two fatal accidents and other difficulties with the type, Australia would subsequently suspend the certificate of airworthiness of the de Havilland 86.

A Savoia-Marchetti SM.73 of the Belgian carrier SABENA, one of which crashed in adverse weather conditions near London. (Philip Jarrett)

Date: 7 October 1935 (*c.*02:20)
Location: Near Silver Crown, Wyoming, US
Operator: United Air Lines (US)
Aircraft type: Boeing 247D (NC-13317)

Operating as Trip 4 and on a US domestic interstate service that had originated at Oakland, California, and last stopped at Salt Lake City, Utah, the twin-engine transport crashed in mountainous terrain some 10 miles (15km) north-west of Cheyenne, where it was to have landed. All twelve persons aboard (nine passengers and three crew members) were killed in the accident.

The aircraft had been proceeding along the direct radio course to the airport and was in a slight descent with its undercarriage still retracted when it struck just below the top of a knoll, then slammed to earth, the accident occurring in early morning darkness. No evidence could be found of any pre-impact mechanical failure, and it was the opinion of the US Bureau of Air Commerce investigative board that the crash resulted from error on the part of the pilots in judging their height above the terrain or distance to the airport, or both.

Date: 10 December 1935 (*c.*16:45)
Location: Near Tatsfield, Kent, England
Operator: Société Anonyme Belge d'Exploitation de la Navigation Aérienne (SABENA) (Belgium)
Aircraft type: Savoia-Marchetti SM.73 (OO-AGN)

All eleven persons aboard (seven passengers and a crew of four) were killed when the tri-motored airliner crashed on a wooded hillside approximately 8 miles (13km) south-east of Croydon Aerodrome, serving London, where it was to have landed at the end of a scheduled international service from Brussels, Belgium. The accident occurred around dusk and during a low overcast, with the cloud base of around 200 to 300ft (60–100m).

It was concluded by the UK Accidents Investigation Branch that the pilot, who did not request bearings from the airport and tried to navigate on his own, had descended out of the clouds prematurely, apparently uncertain of his position. He then must have initiated a steep climbing turn to the left to avoid the surrounding hilltops or after realising that the visible lights were in fact those of Biggin Hill Aerodrome, not Croydon. During the evasive manoeuvre, the SM.73 apparently lost flying speed and stalled, resulting in an uncontrolled descent. And after the stall, some of the passengers may have been thrown forward, causing a weight distribution imbalance that would have hindered the ability of the pilot to regain control. No evidence was found of any prior mechanical or structural failure in the aircraft.

Date: 31 December 1935 (*c.*19:15)
Location: Mediterranean Sea
Operator: Imperial Airways (UK)
Aircraft type: Short S.8 Calcutta (G-AASJ)

The flying boat was forced down less than 1.5 miles (2.5km) from Alexandria, Egypt, its intended destination during a scheduled international service that had originated at Brindisi, Italy, and last stopped at Mirabella, Crete. Among its thirteen occupants (nine passengers and four crew members), only the pilot survived; he was rescued by a ship after spending some five hours in the water.

Apparently as a result of a previous modification of its carburettor jets, G-AASJ had used fuel excessively during the flight, which resulted in the exhaustion of its supply of gasoline, and, in turn, a total loss of power in its three engines. Additionally, the tankage of the Calcutta did not provide an adequate reserve of fuel for this particular operation, except in favourable conditions. The forced landing had been carried out in darkness and rough seas, and the wrecked aircraft sank approximately three hours later, taking with it at least three survivors of the original crash.

Date: 14 January 1936 (*c.*19:30)
Location: Near Forrest City, Arkansas, US
Operator: American Airlines (US)
Aircraft type: Douglas DC-2 (NC-14274)

The twin-engine transport crashed some 90 miles (145km) east-north-east of Little Rock, from where it had taken off earlier, bound for Memphis, Tennessee, one segment of a scheduled US domestic service originating at Newark, New Jersey, with an ultimate destination of Los Angeles, California. All seventeen persons aboard (fourteen passengers and a crew of three) perished.

Proceeding at an unusually low altitude in darkness and good weather conditions, NC-14274 had struck trees before it slammed into a swamp at a recorded air speed of 180mph (290kmh). Despite the break-up of the aircraft, there was no post-impact fire. Although the US Bureau of Air Commerce considered the height at which the DC-2 had been flying as a contributing factor, the agency was unable to determine the underlying cause of the accident. Despite the lack of evidence of interference with the pilots, the Bureau subsequently issued a directive that prohibited entry by passengers into the cockpit of US commercial aircraft at any time during a flight.

Date: 17 January 1936
Location: Near Cochabamba, Bolivia
Operator: Lloyd Aéreo Boliviano SA (Bolivia)
Aircraft type: Junkers Ju.52/3mce

All thirteen persons aboard (ten passengers and three crew members) were killed when the trimotored airliner crashed and burned during a scheduled domestic flight from Cochabamba to La Paz.

Date: 21 January 1936 (*c.*10:00)
Location: Mediterranean Sea
Operator: Compagnie Nationale Air-France
Aircraft type: Chantiers Aéro-Maritime de la Seine (CAMS) 53-1 (F-AJIR)

The twin-engine flying boat, carrying six persons (three passengers and a crew of three), vanished while en route from Marseille, France, to Ajaccio, on Corsica, the first segment of a scheduled international service with an ultimate destination of Tunis, Tunisia. It was believed to have crashed north-west of Ajaccio after transmitting a distress message, the crew reporting power plant trouble.

Date: 10 February 1936
Location: Atlantic Ocean
Operator: Compagnie Nationale Air-France
Aircraft type: Latécoère 301 (F-ANLE)

The four-engine flying boat vanished with six persons aboard, five of them crew members and the sixth an airline employee riding as a passenger, during a transatlantic service from Natal, Brazil, to Dakar, French West Africa (Senegal). In their last message, received at 13:00 Natal time, the crew reported their position as approximately 600 miles (965km) at sea and that they were flying in a storm, but also announced, 'All is well'.

Date: 26 March 1936 (*c.*11:00)
Location: Near Amecameca, Mexico
Operator: Compañía Mexicana de Aviación, SA (Mexico)
Aircraft type: Ford 5-AT-B Tri-Motor (X-ABCO)

Chartered by the Hamburg-American Line and carrying as passengers a group of European tourists, the airliner crashed and burned in a saddle near the Popocatepetl volcano and some 45 miles (70km) southeast of Mexico City, from where it had taken off earlier, bound for the capital of Guatemala. Including the four members of its crew, all fourteen persons aboard the Tri-Motor were killed.

Prior to the accident, X-ABCO had been seen flying at a low altitude, and there was speculation that the pilot, in an attempt to give his passengers a scenic view of the terrain, may have lost control either during a turn or due to an encounter with a strong down draught.

Date: 7 April 1936 (*c.*10:20)
Location: Near Uniontown, Pennsylvania, US
Operator: Transcontinental and Western Air, Inc. (TWA) (US)
Aircraft type: Douglas DC-2 (NC-13721)

Designated as Flight 1 and on a US domestic transcontinental service originating at Newark, New Jersey, with an ultimate destination of Los Angeles, California, the airliner crashed some 40 miles (65km) south-south-east of Pittsburgh and approximately 10 miles (15km) east of Allegheny County Airport, serving that city, where it was to have landed. All but two of the fourteen persons aboard the DC-2 lost their lives in the accident, including both pilots and a passenger who succumbed to his injuries about a week later. Though herself injured, the stewardess hiked down the mountain and led rescuers to the accident scene.

The aircraft had slammed into a wooded mountaintop in instrument meteorological conditions (IMC) consisting of light, freezing rain, and low clouds and fog that covered the mountaintops. Prior to the crash, it had turned from a southerly on to a westerly heading up a small valley, and while proceeding at a low altitude. The pilot then apparently initiated a climb to avoid the terrain, but at a point near the top of the ridge, and while turning to the right, the DC-2 struck a number of trees, after which it slammed to earth.

Blamed for the accident was poor judgement on the part of the pilot-in-command for flying by reference to the ground after having descended through the overcast and over the hazardous terrain without determining his position. His failure to follow the radio range course while operating in IMC violated both his company's and US Department of Commerce's regulations. An additional factor was that NC-13721 had encountered crosswind drift, and at the time of impact had been about 15 miles (25km) south of the intended track, its crew apparently unaware of the discrepancy. No evidence was found of any prior mechanical failure in the aircraft or malfunctioning of the ground navigational aids.

Subsequent to this crash, the Department of Commerce modified the Pittsburgh radio range, discontinuing the simultaneous voice broadcasts, moved the loop-type radio range beacon from that location to Akron, Ohio, and increased the power at the station located at Buckstown, Pennsylvania.

Date: 16 June 1936 (*c.*07:00)
Location: Near Kyrkjebø, Sogn og Fjordane, Norway
Operator: Det Norske Luftfartselskap Fred Olsen & Bergenske A/S (Norwegian Air Lines)
Aircraft type: Junkers Ju.52 (LN-DAE)

All seven persons aboard (three passengers and a crew of four) were killed when the float-equipped airliner crashed and burned in the vicinity of Sognefjord, and some 50 miles (80km) north-east of Bergen, from where it had taken off earlier. Operating on a scheduled domestic service to Trondheim, LN-DAE had struck Lihesten Mountain while proceeding in cloudy weather conditions.

Date: 31 July 1936 (*c.*19:30)
Location: English Channel
Operator: Jersey Airways (UK)
Aircraft type: Saro Cloud (G-ABXW)

The twin-engine amphibian was forced down during a scheduled service between two of the Channel Islands, from Guernsey to Jersey. Carried out shortly before sunset and in weather conditions consisting of intermittent rain and drizzle, a visibility of 1 to 3 miles (*c.*1.5–5km) and winds approaching 40 knots, the ditching was apparently successful, but the aircraft must have capsized in the rough water and was subsequently smashed to pieces on a reef. As a result, none of the ten persons aboard G-ABXW (eight passengers and two crew members), survived; the occupants had donned lifebelts and must have escaped from the cabin, only to drown. Considerable wreckage was subsequently recovered, as were the bodies of all but one of the victims.

It was theorised that the flight in turbulent conditions may have caused a small quantity of fuel in the bottom of the tank to surge sufficiently to uncover the tank outlet temporarily, and thus cause one or both fuel pumps to become air-locked. The aircraft's undercarriage had been extended at the time of the ditching, suggesting that the pilot had tried to reach land after the failure of one or both power plants. Rescue efforts had been hampered by the heavy seas and the fact that G-ABXW was not equipped with radio equipment, which could have been used to establish its position. It was in fact noted in the report of the UK Accidents Investigation Branch that the dispatch of an aircraft without a radio violated established directives.

Date: 5 August 1936 (*c.*22:00)
Location: Near St Louis, Missouri, US
Operator: Chicago & Southern Air Lines (US)
Aircraft type: Lockheed 10B Electra (NC-16022)

The twin-engine aircraft crashed and burned approximately 3 miles (5km) north of Lambert Field, serving St Louis, from where it had taken off less than 15 minutes earlier and which was an en route stop during a scheduled US domestic service originating at New Orleans, Louisiana, with an ultimate destination of Chicago, Illinois. All eight persons aboard (six passengers and two pilots) were killed.

For undetermined reasons, NC-16022 was attempting to return to the airport when one wing struck the ground, the accident occurring in darkness and during a fog and low overcast, with a visibility of less than 1 mile (1.5km). There was no evidence of prior mechanical failure in the aircraft, and the US Bureau of Air Commerce concluded that the crash had resulted from the failure of the pilot to either maintain or increase altitude after he decided to turn back.

Date: 5 September 1936 (*c.*22:00)
Location: Near Pittsburgh, Pennsylvania, US
Operator: Pittsburgh Skyways, Inc. (US)
Aircraft type: Stinson SM-6000B (NC-11175)

Ten persons aboard lost their lives, including the lone pilot, when the aeroplane crashed shortly after taking off from Allegheny County Airport, on a non-scheduled sight-

A Junkers Ju.52/3m, widely used by Deutsche Luft Hansa during the 1930s and the type that crashed in the Thuringian Forest of Germany. (Smithsonian Institution)

seeing flight. The sole surviving passenger, a seventeen-year-old girl, escaped serious injury.

Its three engines had failed after the fuel supply was cut off, and there were indications that the pilot had then allowed the Stinson to lose flying speed while attempting an off-airport forced landing, the accident occurring in darkness. It was considered possible by the US Bureau of Air Commerce that the passenger who had been sitting on two flare containers in the cockpit had precipitated the crash by inadvertently switching off the fuel selector valve with her heel.

Date: 28 September 1936
Location: Benghazi, Libya
Operator: Ala Littoria SA (Italy)
Aircraft type: Cant Z.506 (I-RODI)

The float-equipped, trimotored airliner crashed while preparing to land in the harbour at Benghazi, which was an en route stop during a flight from Addis Ababa, Ethiopia, to Rome, Italy. All but one of the ten persons aboard were killed, and the survivor was seri-ously injured; according to press accounts, the occupants were either crew members or technicians employed by the carrier. Reportedly, I-RODI experienced engine failure during its approach, and subsequently struck the mast of a ship and then plummeted into the Mediterranean Sea.

Date: 1 November 1936 (*c.*15:00)
Location: Near Tabarz, Thuringia, Germany
Operator: Deutsche Luft Hansa AG (Germany)
Aircraft type: Junkers Ju.52/3m (D-APOO)

Operating on a regular domestic service from Frankfurt-am-Main to Erfurt, the tri-motored airliner crashed and burned in the Thuringian Forest some 10 miles (15km) south-east of Eisenach, and ten persons aboard were killed, including the three members of its crew. Three passengers survived with injuries. It was believed that the pilot had 'lost his bearings' while flying in a heavy fog, resulting in either a controlled impact with the terrain or an uncontrolled descent into the ground.

Date: 6 December 1936
Location: Near Moscow, USSR
Operator: Deutsch-Russische Luftverkehrs AG
(Deruluft) (German-Russian Airlines)
Aircraft type: Tupolev A.N.T.9 (SSSR-D311)

Nine persons were killed in the crash of the trimotored aeroplane, while five others aboard SSSR-D311 survived the accident.

Date: 9 December 1936 (*c.*10:55)
Location: London, England
Operator: Koninklijke Luchtvaart
Maatschappij voor Nederland en Kolonien
(KLM) (the Netherlands)
Aircraft type: Douglas DC-2 (PH-AKL)

Operating on a scheduled international service to Amsterdam, the Netherlands, the transport crashed while taking off from Croydon Aerodrome. All but two of the seventeen persons aboard lost their lives in the accident, including both pilots; the stewardess and sole surviving passenger were injured, as

was a fireman fighting the post-impact blaze. Among the passengers killed was Juan de la Cierva, who developed the autogyro, and Arvid Achates Lindman, a former Swedish Prime Minister.

The crash occurred during a heavy fog after the aircraft had begun its take-off roll and travelled some 600ft (180m) down the runway, along a white line used for guidance in such conditions. Swerving to the left at an approximate angle of 90 degrees, the DC-2 had just become airborne when its extended undercarriage wheels tore down a fence and wire netting surrounding a tennis court. It continued in flight for about 1,500ft (500m) before it struck the roof of one house, ploughed into another semi-detached house and burst into flames.

It was determined by the UK Accidents Investigation Branch that the pilot had failed to maintain directional control of the aircraft, and also demonstrated 'poor judgement' in not throttling down the engines and abandoning the take-off after it had departed the runway.

The crash against a house near London claimed the lives of all but two of the seventeen persons aboard the KLM Douglas DC-2. (Getty Images)

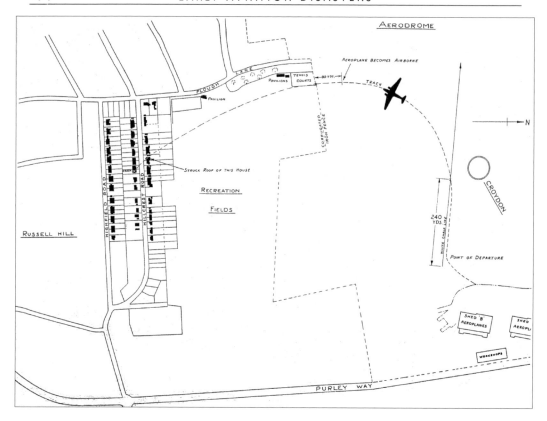

Diagram indicates path of PK-AKL, which crashed during attempted take-off from Croydon Aerodrome, serving the British capital at the time. (Accidents Investigation Branch)

Date: 15 December 1936 (*c.*04:00)
Location: Near Alpine, Utah, US
Operator: Western Air Express (US)
Aircraft type: Boeing 247D (NC-13370)

All seven persons aboard (four passengers and a crew of three) were killed when the twin-engine airliner crashed in the Wasatch range of mountains around 20 miles (30km) south of Salt Lake City, which was its destination during a scheduled US domestic service originating at Los Angeles, California. The wreckage of NC-13370 was located the following June on Lake Hardy Ridge.

Occurring in pre-dawn darkness and cloudy weather conditions, with possible snowfall, the accident was probably related to the inability of the pilots to identify the radio range course because static had adversely affected radio reception.

Date: 27 December 1936 (*c.*19:40)
Location: Near Newhall, California, US
Operator: United Air Lines (US)
Aircraft type: Boeing 247D (NC-13355)

Designated as Trip 34 and on a US domestic intra-state service that had originated at Oakland and last stopped at San Francisco, the transport crashed in the Santa Susana Mountains some 25 miles (40km) north-west of downtown Los Angeles, and approximately 20 miles (30km) from Union Air Terminal, where it was to have landed. All twelve persons aboard (nine passengers and a crew of three) were killed in the accident.

Its undercarriage down, the aircraft was either in level flight or slightly descending and banked 28 degrees to the right at the moment of initial impact. Slashing through several trees, which tore off both wings and starboard horizontal stabiliser, it then slammed into a ridge and slid to the bottom of Rice Canyon. The accident occurred in darkness, and the meteorological conditions in the area at the time were believed to have consisted of rain and a low overcast.

The crash was attributed to error on the part of the pilot, who must have tried to navigate through Newhall Pass at an altitude lower than the surrounding terrain without first determining the existing weather with his radio (which had probably been affected by static). It was believed that just before impact he initiated a turn in an attempt to fly out of the pass after deciding against proceeding any further by visual means and instead initiate an instrument approach from a more favourable position.

Date: 11 January 1937 (*c*.10:30)
Location: Near Playa Vicente, Veracruz, Mexico
Operator: Compañía Mexicana de Aviación, SA (Mexico)
Aircraft type: Lockheed 10E Electra (X-ABEO)

Nine persons aboard (six passengers and a crew of three) lost their lives when the airliner, on a regular domestic service from Mexico City to Mérida, Yucatán, crashed and burned in mountainous terrain some 80 miles (130km) west of Minatitlan, which was an en route stop. There were no survivors from the accident, which occurred in adverse weather conditions.

Date: 12 January 1937 (*c*.11:00)
Location: Near Newhall, California, US
Operator: Western Air Express (US)
Aircraft type: Boeing 247D (NC-13315)

The second fatal airline accident in the same general area in only about two weeks involved the same type of aircraft and occurred under remarkably similar circumstances; only the carrier and the number of fatalities were different. Including those who succumbed later, five persons aboard lost their lives when the transport crashed in the San Gabriel Mountains some 15 miles (25km) north-west of Union Air Terminal, in Burbank, where it was to have landed at the end of a US domes-

A Lockheed 10 Electra of the type operated by the carrier Mexicana that crashed during a Mexican domestic flight. (Smithsonian Institution)

tic service from Salt Lake City, Utah, as Flight 7. Those killed included the aircraft's co-pilot; two other crew members and six passengers survived with injuries.

As with the earlier crash, this one took place in adverse meteorological conditions, with fog and rain, and apparently resulted from error by the pilot, who must have descended to a dangerously low altitude without determining his position using the available radio-navigational facilities on the ground.

Date: 26 January 1937 (*c.*17:30)
Location: Near Oran, Algeria
Operator: Société Anonyme Belge d'Exploitation de la Navigation Aérienne (SABENA) (Belgium)
Aircraft type: Savoia-Marchetti SM.73 (OO-AGR)

All twelve persons aboard (eight passengers and four crew members) perished when the trimotored airliner crashed shortly before it was to have landed at the Oran airport, which was an en route stop during a scheduled international service originating in the Belgian Congo, with an ultimate destination of Brussels, Belgium.

For undetermined reasons, OO-AGR plummeted to the ground from an approximate height of 2,500ft (750m) after the crew reported their intentions to land, the accident occurring shortly before sunset.

Date: 9 February 1937 (*c.*20:50)
Location: Near San Francisco, California, US
Operator: United Air Lines (US)
Aircraft type: Douglas DC-3A (NC-16073)

Operating as Trip 23 and on a US domestic intra-state service originating at Los Angeles and ultimately bound for Oakland, the twin-engine transport crashed in San Francisco Bay about 2 miles (3km) north-east of Mills Field, serving San Francisco, which was a scheduled en route stop. All eleven persons aboard (eight passengers and a crew of three) were killed in the accident.

The aircraft had circled the airport in a clockwise direction, in preparation for landing on the east–west runway, before going into a rapid descent from an approximate height of 400ft (120m) and at an angle of 35–40 degrees. Its undercarriage extended, the DC-3 initially struck the surface of the bay with its starboard wing, which was sheared off in the impact, and came to rest inverted in water that was around 20ft (6m) deep. Both power plants had apparently been switched off just before the crash, and the aircraft's propellers were in slow rotation at the moment of impact. The accident occurred in darkness but good weather conditions; the wind was virtually calm.

Subsequently, most of the wreckage was recovered, as were the bodies of at least seven victims, and in every case death was due to drowning. Examination of the wreckage revealed no evidence of prior technical or structural failure in the aircraft. However, damage to the components indicated that the co-pilot's microphone had become lodged between his control column and the seat rail support; this would have had the effect of jamming the elevators in a nose-down position, and could not have been overcome even with both pilots pulling back their respective control wheels.

The manufacturer subsequently re-designed the socket of the control column in order to prevent a recurrence of this freakish accident.

Date: 19 February 1937 (*c.*13:50)
Location: Queensland, Australia
Operator: Airlines of Australia, Ltd
Aircraft type: Stinson Model 'A' (VH-UHH)

The trimotored airliner crashed and burned around 50 miles (80km) south-east of Brisbane, from where it had taken off earlier, on a scheduled domestic service to Sydney, New South Wales. Two surviving passengers were found nine days later, but five others who had been aboard the Stinson lost their lives, including both pilots; one of the passengers was killed in a fall searching for help.

Prior to the accident, VH-UHH was being flown at a low altitude and under the cloud level, its pilot apparently trying to maintain visual contact with the ground, and the crash occurred when it encountered winds of up to 60 knots, which created a strong down draught that exceeded its ability to climb. And strangely, six years after the 'Southern Cloud' accident (21 March 1931), VH-UHH lacked a two-way radio, which would have given the crew the opportunity to transmit position reports.

Date: 24 March 1937 (*c*.14:00)
Location: Near Ouroux-sur-Saône, Burgundy, France
Operator: Imperial Airways (UK)
Aircraft type: Short S.23 'Empire' (G-ADVA)

Five persons aboard were killed, including the lone designated passenger, when the four-engine flying boat crashed on a mountain some 70 miles (110km) north-west of Lyon. The sole surviving crew member, who was the aircraft's radio operator, escaped serious injury.

During a scheduled international service from Southampton, England, to Brindisi, Italy, with an ultimate destination of Durban, South Africa, the crew reported having 'lost their bearings' while flying in a snowstorm. Moments later, radio contact with G-ADVA abruptly ended.

Date: 25 March 1937 (*c*.18:40)
Location: Near Pittsburgh, Pennsylvania, US
Operator: Transcontinental and Western Air, Inc. (TWA) (US)
Aircraft type: Douglas DC-2 (NC-13730)

Designated as Flight 15A and on US domestic service originating at Newark, New Jersey, with an ultimate destination of Chicago, Illinois, the airliner crashed some 5 miles (10km) west of the Pittsburgh airport, which was a scheduled en route stop. All thirteen persons aboard (ten passengers and three crew members) were killed. As it was pre-

paring to land, the DC-2 rolled to one side before plunging to earth from an approximate height of 500ft (150m), the accident occurring around sunset and in conditions conducive to icing, with a low overcast. There was no fire after impact.

It was determined by the US Bureau of Air Commerce that ice had built up on its wings and in the slot between the edge of its ailerons and the wing tips, and that the latter condition must have changed the airfoil contour and disrupted the flow of air around the structure, leading to a loss of control. Soon after this accident, improved de-icing equipment was announced to help deal with the threat to aircraft caused by the build up of ice.

Date: 3 April 1937 (*c*.15:30)
Location: Near McNary, Arizona, US
Operator: Koninklijke Luchtvaart Maatschappij voor Nederland en Kolonien NV (KLM) (the Netherlands)
Aircraft type: Douglas DC-3 (PH-ALP)

The twin-engine transport had been en route from Southern California to Kansas City, Missouri, the first segment of a transcontinental US flight with an ultimate destination of New York, New York, preparatory to its delivery to the carrier, when it crashed in a blizzard. Its wreckage was found three days later on Baldy Peak, some 150 miles (250km) north-east of Phoenix, with no survivors among its eight occupants.

Date: 6 May 1937 (*c*.19:25)
Location: Near Lakehurst, New Jersey, US
Operator: Deutsche Zeppelin Reederei GmbH (German Zeppelin Transport Company)
Aircraft type: Zeppelin Hindenburg (LZ-129)

Undoubtedly the best known airline accident prior to 1950, this remains even today one of history's most famous non-natural disasters. It also may be one of the best-documented disasters, recorded not only in still pictures but by motion picture film and even in a recorded radio broadcast.

The initial blast is captured on film during sequence that led to the fiery destruction of the German airship Hindenburg. (Smithsonian Institution)

Along with its sister dirigible, the Graf Zeppelin, the Hindenburg had revolutionised air travel in the mid-1930s with their ability to carry a relatively large number of passengers in steamship-style comfort over great distances. Measuring 803ft (244m) long, it remains the largest commercial aircraft, at least in terms of length, ever built. On this date, LZ-129 had completed its first scheduled transatlantic North American flight of the year, which had originated at Frankfurt, Germany, with a planned landing at Lakehurst Naval Air Station, located some 50 miles (80km) south-south-west of New York City.

Lines had just been dropped in preparation for mooring and the airship was at a height of around 100ft (30m) when an explosion occurred. Following the initial blast, the dirigible crashed tail-first, after which the front section, including the cabin portion, settled to the ground. The entire airship

was then gutted in seconds. Killed in the disaster were thirty-five of the ninety-seven persons aboard the Hindenburg (thirteen passengers and twenty-two crew members, the latter including one of the two assigned aircraft commanders), plus a member of the ground crew. Two others on the ground and some thirty of the survivors suffered injuries, many of whom were seriously burned, though about the same number escaped with little or no injury. The crash occurred late in the afternoon, and as a light rain was falling, and although the weather was not adverse, it could have been a contributing factor.

The initial explosion was attributed to the ignition of a combustible mixture of free hydrogen and air that had formed in considerable quantity in the stern section of the dirigible. This condition was believed to have been precipitated by a leak of the highly volatile gas that probably occurred after a

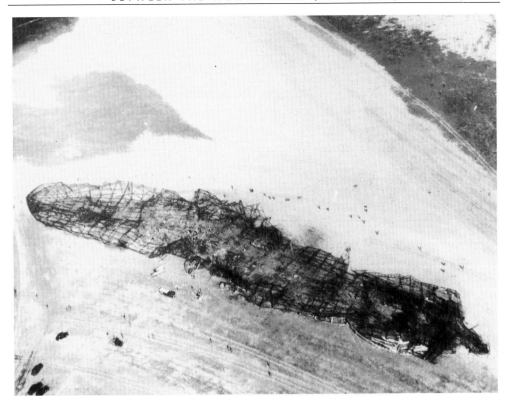

The charred remains of the Hindenburg lie at Lakehurst Naval Air Station after the disaster that claimed thirty-six lives. (Smithsonian Institution)

bracing wire, which apparently broke when the airship made a sharp turn in preparation for landing, and tore a gash in one of its stern hydrogen cells. In its official report, the US Bureau of Air Commerce considered that the 'most probable' cause of ignition was a brush discharge, also known as Saint Elmo's Fire. The static electricity could have been built up when the mooring ropes were dropped on to the wet ground less than 5 minutes before the explosion. Though initially dry, the ropes soon became damp, increasing their conductivity and equalising the potential between the aircraft and the ground. Eventually, however, the potential gradient between the dirigible and the surrounding airspace was sufficient to generate static sparks. Another hypothesis that came to light in the late twentieth century was that a static discharge had actually ignited the skin of the Hindenburg, which itself was composed of volatile elements. Despite rumours, no evidence was ever found of sabotage.

Shortly after the disaster, the Graf Zeppelin would be retired from service, marking the end of lighter-than-air passenger service. Although the safety record of the great airships will always be tarnished by the tragedy at Lakehurst, the fact remains that the thirteen killed on the Hindenburg are the only passengers to lose their lives in commercial dirigible operations.

Date: 2 June 1937
Location: Chile
Operator: Línea Aérea Nacional de Chile (LAN-Chile)
Aircraft type: Sikorsky S-43

The twin-engine flying boat vanished over the Sea of Chiloé during a regular domestic service between two Chilean cities, from Puerto Montt to Magallanes (Punta Arenas), with nine persons aboard. Subsequently, one piece of wreckage and the bodies of two victims were recovered on one of the Desertores Islands; there were no survivors from the crash.

Date: 28 July 1937 (*c*.10:30)
Location: Near Beert (Brages), Brabant, Belgium
Operator: Koninklijke Luchtvaart Maatschappij voor Nederland en Kolonien NV (KLM) (the Netherlands)
Aircraft type: Douglas DC-2 (PH-ALF)

Operating on a scheduled international service from Amsterdam, the Netherlands, to Paris, France, the transport crashed and burned approximately 10 miles (15km) south-west of Brussels, from where it had taken off shortly before and which was an en route stop. All fifteen persons aboard (eleven passengers and a crew of four) were killed.

The accident had been precipitated by an in-flight fire that may have itself resulted from a lightning strike that occurred while the DC-2 was flying through an area of thunderstorm activity. However, the lightning theory could not be proven. Parts that shed from PH-ALF were strewn along a path more than 3 miles (5km) long as the blaze continued to spread. Additionally, an airline employee's cap was found approximately 2 miles (3km) from the crash site, indicating that the flight crew had opened their windows in an attempt to see out of the smoke-filled cockpit. However, this action would have produced an airstream flowing through the fuselage, which could in turn have intensified the blaze, as would the flammable material being carried aboard the DC-2. Eventually, the flames would have damaged the aircraft's rudder and elevator surfaces, leading to a loss of control.

Date: 2 August 1937 (*c*.05:30)
Location: Near Wadi Halfa, Anglo-Egyptian Sudan
Operator: Ala Littoria SA (Italy)
Aircraft type: Savoia-Marchetti SM.73 (I-SUSA)

All nine persons aboard (five passengers and four crew members) were killed when the tri-motored airliner crashed and burned near the local airport, where it was to have landed during a scheduled international service originating at Rome, Italy, with an ultimate destination of Asmara, Ethiopia. The accident occurred in pre-dawn darkness after I-SUSA was observed to abandon its landing approach and apparently attempt an overshoot manoeuvre.

Date: 2 August 1937 (*c*.19:40)
Location: Near Colón, Panama Canal Zone
Operator: Pan American-Grace Airways (Panagra) (US)
Aircraft type: Sikorsky S-43 (NC-15065)

The flying boat, carrying fourteen persons (eleven passengers and a crew of three), crashed in the Golfo de los Mosquitos approximately 35 miles (55km) west of Cristóbal, located near the city of Colón and where it was to have landed. Some wreckage was recovered from the water, but no survivors or bodies were found.

Operating on a scheduled international service that had originated at Guayaquil, Ecuador, and had last stopped at Cali, Colombia, the aircraft was preparing to land at France Field, serving the Canal Zone, when it plummeted into the sea some 10 miles (15km) off shore. In the last message from the crew, NC-15065 was reported 'spiralling down over water'. The subsequent crash occurred in darkness and during a heavy rain. Examination of the recovered debris indicated that after the impact, which was estimated to have been at a speed of at least 90mph (145kmh), a fire had burned on the surface of the water.

Two scenarios were considered as 'most probable' in contributing to the accident. The first was the failure of one or both power plants that must have occurred during the spiralling manoeuvre mentioned in the last radio transmission. With regard to this issue, investigation revealed that due to a design defect in the type aircraft, the depletion of gasoline from the auxiliary tanks through seepage could result in air being sucked by the fuel pumps through the fuel lines. This in turn could lead to engine stoppage by cutting off the supply of gasoline. The other possible contributing factor leading to the crash was the adverse weather encountered during the descent, which reduced or eliminated forward visibility.

Date: 17 October 1937 (c.21:00)
Location: Near Oakley, Utah, US
Operator: United Air Lines (US)
Aircraft type: Douglas DC-3A (NC-16074)

Designated as Trip 1 and en route from Cheyenne, Wyoming, the twin-engine transport crashed in the Uinta Mountains about 50 miles (80km) east of Salt Lake City, which was its next scheduled stop during a US domestic transcontinental service originating at Newark, New Jersey, with an ultimate destination of Oakland, California. All nineteen persons aboard (sixteen passengers and a crew of three) were killed.

The DC-3 was in level flight and on a compass heading of around 235 degrees while some 15 miles (25km) to the south of the radio range course when it slammed into Humpy Ridge, below Hayden Peak, at an approximate elevation of 10,000ft (3,000m). Its partially burned wreckage was located in deep snow from the air the following day. The accident occurred in darkness, and prior to the crash the aircraft must have encountered light to moderate snow and, probably, snow static. Based on a review of its flight analyser, it had also been in turbulence for the last 10 minutes before impact. The cloud conditions in the area at the time were not known.

A combination of factors were believed to be responsible for the crash: 1) Static conditions that rendered reception of radio signals unintelligible; 2) The continuation of the flight at a height below the terrain without the aid of either ground visibility or radio signals to definitely establish the position of the aircraft; and 3) A change in the weather caused by the approach of an unpredicted cold front.

Date: 26 October 1937 (c.04:30)
Location: Off Western Africa
Operator: Compagnie Nationale Air-France
Aircraft type: Dewoitine D.333 (F-ALQA)

The trimotored airliner vanished with six persons aboard (three passengers and three crew members) during a scheduled international service from Dakar, French West Africa (Senegal), to Casablanca, Morocco, in pre-dawn darkness and after transmitting an SOS message. Two mailbags identified as belonging to F-ALQA were subsequently recovered, one from the Atlantic Ocean and another on a beach near Salé, Morocco. However, no survivors or bodies were found.

Date: 12 November 1937 (c.16:50)
Location: Near Mannheim, Baden, Germany
Operator: Deutsche Luft Hansa AG (Germany)
Aircraft type: Heinkel He.111 (D-AXAV)

The twin-engine transport crashed while preparing to land at the Mannheim airport, at the end of a scheduled domestic service from Berlin, the accident occurring during a fog. Ten persons aboard the aircraft were killed in the crash, including the three members of its crew; two passengers survived with injuries.

Date: 16 November 1937 (c.14:30)
Location: Near Ostende, West Flanders, Belgium
Operator: Société Anonyme Belge d'Exploitation de la Navigation Aérienne (SABENA) (Belgium)
Aircraft type: Junkers Ju.52/3m (OO-AVB)

Operating on a scheduled international service originating at Frankfurt, Germany, with an ultimate destination of London, the airliner crashed while attempting to land at the Ostende airport, to where it had been diverted due to bad weather at Brussels. Killed in the tragedy were twelve persons aboard the Ju.52, including three crew members and an infant who was apparently stillborn to one of the passengers as a result of the crash; the accident also claimed the lives of five members of the German Grand Ducal von Hesse family on their way to Great Britain to attend a wedding. There were no survivors.

While approaching to land in a fog, OO-AVB struck the chimney of a factory approximately 2 miles (3km) from the airport, the impact shearing off one wing, then slammed to earth and burst into flames. An airport employee was blamed for not adequately assisting the pilot down in the conditions of poor visibility, even though rockets had been fired from the ground in an attempt to do so.

Date: 10 January 1938 (*c.*15:05)
Location: Near Bozeman, Montana, US
Operator: Northwest Airlines (US)
Aircraft type: Lockheed 14H Super Electra (NC-17388)

Ten persons aboard (eight passengers and two pilots) were killed when the twin-engine aircraft crashed and burned some 80 miles (130km) south-east of Butte, from where it

had taken off earlier. There were no survivors from the accident.

Designated as Trip 2 and bound for Billings, Montana, one segment of a US domestic service originating at Seattle, Washington, with an ultimate destination of Chicago, Illinois, NC-17388 was last reported cruising at an altitude of 9,000ft (*c.*2,700m) before it plunged into Bridger Canyon. According to witnesses, it had assumed a stall attitude before it fell steeply to the ground while in a spin or tight spiral. The crash occurred in meteorological conditions consisting of strong winds and an overcast sky, with snow flurries in the area.

Investigation revealed that the upper portion of both the aircraft's right and left vertical tail fins had separated in the air, resulting in a loss of control. It was further determined that through fatigue, distortion or a collision with an object, such as a bird, the structures had been weakened to the point that they became susceptible to flutter, which apparently caused their final failure.

The following day, and as soon as flutter became suspected as a factor in the crash, the US Department of Commerce grounded

A Lockheed 14 Super Electra of the type flown by Northwest Airlines that crashed after flutter-induced in-flight structural failure. (Smithsonian Institution)

all aeroplanes of this type. The government agency also launched a research programme to study the effects of flutter, and would later acquire new equipment for measuring natural periods of vibration. Lockheed would itself take steps to eliminate the threat to the Super Electra by redesigning its tail surfaces so to make the components as far apart as physically possible.

Date: 11 January 1938 (*c.*08:30)
Location: South Pacific Ocean
Operator: Pan American Airways System (US)
Aircraft type: Sikorsky S-42B (NC-16734)

All seven crewmen (and its only occupants) lost their lives when the flying boat crashed approximately 15 miles (25km) north-west of Pago Pago, on the island of Tutuila, in American Samoa, from where it had taken off earlier, bound for Auckland, New Zealand. The pilot was Edwin Musick, who in 1935 had piloted the 'China Clipper' on the first scheduled transpacific airline service.

The aircraft had been on a scheduled international mail service originating at Honolulu, US Territory of Hawaii, and had turned back towards Pago Pago due to an oil leak in one of its four engines. It was theorised that gasoline vapours had become trapped by a wing flap when it was extended after the crew began dumping fuel in preparation for landing, causing an in-flight fire and/or explosion. Searchers recovered only bits of wreckage, and none of the victims' bodies.

Date: 9 February 1938
Location: Near Marseille, Provence, France
Operator: Compagnie Nationale Air-France
Aircraft type: Liore-et-Olivier LeO H-47 (F-ANPB)

The four-engine flying boat crashed in the harbour, and eight persons aboard were killed, including three members of its crew. Four passengers and two other crew members survived the morning accident, none of whom were seriously injured.

Taking off on a regular service to Ajaccio, Corsica, F-ANPB struck the submerged portion of a pier that the pilot was unable to see in the foggy weather conditions, then caught fire and sank.

Date: 13 February 1938
Location: Mediterranean Sea
Operator: Ala Littoria SA (Italy)
Aircraft type: Cant Z.506 (I-ORIA)

The float-equipped trimotored transport vanished between the (Spanish) Balearic Islands and Sardinia, Italy, with fourteen persons aboard (ten passengers and a crew of four). Operating on a regular international service from Cadiz, Spain, to Rome, Italy, I-ORIA had last stopped at Pollensa, on the Spanish island of Majorca, and was lost some time after its last radio transmission, received at 14:30 local time, while flying in a storm.

Date: 1 March 1938 (*c.*21:30)
Location: Near Wawona, California, US
Operator: Transcontinental and Western Air, Inc. (TWA) (US)
Aircraft type: Douglas DC-2 (NC-13789)

Nine persons aboard (six passengers and three crew members) lost their lives when the twin-engine transport crashed in Yosemite National Park, some 60 miles (100km) north-north-east of Fresno. There were no survivors. The wreckage of NC-13789 and the victims' remains were found three months later, the DC-2 having slammed into Buena Vista Peak at an approximate elevation of 8,000ft (2,500m).

The aircraft had been flying between two cities in California, from San Francisco to Los Angeles, when it encountered an area of adverse meteorological conditions. According to the US Bureau of Air Commerce, the pilot must have temporarily lost his bearings due to a change in the direction of the wind and a sharp increase in its velocity, unbeknown to him, leading to confusion as to his position relative to the

Fresno radio range course. The subsequent crash occurred in darkness and, apparently, in an area of heavy snowfall.

Date: 23 March 1938 (*c*.07:00)
Location: Near Corsavy, Roussillon, France
Operator: Compagnie Nationale Air-France
Aircraft type: Dewoitine D.338 (F-AQBB)

All seven occupants (four passengers and a crew of three) were killed when the tri-motored airliner crashed on a peak in the Pyrenees approximately 20 miles (30km) south-south-west of Perpignan. The D.338 had been on a scheduled international service from Casablanca, Morocco, to Paris, France, when the accident occurred, reportedly in blizzard conditions.

Date: 30 April 1938 (*c*.14:00)
Location: Near Formia, Latium, Italy
Operator: Ala Littoria SA (Italy)
Aircraft type: Savoia-Marchetti SM.73 (I-BAUS)

Operating on a regular domestic service from Brindisi to Rome, the trimotored airliner crashed and burned some 75 miles (120km) south-east of its destination, killing all nineteen persons aboard (fourteen passengers and five crew members). The aircraft had struck cloud-obscured Mount Maranola only minutes after sending a radio message, in which the crew requested navigational assistance. Considered as contributory were the adverse weather conditions in which the accident had occurred.

Date: 16 May 1938 (*c*.14:00)
Location: Near Palmdale, California, US
Operator: Northwest Airlines (US)
Aircraft type: Lockheed 14H Super Electra (NC-17394)

The twin-engine transport crashed and burned in the Sierra Pelona range of mountains some 30 miles (50km) north of Los Angeles, California, and all nine persons aboard lost their lives; the victims were mostly employees of either the carrier or the manufacturer, but also included the dependants of one of them.

Having taken off earlier from Union Air Terminal, in Burbank, NC-17394 had been on a US domestic flight to Las Vegas, Nevada, where it was to be officially delivered to the airline. The Super Electra had been cruising in a low overcast when it slammed into a mountain, near its crest and at an approximate elevation of 3,300ft (1,005m), just above Mint Canyon.

The accident was attributed to faulty judgement by the crew, who had must have tried to navigate in the adverse meteorological conditions by visual reference to the ground and proceeded at an insufficient altitude over the hazardous terrain. A possible contributing factor was improper pre-flight planning by the pilot, who had apparently failed to obtain sufficient weather information prior to departure.

Date: 24 May 1938 (*c*.22:15)
Location: Near Cleveland, Ohio, US
Operator: United Air Lines (US)
Aircraft type: Douglas DST-A (DC-3) (NC-18108)

Designated as Trip 9 and on a US domestic service originating at Newark, New Jersey, with an ultimate destination of Chicago, Illinois, the twin-engine transport crashed and burned approximately 8 miles (13km) east of Cleveland Municipal Airport, where it was scheduled to land. Ten persons aboard (seven passengers and a crew of three) lost their lives in the accident; there were no survivors.

It was believed that the pilot had been attempting a gear-down forced landing in a field due to an uncontrollable fire in the aircraft's starboard power plant when NC-18108 clipped the top of a tree and then slammed into a wooded area, the accident occurring in darkness. A US Department of Commerce investigative board determined that the blaze had been precipitated by the failure of the engine's No.3 cylinder barrel. In the following sequence, the skirt of the corresponding piston apparently caught on the broken edge of the lower portion of the failed cylinder barrel during a down stroke, and as a result of the sudden stoppage of the piston, the link rod piston pin came loose, permitting the rod on its next up stroke to drive the piston against the head of the cylinder. The excessive upward travel of the piston lifted the upper portion of the cylinder and pulled the intake pipe out of the blower section. It also caused the exhaust pipe sleeve, which connected the cylinder to the pipe itself, to become canted, leaving an opening through which exhaust flame could escape.

The displacement of parts created numerous possibilities for the ignition of fuel, oil or their vapours. Fed by the oil supply of the engine, the blaze then spread throughout the power plant. Subsequent to this accident, both the Department of Commerce and United Air Lines worked to develop a diaphragm for use between the power and accessory sections of aircraft engines to prevent fire from travelling from one to another under circumstances similar to what happened to NC-18108, and thus leading to a similar disaster.

Date: 14 July 1938 (*c*.08:00)
Location: Tyrrhenian Sea
Operator: Ala Littoria SA (Italy)
Aircraft type: Savoia-Marchetti SM. 66 (I-VOLO)

The three-engine flying boat crashed some 90 miles (145km) off the eastern coast of Sardinia during a scheduled service from Cagliari, on the island, to Rome, the accident occurring during a heavy fog. Searchers subsequently recovered wreckage and the bodies of at least six victims, but there were no survivors among the twenty persons who had been aboard the aircraft (sixteen passengers and four crew members).

Date: 22 July 1938 (*c*.17:40)
Location: Near Stulpicani, Transylvania, Romania
Operator: Polskie Linje Lotnicze (LOT) (Poland)
Aircraft type: Lockheed 14H Super Electra (SP-BNG)

The twin-engine transport crashed approximately 200 miles (320km) north of Bucharest, which was its destination during a scheduled international service from Warsaw, Poland. All fourteen persons aboard (ten passengers and a crew of four) lost their lives in the accident, which occurred during a thunderstorm that was accompanied by rain and a low overcast. The aircraft may have been struck by lightning.

Date: 29 July 1938
Location: North Pacific Ocean
Operator: Pan American Airways System (US)
Aircraft type: Martin M-130 (NC-14714)

Operating as Trip 229 and carrying fifteen persons (six passengers and nine crew members), the four-engine flying boat vanished while en route from Guam to Manila, in the Philippines, the final segment of a transpacific crossing that had originated at San Francisco, California, US, and also stopped at the US Territory of Hawaii.

The 'Hawaii Clipper' was last heard from shortly after 13:00 local time, when at a reported position of approximately 670 miles (1,080km) east-south-east of its destination, and flying at a height of around 9,000ft (2,700m) in rain, clouds and rough air conditions. Radio contact was abruptly lost after the aircraft's radio operator had requested a 1-minute delay in a routine weather report from a station in the Philippines due to 'rain static'. No trace of NC-14714 was found, and despite various theories, including a criminal act, no reasonable explanation for its disappearance has ever been made.

A Pan American Airways System Martin M-130 flying boat, identical to the 'Hawaii Clipper' that was mysteriously lost over the Pacific Ocean. (Pan Am)

Date: 10 August 1938
Location: Near Debrecen, Hungary
Operator: Magyar Legiforagalmi Reszvenytarsasag (MALERT) (Hungary)
Aircraft type: Fokker F.VIII (HA-FNC)

All twelve persons aboard (nine passengers and a crew of three) lost their lives when the twin-engine airliner, on a domestic service to Debrecen from Budapest, crashed and burned approximately 120 miles (190km) east of the Hungarian capital, the accident occurring during a thunderstorm.

Date: 12 August 1938 (*c.*12:30)
Location: Near San Andres Tuxtla, Veracruz, Mexico
Operator: Compañía Mexicana de Aviación SA (Mexico)
Aircraft type: Lockheed 10E Electra (X-ABAS)

The aircraft crashed and burned while en route to the city of Veracruz from Villahermosa, Tabasco, one segment of a regular service with an ultimate destination of Mexico City. All eleven persons aboard (eight passengers and a crew of three) were killed in the accident. In its last message, X-ABAS was reported flying at 11,000ft (*c.*3,400m) in heavy rain, with the adverse weather conditions that almost certainly caused or contributed to the crash related to a hurricane affecting the region.

Date: 13 August 1938 (*c.*11:00)
Location: Near Offenburg, Baden, Germany
Operator: Ceskoslovenske Statni Aerolinie (CSA) (Czechoslovakia)
Aircraft type: Savoia-Marchetti SM.73 (OK-BAG)

Operating on a scheduled international service from Prague, Czechoslovakia, to Strasbourg, France, with an ultimate destination of Paris, the trimotored airliner struck a hilltop in the Black Forest and burst into flames, the crash occurring in a heavy fog. Killed in the accident were seventeen persons aboard the aircraft, comprising of thirteen passengers and four members of the crew; the victims included a stewardess, who succumbed the following day to injuries sustained in the accident.

Date: 15 August 1938
Location: Near Rio de Janeiro, Brazil
Operator: Sindicato Condor Ltda (Brazil)
Aircraft type: Junkers Ju.52/3mfe (PP-CAT)

Nine persons aboard (five passengers and a crew of four) lost their lives when the float-equipped airliner crashed and sank in Guanabara Bay as it was taking off from the water, on a scheduled domestic service to Vitoria, Espirito Santo. The morning accident left no survivors.

Date: 18 August 1938 (*c*.17:00)
Location: Near Mornago, Lombardy, Italy
Operator: Macchi (Italy)
Aircraft type: Macchi M.C.94 (I-NILO)

The twin-engine commercial flying boat crashed some 30 miles (50km) north-west of Milan, while on a test flight, and all fifteen persons aboard the aircraft were killed. Besides the designated two-member flight crew, the victims consisted of technicians and engineers.

Date: 24 August 1938
Location: Tokyo, Japan
First aircraft:
Operator: Nippon Koku Yuso Kabushiki Kaisha (Japan Air Transport Company)
Type: Unknown
Second aircraft:
Operator: Japan Flying School
Type: Unknown

The worst civilian aviation disaster occurring prior to the Second World War was this mid-air collision between a twin-engine transport carrying no passengers, and possibly either a Nakajima A.T. or a Nakajima-Douglas DC-2, and a smaller aeroplane. After they hit, both aircraft fell into a Tokyo suburb, one of them striking a foundry and bursting into flames.

Most of the fifty-eight persons reportedly killed in the morning accident were on the ground, but also included all three occupants of the larger aircraft and both men aboard the trainer. Approximately 100 others suf-fered injuries. The post-impact fire spread to four machine shops and several nearby houses. Soon after the tragedy, training flights over Tokyo were banned.

Date: 24 August 1938 (*c*.08:30)
Location: Near Wangmoon, Kwantung, China
Operator: China National Aviation Corporation
Aircraft type: Douglas DC-2 (32)

Operating on a scheduled service from Hong Kong to Chungking, China, the twin-engine transport was attacked by a group of Japanese fighter aircraft, then strafed after it had ditched in the Pearl River, west of Canton. All but three of the seventeen persons aboard the DC-2 lost their lives in the hostile incident; one passenger and two members of its crew of four, the pilot and radio operator, survived. The aircraft itself would be rebuilt, only to be shot down again by the Japanese two years later (29 October 1940).

Date: 1 October 1938
Location: Near Soglio, Grisons (Graubunden), Switzerland
Operator: Deutsche Lufthansa AG (Germany)
Aircraft type: Junkers Ju.52/3m (D-AVFB)

The trimotored airliner, carrying thirteen persons (ten passengers and a crew of three), vanished in the afternoon during a sched-uled international service from Frankfurt, Germany, to Milan, Italy. Its disappearance would remain a mystery until a mountain guide located debris identified as belong-ing to D-AVFB at an elevation of more than 11,000ft (3,300m) on the Cengalo Glacier, near the Italian border, in July 1952. However, the circumstances of the non-sur-vivable crash would remain unknown.

Date: 10 October 1938 (*c*.11:00)
Location: Near Soest, Westphalia, Germany
Operator: Société Anonyme Belge d'Exploitation de la Navigation Aérienne (SABENA) (Belgium)
Aircraft type: SABCA SM.73 (OO-AGT)

Operating on a scheduled international service to Berlin from Brussels, Belgium, the trimotored transport crashed around 30 miles (50km) east-north-east of Dortmund. All twenty persons aboard (sixteen passengers and four crew members) were killed in the accident.

The aircraft was last reported cruising at 5,000ft (*c.*1,500m) before it plummeted to earth, the crash occurring in adverse weather conditions, with rain and fog. There was speculation that a propeller may have broken, tearing loose an engine, or that the pilot may have attempted a sudden pullout from a rapid descent, the manoeuvre overstressing a wing and causing its failure.

Date: 25 October 1938 (*c.*13:45)
Location: Near Melbourne, Victoria, Australia
Operator: Australian National Airways
Aircraft type: Douglas DC-2 (VH-UYC)

The transport, which had been on a scheduled domestic intra-state flight from Adelaide, South Australia, struck Mount Dandenong and burned some 25 miles (40km) south-east of Essendon Aerodrome, serving Melbourne and where it was to have landed. All eighteen persons aboard (fourteen passengers and a crew of four) perished. An apparent navigational error must have led the pilots to believe that they had been 20 to 25 miles (*c.*30–40km) closer to their destination than was actually the case, resulting in their overshooting of the airport. The DC-2 had continued to descend on a straight course, the crew evidently expecting to break through the clouds covering the terrain, until its impact at an approximate elevation of 1,870ft (570m), or less than 100ft (30m) from the crest of the ridge.

The following deficiencies were identified as contributing to the accident: 1) The aircraft's navigational log was either not kept or had not been properly utilised during the latter part of the flight, as required by the carrier; 2) The company's procedure for descent through an overcast into this airport was not adopted, and 3); A request for a bearing from

the aircraft was not received by the radio operator at the airport nor logged at any other operating station.

Also noted in the investigative report was the lack in Australia of an ultra-high frequency (UHF) beacon network, and indeed, the crash of VH-UYC would prove pivotal in the development of the nation's airway system.

Date: 4 November 1938 (*c.*10:55)
Location: Jersey, Channel Islands
Operator: Jersey Airways (UK)
Aircraft type: de Havilland 86 (G-ACZN)

The four-engine airliner crashed in the vicinity of St Helier approximately a minute after taking off from the island airport, on a scheduled service to Southampton, England. Killed in the accident were all thirteen persons aboard the aircraft (eleven passengers and two crew members), plus a man working in the field in which the crash occurred.

It was believed that the pilot had allowed the de Havilland to fall into a side-slip while climbing through a low overcast, and at an insufficient altitude for him to regain control. The aircraft was seen to emerge from the cloud base at a height of around 120ft (40m) and plunge to earth, and after impact it slid across the ground until it struck a solid earth bank, whereupon it burst into flames.

Date: 14 November 1938 (*c.*18:40)
Location: Near Amsterdam, the Netherlands
Operator: Koninklijke Luchtvaart Maatschappij voor Nederland en Kolonien NV (KLM) (the Netherlands)
Aircraft type: Douglas DC-3 (PH-ARY)

Operating on a scheduled international service from Berlin, Germany, the aircraft crashed while attempting to land at Schiphol Airport, serving Amsterdam. Six of the eighteen persons aboard were killed, including the four members of its crew, while the twelve surviving passengers suffered various injuries.

Its undercarriage down but flaps still retracted, the DC-3 had struck a dyke after descending below a safe height during its approach, coming to rest in a ditch. There was no fire. The accident occurred in darkness and weather conditions consisting of a low overcast, although the visibility would have been greater beneath the clouds. No evidence was found of any pre-impact technical failure in the aircraft, and the crash apparently resulted from pilot error.

Date: 26 November 1938 (c.15:20)
Location: Near Bathurst (Banjul), Gambia
Operator: Deutsche Luft Hansa AG
(Germany)
Aircraft type: Junkers Ju.90V2 (D-AIVI)

The four-engine airliner crashed, killing twelve of the fifteen persons aboard and injuring the survivors; the occupants consisted of crew members and technicians. Taking off from the Bathurst airport on a flight in which it was being tested in a tropical environment, D-AIVI lost height after the failure of two power plants on one side, then struck a tree, slammed to earth and caught fire.

Date: 29 November 1938 (c.05:30)
Location: Near Point Reyes, California, US
Operator: United Air Lines (US)
Aircraft type: Douglas DC-3A (NC-16066)

Five persons lost their lives after the transport was ditched in the Pacific Ocean some 35 miles (55km) north-west of San Francisco. The victims included two members of its crew; only the captain and one passenger survived.

Designated as Trip 6, NC-16066 had been on a US domestic service originating at Seattle, Washington, with an ultimate destination of Los Angeles, California. After the gear-up water landing was accomplished in pre-dawn darkness approximately 1 mile (1.5km) off shore, its occupants climbed to the top of the aircraft through the emergency hatch in the flight deck. Subsequently, however, the DC-3 was swept shoreward and battered to destruction on the rocks. The bodies of only two of the victims were found.

The pilot had apparently failed to resolve an orientation problem and definitely establish his position while en route from Medford, Oregon, to Sacramento, California, which was one segment of the flight. As a result, NC-16066 deviated from the proper radio range course and on to a westerly heading, and was later forced down by fuel exhaustion. In addition to the pilot, company personnel were blamed for not adequately safeguarding the flight, including the failure to offer assistance when it became overdue. The competency ratings of the former and two of the latter would later be revoked.

Date: 2 December 1938 (c.07:55)
Location: Mexico City, Mexico
Operator: Compañía Mexicana de Aviación
SA (Mexico)
Aircraft type: Lockheed 10E Electra
(X-ABAU)

All eight persons aboard (five passengers and a crew of three) were killed when the twin-engine transport crashed and burned on a hill in the Peñón de los Baños district shortly after its departure from the Mexico City airport, on a scheduled domestic service to Mérida, Yucatán.

The accident was attributed to the foggy weather conditions in which it had occurred, in combination with human error. Specifically, the highly experienced pilot of X-ABAU had proceeded with the flight despite the fact that aircraft were not being authorised to take off due to the poor visibility. During the ground roll, the Electra had deviated to the left of the runway, and after becoming airborne assumed a heading that took it towards the rapidly-rising terrain. There was no evidence of significant technical failure in the aircraft that could have factored in the crash.

Date: 8 December 1938 (c.09:00)
Location: East China Sea
Operator: Nihon Koku Yuso (Japan Aviation Corporation)
Aircraft type: Nakajima A.T.2 (J-BDOH)

Ten persons lost their lives when the twin-engine transport crashed in the region of the Loochoo (Ryukyu) Islands, during a scheduled service from Fukuoka, Japan, to Taihoku (Taipei), on Japanese-occupied Formosa, falling into the ocean after experiencing power plant failure. The victims included the three members of its crew; two passengers survived.

Date: 7 January 1939 (*c.*16:30)
Location: Near Senlis, Ile-de-France, France
Operator: Swissair AG
Aircraft type: Douglas DC-2 (HB-ITA)

Five persons aboard lost their lives, including the entire crew of three, when the airliner crashed some 15 miles (25km) north-east Le Bourget Field, serving Paris, where it was to have landed at the end of a scheduled international service from Zurich, Switzerland. Four passengers survived the accident with various injuries. The DC-2 had slammed to earth while apparently trying to break out of a low overcast during its landing approach, or possibly after a low-altitude stall. There was no fire after impact.

Date: 13 January 1939
Location: Near Rio Bonito, Rio de Janeiro, Brazil
Operator: Syndicato Condor Ltda (Brazil)
Aircraft type: Junkers Ju.52/3mge (PP-CAY)

Operating on a regular domestic service to the city of Rio de Janeiro from Vitoria, Espirito Santo, the trimotored airliner crashed and burned on a mountain approximately 30 miles (50km) east of its destination. All ten persons aboard (five passengers and a crew of five) were killed in the afternoon accident, which occurred in adverse weather conditions, with gale-force winds.

Date: 12 February 1939 (*c.*14:15)
Location: Territory of Alaska, US
Operator: Marine Airways (US)
Aircraft type: Fairchild 71

All six occupants (five passengers and the pilot) were killed when the amphibious aeroplane, which was on an air-taxi service within Alaska, from Ketchikan to Juneau, crashed on Grand Island about 20 miles (30km) southeast of its destination, the accident occurring in adverse meteorological conditions. The wreckage of the Fairchild and the bodies of the victims were found the following month.

Date: 24 February 1939 (*c.*09:45)
Location: Near Beuil, Provence, France
Operator: Deutsche Luft Hansa AG (Germany)
Aircraft type: Junkers Ju.52/3m (D-ALUS)

The trimotored airliner crashed and burned while on a regular service to Berlin, Germany, from Barcelona, Spain, via Rome, Italy. Its wreckage was found about a week later in mountainous terrain some 40 miles (65km) north-north-west of Nice, with no survivors among its ten occupants, including two crew members; the passengers were German service personnel.

Engine trouble may have factored in the accident, which occurred in adverse weather conditions, with fog and falling snow in the area.

Date: 18 March 1939 (*c.*13:30)
Location: Near Adler, Washington, US
Operator: Boeing Airplane Company (US)
Aircraft type: Boeing 307 Stratoliner (NC-19901)

The newly built four-engine airliner crashed about 50 miles (80km) south of Seattle, from where it had taken off about half an hour earlier, and all ten men aboard were killed. As it was undergoing stability testing with two of its four engines having been intentionally shut down, the Stratoliner apparently stalled and went into a spin. The aircraft then broke up at an altitude of between 3,000 and 5,000ft (*c.*1,000–1,500m) during an attempted pull out from the uncontrolled descent.

The Boeing 307, the world's first pressurised airliner, which suffered a fatal accident during a developmental test flight in March 1939. (Boeing)

Date: 26 March 1939 (*c.*02:50)
Location: Near Oklahoma City, Oklahoma, US
Operator: Braniff Airways (US)
Aircraft type: Douglas DC-2 (NC-13727)

Designated as Trip 1 and on a US domestic service originating at Chicago, Illinois, with an ultimate destination of Dallas, Texas, the transport crashed and burned at the Oklahoma City municipal airport, which was one of three en route stops. The accident killed eight persons aboard the DC-2, including the hostess; both pilots and two passengers survived with injuries.

Its port engine had lost power immediately after NC-13727 had taken off, and subsequently failed completely as the crew was attempting to return to the airport. The aircraft had nearly completed an anti-clockwise circle when it slammed to earth after its port wing tip struck the ground, coming to rest on airport property. The crash occurred in pre-dawn darkness, and the local weather conditions at the time consisted of a low overcast, with a ceiling of 700ft (*c.*200m) and a visibility of more than 10 miles (15km) in light rain.

The investigation by the US Air Safety Board revealed that during the left turn, the No.6 cylinder of the malfunctioning power plant was forced out, carrying with it the lower one-third of the engine ring cowl. The corresponding piston was then thrown clear, and shortly afterwards there was a further displacement of the engine cowling, which caused buffeting. This, combined with the severe vibration generated by the windmilling of the port propeller and the necessary rudder and aileron control inputs required to maintain direction, produced excessive drag, causing the aircraft to yaw violently to the left and stall, resulting in a loss of control from which the crew was unable to effect recovery.

Contributing to the crash was the absence on the DC-2 of full-feathering propellers or a similar propeller control mechanism, and the installation of such equipment on multi-engine air carrier aircraft was recommended by the Board. They had in fact already been installed on a number of commercial transports even before completion of the Board's report, and would soon thereafter become a standard safety feature.

Date: 2 May 1939 (*c.*15:30)
Location: Near Taroudant, Morocco
Operator: Compagnie Nationale Air-France
Aircraft type: Dewoitine D.338 (F-ARIC)

All nine persons aboard (six passengers and a crew of three) were killed when the tri-motored airliner crashed and burned on a hillside about 100 miles (150km) south-west of Marrakech. The accident occurred during a scheduled international service from Casablanca, Morocco, to Dakar, Senegal, and after the crew of F-ARIC had reported 'ice' while flying in adverse weather conditions.

Date: 20 July 1939 (*c.*18:50)
Location: Near Konstanz, Baden, Germany
Operator: Swissair AG
Aircraft type: Junkers Ju.86 (HB-IXA)

Operating on a scheduled international service from Vienna, Austria, to Zurich, Switzerland, the twin-engine airliner crashed some 25 miles (40km) north-east of its destination, and in the vicinity of Bodensee (Lake Constance). All six occupants (four passengers and two crew members) were killed.

It was believed that the Ju.86 had experienced a malfunction in its port power plant, and while attempting a forced landing it plunged to earth from an approximate height of 150ft (50m), striking the ground about half a mile (0.8km) from the local airport. The accident apparently resulted from a loss of flying speed during a one-engine operation, and as HB-IXA was making a left turn with its undercarriage extended. The small size of

the airport accounted for the pilot's need to land at a slower speed. However, he must have unintentionally exceeded the stalling velocity of the aircraft at an altitude too low to increase speed by initiating a dive.

Date: 13 August 1939 (*c.*16:35)
Location: Near Rio de Janeiro, Brazil
Operator: Pan American Airways System (US)
Aircraft type: Sikorsky S-43B (NC-16933)

The twin-engine flying boat crashed in Guanabara Bay off the island of Cobres, killing fourteen persons aboard, including its entire crew of four. Two passengers survived the accident with injuries. The bodies of the victims and most of the wreckage would subsequently be retrieved from either the surface or bottom of the bay.

Having nearly completed a scheduled international service that had originated at Miami, Florida, US (though not with the same aircraft), NC-16933 was approaching to land from a south-easterly direction when it suddenly yawed to the left at an approximate height of 150ft (50m), apparently after its port power plant malfunctioned for undetermined reasons. It then began a gradual descending turn in the same direction and stalled just before striking a caisson, whereupon it broke apart and burst into flames. Despite the good weather conditions at the time, with unlimited visibility, the water was described as 'choppy'.

There was evidence that the pilot had tried to land the aircraft to the left of the original flight path, which proved beyond its operating capabilities under the circumstances. Experience by the airline indicated that the S-43 would lose altitude rapidly and yaw towards the inoperative power plant during single-engine flight with the flaps extended. Each main tank on the S-43 had a float valve designed to prevent an air-lock in the fuel lines, although the carrier had initiated a change in the system in order to give pilots more flexibility in selecting the tanks from which gasoline could be utilised. However,

A Pan American Airways System Sikorsky S-43 flying boat, one of which crashed in the bay near Rio de Janeiro, Brazil. (Pan Am)

the revised system had not been incorporated into NC-16933, so the chance of an air-lock should have been greatly reduced by the presence of the float valve.

Date: 15 August 1939 (*c.*13:00)
Location: Near Vordingborg, Denmark
Operator: British Airways Ltd
Aircraft type: Lockheed 10A Electra (G-AESY)

Five persons aboard lost their lives when the twin-engine aircraft was forced to ditch in the channel between the islands of Sjælland and Falster, and about half a mile (0.8km) from the Strorstrøm bridge. Those killed included one crew member; only the pilot survived the accident. The wreckage and the bodies of the victims were recovered.

The Electra had been on a scheduled international service from London to Stockholm, Sweden, when fuel vapour ignited either in its cabin or the space in its port wing, necessitating the forced landing. The blaze was attributed to the leakage of gasoline from the overflow boxes, which in turn must have resulted from the overfilling of its fuel tanks. However, the cause of the ignition of the fuel could not be determined.

Date: 18 December 1939
Location: Strait of Gibraltar
Operator: Concessionaria Líneas Aéreas Subvencionadas SA (Iberia) (Spain)
Aircraft type: Junkers Ju.52/3m (M-CABA)

Operating on a scheduled international service from Sevilla, Spain, to Tetuan, Morocco, the trimotored airliner was shot down by British anti-aircraft fire, falling into the sea approximately 5 miles (10km) south of Europa Point, Gibraltar. There were no survivors among the ten persons aboard the Ju.52 (seven passengers and a crew of three).

Date: 21 December 1939 (*c.*13:00)
Location: Mediterranean Sea
Operator: Imperial Airways (UK)
Aircraft type: Lockheed 14 Super Electra (G-AFYU)

The twin-engine airliner was ditched off the northern coast of Africa and some 300 miles (480km) north-west of Alexandria, Egypt. Among its eleven occupants, a ship rescued six survivors, including the pilot and two other members of its crew; the bodies of the five persons killed (three passengers and two crew members) were not recovered.

Having taken off earlier from Alexandria, G-AFYU had last stopped at As Sallum, also in Egypt, bound for Malta, one segment of a scheduled international service with an ultimate destination of London, and was forced down less than an hour after its last radio transmission, received at 12:20 Egyptian time. Though not specified in available press reports, the reason for the ditching was apparently related to some technical defect or malfunction.

Date: 24 December 1939 (*c.*08:00)
Location: Near Mogador, Morocco
Operator: Linee Aeree Transcontinentali Italiane SA (LATI) (Italy)
Aircraft type: Savoia-Marchetti SM. 83 (I-ARPA)

All seven occupants were killed when the trimotored airliner crashed and burned some 100 miles (150km) west-south-west of Marrakech. The victims included three journalists in addition to the crew.

The transport struck a mountain and burst into flames while attempting a forced landing, apparently due to the adverse meteorological conditions it had encountered while flying from Villa Cisneros, Spanish Sahara, to Seville, Spain, one segment an inaugural airmail service to Rome from Rio de Janeiro, Brazil.

THE SECOND WORLD WAR (1940–1945)

Whereas governments had played a role in the development of commercial aviation in the 1920s and 1930s, warlike governments helped disrupt airline travel, along with virtually everything else, during the first half of the 1940s. Some services were able to continue, particularly those in the US and the Americas, and even Air France was able to conduct limited operations, despite the occupation of its home country by Nazi Germany, by moving the centre of its operations to another continent.

Occasionally during this period, air travel was not only disrupted, but became the direct target of hostilities. A number of airline crashes recounted in this chapter were not accidents, but involved hostile action. The most famous of these incidents, and which involved a famous personality, involved the downing of a British airliner by German warplanes in 1943.

Despite the threats, air travel would continue to thrive during this period, with the airline industry actually playing an important role in aiding the war effort. This was particularly true in the US, where commercial airliners and their crews saw wide use in supplementing military forces in the transport of personnel.

The most recognisable aircraft during this time was the Douglas DC-3, which had been developed during the 1930s and would at one time or another be used by virtually every major airline during and long past the end of the war, with many of the transports becoming available after their use by military forces.

Information on crashes during this time would be greatly affected by wartime censorship. This and the disruption of commercial aviation by the worldwide conflict account for the fact that most of the incidents described here in considerable detail involved US and UK operators.

Date: 10 February 1940
Location: Near Cosenza, Calabria, Italy
Operator: Ala Littoria SA (Italy)
Aircraft type: Savoia-Marchetti SM.75 (I-LEAL)

Operating on a scheduled domestic service from Brindisi to Rome, the trimotored airliner crashed and burned on a hillside, and all ten persons aboard (four passengers and a crew of six) were killed. The accident occurred in adverse weather conditions, with fog and a low overcast, and after the crew had reported an accretion of ice on the aircraft's wings.

Date: 27 February 1940 (*c.*10:00)
Location: Near Bucaramanga, Santander, Colombia
Operator: Sociedad Colombo-Alemana de Transportes Aéreos (SCADTA) (Colombia)
Aircraft type: Boeing 247D (C-79)

The Handley Page H.P. 42E, serial number G-AAGX, was the aircraft operated by Imperial Airways that vanished over the Gulf of Oman. (Philip Jarrett)

The aircraft crashed in the Andes during a scheduled domestic service from Bogotá to Cucuta, in Norte de Santander, killing all eleven persons aboard (nine passengers and two pilots). It was believed that the crew had lost their bearings after encountering an area of heavy fog, and subsequently C-79 struck a mountain and burst into flames.

Date: 1 March 1940 (*c.*13:20)
Location: Gulf of Oman
Operator: Imperial Airways (UK)
Aircraft type: Handley Page H.P. 42E (G-AAGX)

Operating on the service CW197 and en route from Jiwani, Pakistan, to Sharjah, Trucial States (United Arab Emirates), the four-engine airliner vanished with eight persons aboard (four passengers and a crew of four). Search for G-AAGX was abandoned a week later.

The Handley Page apparently went down some 35 miles (55km) east of Dibah, Muscat and Oman, and may have plummeted into the sea or crashed during an attempted forced landing atop the water, in either case with the wreckage sinking without a trace. The visibility and overall weather conditions in the area at the time must have been good. There were no indications of trouble in their last routine wireless transmission, although what may have been a 'partial' SOS message that was received may have been sent by the crew.

No evidence has ever come to light that could help in determining the reason for the loss of G-AAGX. The UK Air Ministry considered as improbable that the crash had resulted from sabotage, hostile action or in-flight fire. Also considered improbable was complete fuel exhaustion, although the starvation of the supply of gasoline attributed to improper activation of the corresponding controls could not be ruled out. Other possible causes were a bird strike damaging a propeller and leading to the failure of the engine mounting or even an entire wing; some type of structural failure, especially considering the age of aircraft and the history of vibration experienced with the type, or multiple power plant malfunction, which also could have preceded structural failure.

Two months after the disappearance, and in following one of the recommendations made in the investigative report, it was announced by the British government that the H.P. 42 would no longer be used in passenger operations. It was also recommended that commercial aircraft used in long over-water flights be equipped with personal and group life-saving gear, which would later be standard throughout the industry.

Date: 16 March 1940
Location: Near San Vicenzo, Italy
Operator: Ala Littoria, SA (Italy)
Aircraft type: Savoia-Marchetti SM.73 (I-SUTO)

The trimotored airliner crashed on Stromboli, a volcanic island in the Lipari group, during a scheduled international flight that had originated at Tripoli, Libya, and last stopped at Catania, on Sicily, with an ultimate destination of Milan, Italy. All fourteen persons aboard (ten passengers and a crew of four) were killed in the accident, which occurred in evening darkness and stormy weather conditions.

Date: 14 June 1940 (*c.*15:00)
Location: Gulf of Finland
Operator: Aero O/Y (Finland)
Aircraft type: Junkers Ju.52/3m (OH-ALL)

The trimotored airliner was shot down by two Soviet military aircraft some 25 miles (40km) north-north-east of Tallinn, Estonia, from where it had taken off earlier, on a scheduled international service to Helsinki, Finland. All nine persons aboard the Ju.52 (seven passengers and two crew members) were killed in the incident, which occurred at the beginning of a Soviet military blockade on Estonia, and two days before the former province of Imperial Russia was invaded by military forces of the USSR.

Date: 23 August 1940
Location: Near Cluj, Transylvania, Romania
Operator: Liniile Aeriene Române Exploatate cu Statul (LARES) (Romania)
Aircraft type: Douglas DC-3 (YR-PIF)

The aircraft crashed approximately 200 miles (320km) north-west of Bucharest, from where it had taken off earlier, on a scheduled international service to Vienna, Austria. All fifteen persons aboard (twelve passengers and a crew of three) were killed in the accident, which occurred during a thunderstorm.

Date: 31 August 1940 (*c.*14:40)
Location: Near Lovettsville, Virginia, US
Operator: Pennsylvania Central Airlines (US)
Aircraft type: Douglas DC-3A (NC-21789)

Designated as Trip 19 and on a US domestic service to Pittsburgh, Pennsylvania, the transport crashed some 35 miles (55km) north-west of Washington, DC, from where it had taken off earlier. All twenty-five persons aboard perished, including a crew of three; among the passengers was US Senator Ernest Lundeen, who represented the state of Minnesota, and the recently-hired secretary to the airline's district traffic manager, the latter of whom was riding in the cockpit jump-seat.

The DC-3 had reportedly been cruising at a height of 6,000ft (*c.*1,800m) before it plunged into farmland, descending in a nearly wings-level attitude at an estimated angle of 30 degrees and hitting the ground at a speed of around 300mph (480kmh), then disintegrated and burst into flames. Flying through a thunderstorm, NC-21789 had just entered an area of rain described as 'exceptionally heavy,' and witnesses reported an extremely violent stroke of lightning seconds before the crash.

By examining the known facts, the US Civil Aeronautics Board (CAB) concluded that the observed lightning, though not actually striking it, could have damaged the aircraft and/or temporarily disabled the two pilots, resulting in a loss of control. Had the cockpit windows been smashed, the crew would have been subjected to flying glass and torrents of water. Or they could have suffered from acoustical shock, concussion or the impairment of vision. Additionally, the jump-seat occupant could have been thrown forward, hampering the ability of the pilots to regain control. There was no evidence that turbulence alone had caused the crash, nor of any pre-impact mechanical or structural failure in NC-21789. The Board regarded this as an 'extremely unusual occurrence,' and indeed, such an accident has not been repeated since in the operations of the US airline industry.

In its report, the CAB report recommended continued research into the effects on aircraft of both lightning and turbulence and the exploration of ways to improve the dissemination of hazardous weather information to pilots. Much progress has been made in these areas over a period of years and decades, but thunderstorms still remain a threat to commercial aviation, even in modern times.

Date: 29 October 1940
Location: Near Changyi, Yunnan, China
Operator: China National Aviation Corporation
Aircraft type: Douglas DC-2 (39)

Operating on a scheduled domestic service from Chungking to Kunming, the transport was attacked by Japanese military aircraft, then strafed on the ground after making a crash-landing some 75 miles (120km) north-east of its destination. Nine persons aboard the DC-2 were killed, while three passengers, the co-pilot and one other crew member survived.

Date: 4 November 1940 (c.04:40)
Location: Near Centerville, Utah, US
Operator: United Air Lines (US)
Aircraft type: Douglas DC-3A (NC-16086)

Designated as Trip 16, the transport crashed about 10 miles (15km) north-east of Salt Lake City, where it was to have landed at the end of a US domestic service from Oakland, California, and all ten persons aboard (seven passengers and a crew of three) were killed.

The DC-3 was in level flight and on a south-easterly heading when it struck Bountiful Peak, in the Wasatch mountain range, the accident occurring in pre-dawn darkness and adverse meteorological conditions, with a low overcast and possible snow flurries.

It was determined by the US Civil Aeronautics Board (CAB) that the radio range being used by the United crew in the let-down procedure had not been functioning normally at the time, with the north leg of the airway having been displaced to the east of the published course. Contributing to the crash was the failure of the pilot to follow the established radio range technique. Specifically, NC-16086 had probably begun descending while on a north-westerly heading east of the normal position for such a procedure before assuming the reciprocal track. This was done despite the fact that the pilot had apparently not located the north leg of the radio range, having previously proceeded towards the station and into the 'twilight' area without definitely locating the west leg. That he continued for approximately 3 minutes directly towards the high terrain while 'searching' for the north leg indicated his trust in the proper operation of the ground facilities. There had been no notification regarding the malfunction of the radio range due to improper procedures by communications operators on the ground, although static had partially affected their ability to carry out their monitoring duties. Wet snow had probably caused the misalignment of the radio range.

Recommendations in the CAB report included the implementation of ultra-high frequency radio ranges and possible changes of regulations then in effect or the introduction of new ones with regard to instrument flight. The development after the Second World War of very-high-frequency omnidirectional range (VOR) systems, which are less sensitive to atmospheric interference and aberrations, would help prevent these types of accidents.

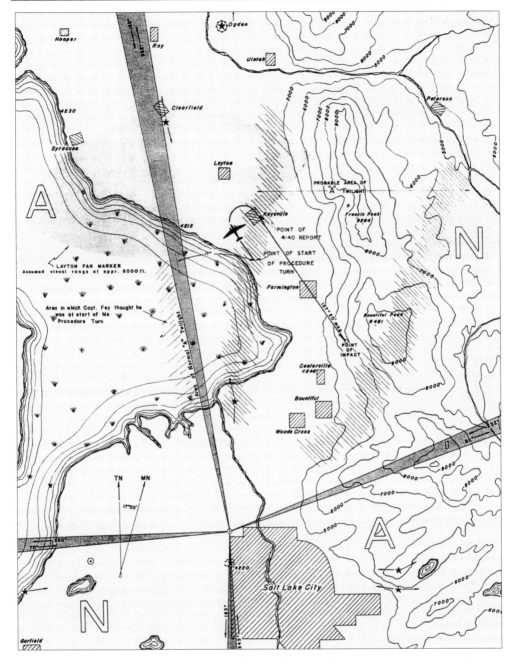

Chart showing displaced flight track of the United Air Lines Douglas DC-3, leading to its crash in the Wasatch Mountains of Utah. (Civil Aeronautics Board)

Date: 4 November 1940
Location: Near Rincón, Santa Cruz, Bolivia
Operator: Lloyd Aéreo Boliviano SA
Aircraft type: Junkers Ju.52/3mce (CB-17)

All seventeen persons aboard were killed when the airliner crashed during a storm some 250 miles (400km) east of the city of Santa Cruz, from where it had taken off earlier, on a scheduled international service to Corumba, Brazil. The wreckage of CB-17 and the remains of the victims were found 15 months later.

Prior to the accident, the Ju.52 had apparently altered its course in order to land somewhere other than at its intended destination, possibly due to the weather.

Date: 8 November 1940
Location: Near Kamenz, Brandenburg, Germany
Operator: Deutsche Luft Hansa AG (Germany)
Aircraft type: Junkers Ju.90A-1 (D-AVMF)

The four-engine airliner crashed some 25 miles (40km) north-east of Dresden during a scheduled international service from Berlin, Germany, to Budapest, Hungary. All twenty-nine persons aboard (twenty-three passengers and a crew of six) were killed in the accident, which apparently resulted from icing of the tail plane.

Date: 8 November 1940
Location: Near Rio de Janeiro, Brazil
First aircraft:
Operator: Viação Aérea São Paulo SA (VASP) (Brazil)
Type: Junkers Ju.52/3mg3e (PP-SPF)
Second aircraft:
Operator: Shell-Mex Argentina Ltda
Type: de Havilland 84 Dragon (LN-KAB)

Operating on a scheduled domestic service to São Paulo, the trimotored airliner had just taken off from Santos Dumont Airport, serving Rio de Janeiro, when it collided with the smaller twin-engine aeroplane in cloudy weather conditions and at an approximate altitude of 1,500ft (500m), and both then crashed, the former in Botafogo Bay. Killed in the accident were all eighteen persons aboard the Ju.52 (fourteen passengers and four crew members), as was the pilot (and sole occupant) of the Dragon.

Date: 4 December 1940 (c.17:50)
Location: Blue Island, Illinois, US
Operator: United Air Lines (US)
Aircraft type: Douglas DC-3A (NC-25678)

Ten persons lost their lives when the transport crashed in close proximity to Chicago Municipal Airport, where it was scheduled to land. Those killed included the aircraft's three crew members; six passengers survived with various injuries.

Designated as Trip 21 and on a US domestic service from New York, New York, NC-25678 had been on its final approach to the north-west runway, with its undercarriage down and flaps extended, when it apparently stalled at an approximate height of 150ft (50m), falling into an incipient spin after its port wing dropped. Power was increased and then retarded in an apparent attempt to minimise the crash just before the DC-3 struck the roof of one house, then slammed into the back yard of another residence in a nose-down, nearly vertical attitude. Small fires that erupted in and around the wreckage were quickly extinguished. The accident occurred in darkness and instrument weather conditions, with a ceiling of around 1,000ft (300m), scattered clouds at about 500ft (150m) and a visibility of less than 1 mile (1.5km) in light fog and light snow. Additionally, mist or wet snow on the windscreen of the aircraft would have further reduced the crew's visibility.

It was ruled by US Civil Aeronautics Board (CAB) that the pilot did not exercise 'a degree of caution' to avert the stall, by failing to maintain adequate flying speed. Contributing to the crash was the accumulation of ice on the leading edge of the aircraft's wings, which would have effectively raised the stalling speed of the transport, in combination with the decision of the pilot to land on a relatively short runway.

Recommendations made in the CAB report included the development of a stall-warning device, systems to prevent icing in and on the pitot tubes that could lead to erroneous instrument indications, and aircraft windscreen wipers, all of which would become standard equipment on aeroplanes. Also recommended was the availability of auxiliary power units for airports, as in this case the crashing aircraft had severed power lines, causing a disruption in lighting and communications facilities.

Date: 10 January 1941
Location: Mediterranean Sea
Operator: Linee Aeree Transcontinentali Italiane SA (LATI) (Italy)
Aircraft type: Savoia-Marchetti SM.83 (I-AREM)

All sixteen persons aboard (twelve passengers and a crew of four) lost their lives when the trimotored airliner crashed at sea during a scheduled international service.

Date: 15 January 1941 (c.16:00)
Location: Atlantic Ocean
Operator: Linee Aeree Transcontinentali Italiane SA (LATI) (Italy)
Aircraft type: Savoia-Marchetti SM.75 (I-BAYR)

The airliner, carrying ten persons, was lost near the Equator approximately 600 miles (965km) north-north-east of Natal, Brazil, from where it had taken off earlier, on a scheduled international service to Italy via the (Portuguese) Cape Verde Islands. In addition to the crew of four, all but two of the passengers were employees of the carrier. Prior to the disappearance of I-BAYR, the crew had reported the failure of one of its three engines, and about an hour after that message radi-

oed that the aircraft was turning back. About three hours later, the crew transmitted an SOS distress message, after which the SM.75 was never heard from again.

Date: 17 January 1941
Location: Near Nagyvarad, Hungary
Operator: Magyar Legiforgalmi Rt. (MALERT) (Hungary)
Aircraft type: Junkers Ju.52/3m (HA-JUA)

The trimotored airliner crashed and burned some 150 miles (250km) south-east of Budapest, from where it had taken off earlier, on a scheduled domestic service to Maros-Vasarhely. Killed in the accident were twelve persons aboard the Ju.52, including the three members of its crew; four passengers survived with injuries.

Date: 6 February 1941 (c.03:50)
Location: Near Armstrong, Ontario, Canada
Operator: Trans-Canada Air Lines
Aircraft type: Lockheed 14-08 Super Electra (CF-TCP)

Designated as Flight 3, the twin-engine aircraft crashed some 200 miles (320km) north of Thunder Bay while approaching to land at Armstrong Airport, which was an en route stop during a domestic service from Toronto, Ontario, to Winnipeg, Manitoba. All twelve persons aboard (nine passengers and a crew of three) were killed.

The accident occurred in pre-dawn darkness and adverse meteorological conditions, with an overcast at around 1,000ft (300m) and a visibility of approximately 1.5 miles (2.5km) in light snowfall, but its cause could not be determined despite 'exhaustive' independent inquiries by both the airline and Canadian government authorities.

Date: 26 February 1941 (c.23:50)
Location: Near Atlanta, Georgia, US
Operator: Eastern Air Lines (US)
Aircraft type: Douglas DST (DC-3) (NC-28394)

Operating as Trip 21 and on a US domestic service originating at New York, New York, with an ultimate destination of Brownsville, Texas, the transport crashed approximately 7 miles (11km) south-east of Candler Field, serving Atlanta, where it was scheduled to land. Eight persons aboard lost their lives in the accident, including the three members of the crew; among the eight surviving passengers, all of whom were injured, was Eddie Rickenbacker, a flying ace of the First World War and who at the time was the president of the airline.

The DST had struck treetops and then slammed into a pine grove, the accident occurring in darkness and instrument weather conditions that at the airport consisted of low clouds, with a ceiling of only 200 to 500ft (c.60–150m), and a visibility of 1 mile (c.1.5km) in fog and light rain. Its wreckage was not located until the following morning. It was concluded by the US Civil Aeronautics Board (CAB) that the captain had apparently failed to cross-check the aircraft's altimeters, one of which may have been incorrectly set, before commencing an instrument approach. Also, Eastern Air Lines was criticised for the absence of an established uniform cockpit procedure by which the flight crew would be required to make a complete check of the controls and instruments during landing operations. Some months later, and at the recommendation of the CAB, the US Civil Aeronautics Administration (CAA) initiated an informal investigation of the carrier's operating procedures.

Date: 28 March 1941 (c.11:45)
Location: Near Elands Bay, South Africa
Operator: South African Airways
Aircraft type: Lockheed 18 Lodestar (ZS-AST)

The twin-engine transport crashed on a mountain approximately 100 miles (150km) north of Cape Town during a scheduled domestic service, and all ten persons aboard (six passengers and a crew of four) were killed.

Date: 3 June 1941 (c.17:00)
Location: North Atlantic Ocean
Operator: Great Western and Southern Air Lines (UK)
Aircraft type: de Havilland 84 Dragon II (G-ACPY)

The twin-engine aeroplane vanished during a scheduled service from the Isles of Scilly to Penzance, Cornwall, with six persons aboard (five passengers and the pilot). It was believed that G-ACPY had been shot down by a German military aircraft less than 20 minutes after take-off.

Date: 18 June 1941
Location: Near Bucharest, Romania
Operator: Liniile Aeriene Române Exploatate cu Statul (LARES) (Romania)
Aircraft type: Douglas DC-3 (YR-PIF)

The transport crashed and burned shortly after taking off from the Bucharest airport, on a scheduled international service to Sofia, Bulgaria, and all fifteen persons aboard were killed.

Date: 21 June 1941
Location: Sea of Japan
Operator: Manskya Koku Kabushiki Kaisha (Manchurian Air Transport Co) (Manchukuo)
Aircraft type: Mitsubishi MC-20 (M-604)

The twin-engine airliner crashed, presumably during a scheduled service between Japan and Japanese-occupied China, and all eighteen persons aboard were killed.

Date: 1 September 1941 (c.13:40)
Location: Near Marseille, Provence, France
Operator: Air France
Aircraft type: Bloch 220 (F-AQNL)

The twin-engine airliner crashed in the Etang de Bolmon lagoon shortly after taking off from Marignane Airport, serving Marseille, on a scheduled domestic service to Toulouse. Killed in the accident were fourteen persons aboard the transport, including the three members of its crew; two passengers survived with injuries.

Following the failure of its port power plant, F-AQNL was attempting to return to the airport, but during a left bank it lost height. One wing then struck the surface of the lagoon, after which the aircraft slammed into the water. The wind at the time was blowing at a speed of around 25mph (40kmh).

Date: 28 October 1941
Location: Near Petrich, Bulgaria
Operator: Deutsche Lufthansa AG (Germany)
Aircraft type: Junkers Ju.52 (D-AUXZ)

All thirteen persons aboard were killed, including a probable crew of three, when the trimotored airliner crashed in the vicinity of the Hungarian/Greek border.

Date: 30 October 1941 (c.02:05)
Location: Near Moorhead, Minnesota, US
Operator: Northwest Airlines (US)
Aircraft type: Douglas DC-3A (NC-21712)

Operating as Trip 5 and on a US domestic service originating at Chicago, Illinois, with an ultimate destination of Seattle, Washington, the transport crashed approximately 5 miles (10km) east of Fargo, North Dakota, which was a scheduled en route stop. All but one of the fifteen persons aboard were killed in the accident, including two members of its crew; the injured survivor was the captain, who had apparently been ejected from the cockpit on impact. The crash occurred in pre-dawn darkness and during a low overcast.

In a subsequent testimony, the pilot said he had just levelled off after descending to a height of around 600ft (180m) in an unsuccessful attempt to break out of the cloud base, in preparation for landing, when the aircraft 'began to act peculiarly'. Full power was applied and its undercarriage retracted, but the DC-3 started to shake and then descended until striking the ground in an area of flat terrain with its tail wheel and propeller tips. It

then jumped over a small ravine, slammed into a bank and burst into flames.

Blamed for the crash was the failure of the aircraft to respond to full power while in a stalled condition. Considered as contributing factors were the accumulation of ice on its wings and other surfaces, which increased drag and raised its stalling speed; the failure of the captain, who had lost confidence in his air speed indicators, to realise that NC-21712 was nearly in a stalled condition; faulty judgement on his part in even attempting a landing at Fargo in known icing and adverse meteorological conditions; and the failure of the airline's dispatcher to recognise the seriousness of the weather situation and direct the pilot to his alternate destination.

Flight tests conducted in the wake of this accident revealed a flight characteristic of the DC-3 that had not been previously known, and the US Civil Aeronautics Board (CAB) subsequently circulated information throughout the industry with respect to the effects of the application of full power under certain conditions. Also, the Board recognised the potential dangers of letting down in adverse weather conditions in an attempt to make visual contact with the ground (i.e. to 'take a look'), and considered a regulation prohibiting this procedure.

Date: 30 October 1941 (c.22:10)
Location: Near Saint Thomas, Ontario, Canada
Operator: American Airlines (US)
Aircraft type: Douglas DC-3 (NC-25663)

Ending what was at the time the deadliest day in the history of American commercial aviation was the crash of Flight 1, which occurred on foreign soil some 110 miles (175km) southeast of Toronto but during a US domestic service originating at New York, New York, with an ultimate destination of Chicago, Illinois. All twenty persons aboard the aircraft (seventeen passengers and a crew of three) perished in the accident.

The DC-3 had been en route from Buffalo, New York, to Detroit, Michigan, one

An American Airlines Douglas DC-3 was one of two aircraft of the same type involved in major accidents during a single day in October 1941. (American Airlines)

segment of the flight, and according to witnesses was proceeding on its normal course and apparently at its last reported cruising height of 4,000ft (c.1,200m) when it suddenly commenced a descending right turn. Recovering from the spiral at a low altitude after about four circles, it was then seen to climb to an approximate height of 200 to 500ft (60–150m) before it apparently stalled and plunged to earth in a steep attitude, bursting into flames on impact. The accident occurred in darkness and during a drizzle, but the weather conditions were not considered to have been a factor.

In its investigation, the US Civil Aeronautics Board (CAB) found no evidence of sabotage, incapacitation of the flight crew, or preimpact fire or technical failure, although the latter could not be completely ruled out. And despite the indications that the aircraft was partially out of control during the descent, the Board was unable to determine the cause of the crash.

Date: 16 January 1942 (c.19:20)
Location: Near Arden, Nevada, US
Operator: Transcontinental and Western Air, Inc. (TWA) (US)
Aircraft type: Douglas DC-3 (NC-1946)

Designated as Flight 3, the airliner crashed in the Spring Mountains some 25 miles (40km) south-west of Las Vegas and about 15 minutes after it had taken off from the city's airport, bound for Los Angeles, California, the final segment of a transcontinental US domestic service that had originated at New York, New York. All twenty-two persons aboard perished, including the three members of its crew; among the passengers were American motion picture actress Carole Lombard, her mother and her press agent.

The DC-3 had been around 7 miles (11km) north of the centreline of the prescribed radio range course when it struck a nearly vertical cliff on Potosi Mountain, less than 100ft (30m) below its peak and at an approximate elevation of 8,000ft (2,500m), bursting into flames on impact. It was dark at the time of the accident, although the meteorological conditions in the area were good, with ceiling and visibility unlimited.

It was concluded by the US Civil Aeronautics Board (CAB) that the captain had apparently not used the available ground navigational facilities, leading to the deviation from the proper course. Considered as contributing factors were the use of an erroneous compass heading; a blackout of most beacons in the area of the accident made necessary by the entry by the US only a month earlier into the Second World War; and the failure of the crew to comply with the airline's directive, issued the previous July, in which its pilots were to confine their flight movements to the on-course signals of the airway being used. With regard to the compass heading, the CAB report noted that the flight plan, which included an inaccurate true course of 234 degrees, had apparently been prepared by the first officer, who had considerably more experience flying out of Boulder City, Nevada, rather than Las Vegas, the latter of which had been an unplanned refuelling stop during this trip. As a result, he may have based his calculations on the outbound course from the former rather than the latter.

The accident revealed the need for more precise and specific procedures and regulatory standards with regard to night contact flight, and among the recommendations made in the CAB report was the inclusion in air carrier operating manuals of such procedures at each airport in order to assure an adequate safety margin during climb-outs and let-downs.

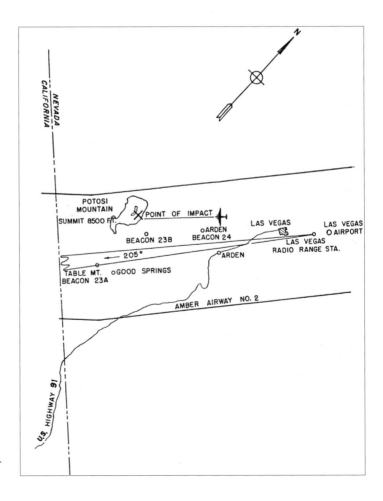

Chart indicates northerly deviation from the radio range course, resulting in crash of the Transcontinental and Western Air Douglas DC-3. (Civil Aeronautics Board)

Date: 30 January 1942 (*c*.08:00)
Location: South Pacific Ocean
Operator: Qantas Empire Airways (Australia)
Aircraft type: Short S.23 'Empire' (G-AEUH)

Operated by Qantas on behalf of the British carrier Imperial Airways and on a service from Darwin, Australia, to Surabaya, Dutch East Indies (Indonesia), the four-engine flying boat was attacked and shot down by a group of Japanese Zero fighters, crashing approximately 3 miles (5km) off the Portuguese island of Timor. Among the eighteen persons aboard the S.23, five survivors were rescued from the sea, including two members of its crew of five.

Date: 15 February 1942 (*c*.08:50)
Location: Near Plymouth, Devon, England
Operator: British Overseas Airways Corporation (BOAC)
Aircraft type: Consolidated Liberator CI (G-AGDR)

All nine persons aboard were killed when the four-engine transport, bound for England from Cairo, Egypt, was inadvertently shot down by two Royal Air Force Spitfire fighters, falling into the English Channel approximately 5 miles (8km) south-west of Eddystone Lighthouse. The victims included a BOAC crew; the passengers consisted of both civilians and military personnel.

The fighters that attacked G-AGDR were being flown by Polish pilots who failed to identify it as a friendly aircraft. Considered as a contributing factor was the failure of higher level personnel to exercise proper and effective control over pilots under their command.

Date: 20 February 1942
Location: Near Brisbane, Queensland, Australia
Operator: Qantas Empire Airways (Australia)
Aircraft type: de Havilland 86 (VH-USE)

The four-engine aircraft crashed into a hillside shortly after taking off from Archerfield Airfield, serving Brisbane, on a scheduled domestic service to Darwin, Northern Territory. All nine persons aboard (seven passengers and two crew members) were killed. It was believed that VH-USE had suffered structural failure while flying in darkness and adverse weather conditions, with rain and a low overcast.

Date: 28 February 1942
Location: Indian Ocean
Operator: Qantas Empire Airways (Australia)
Aircraft type: Short S.23 'Empire' (G-AETZ)

The second loss of a flying boat on a Far Eastern route in less than a month involved an aircraft being operated by Qantas on behalf of British Overseas Airways Corporation (BOAC). This one vanished some 150 miles (250km) from Java, in the Dutch East Indies, from where it had taken off earlier, on a scheduled service to Broome, Western Australia, with twenty persons aboard (sixteen passengers and four crew members). It was believed that G-AETZ had been shot down by Japanese military aircraft.

Date: 14 March 1942 (*c*.21:30)
Location: Near Kunming, Yunnan, China
Operator: China National Aviation Corporation
Aircraft type: Douglas DC-2 (31)

The airliner crashed shortly after its departure from the Kunming airfield, on a scheduled domestic service to Chungking, Sichuan, and thirteen persons aboard were killed, including the three members of its crew. Four passengers survived the accident, which occurred in darkness. Factors cited as causing the crash were engine trouble, combined with the overloading of the DC-2 and the soft, wet ground from which the aircraft had taken off.

Date: 21 April 1942 (*c*.21:30)
Location: Near Annaburoo Station, Northern Territory, Australia
Operator: Guinea Airways (Australia)
Aircraft type: Lockheed 14 Super Electra (VH-ADY)

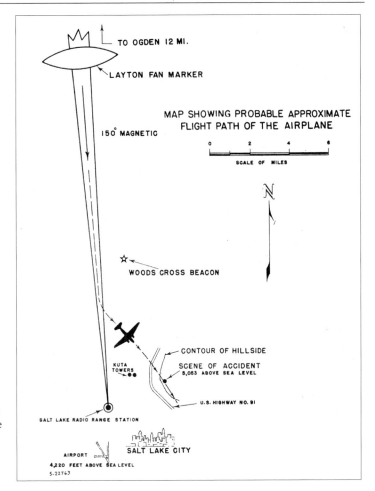

TO OGDEN 12 MI.

LAYTON FAN MARKER

MAP SHOWING PROBABLE APPROXIMATE
FLIGHT PATH OF THE AIRPLANE

150° MAGNETIC

0   2   4   6

SCALE OF MILES

N

WOODS CROSS BEACON

CONTOUR OF HILLSIDE

KUTA
TOWERS

SCENE OF ACCIDENT
5,063 ABOVE SEA LEVEL

U.S. HIGHWAY NO. 91

SALT LAKE RADIO RANGE STATION

AIRPORT

SALT LAKE CITY

4,220 FEET ABOVE SEA LEVEL

5-22763

Chart shows deviation from the correct flight path of the United Air Lines Douglas DST, leading to its impact with the terrain. (Civil Aeronautics Board)

Operating under US military contract and on an internal Australian service to Darwin from Brisbane, Queensland, via Daly Waters and Batchelor, Northern Territory, the twin-engine transport crashed some 60 miles (100km) south-east of its ultimate destination, and its wreckage was found two months later. All twelve persons aboard VH-ADY were killed in the accident, including two civilian crew members; the passengers were American and Australian service personnel. The aircraft slammed into a hill and burned after its pilots apparently became uncertain of their position while trying to find a place to land in the darkness and poor visibility, and while practically out of fuel, after straying considerably off the intended track.

Date: 1 May 1942 (*c*.23:00)
Location: Near Salt Lake City, Utah, US
Operator: United Air Lines (US)
Aircraft type: Douglas DST-A (DC-3) (NC-18146)

Designated as Trip 4 and on a transcontinental US domestic service originating at San Francisco, California, with an ultimate destination of New York, New York, the aircraft crashed and burned on a hill approximately 4 miles (6.5km) north-east of the Salt Lake City municipal airport, where it was scheduled to land. All seventeen persons aboard (fourteen passengers and three crew members) were killed.

The DC-3 had been flying in a south-easterly direction when its propellers and extended undercarriage struck the ground at an approximate elevation of 5,000ft (1,500m), and the aircraft then 'ricocheted' across a gully, coming to rest some 300ft (100m) beyond the point of initial impact. It was dark at the time of the accident, and the airport weather consisted of a low ceiling, with a solid overcast at 2,000ft (c.600m) and broken clouds down to 1,200ft (c.350m), a visibility of 8 miles (c.13km) and light to moderate rain.

Proceeding on the north leg of the radio range course on a magnetic heading of 150 degrees, NC-18146 began to deviate to the left of the proper route, for reasons that could not be determined, after switching to contact flight procedures within 10 miles (c.15km) of the airport. There was no evidence of mechanical failure in the aircraft, and the available navigational aids were functioning properly at the time of the crash.

The US Civil Aeronautics Board (CAB) investigation of the accident brought to light the need for more precise and specific operational procedures at airports surrounded by hazardous terrain. It was recommended by the CAB that such procedures be established administratively for arriving and departing aircraft operating under night-time contact flight, as they already existed for instrument operations, especially in cases where an approach began under instruments and the pilot then continued visually.

Date: 19 May 1942
Location: Near Rome, Italy
Operator: Linee Aeree Transcontinentali Italiane SA (LATI) (Italy)
Aircraft type: Savoia-Marchetti SM. 75 (I-MELE)

All twenty persons aboard were killed when the trimotored airliner struck trees, then crashed and burned, the accident occurring immediately after it had taken off from the Rome airport, on a scheduled international service to Tripoli, Libya.

Date: 22 August 1942 (c.13:00)
Location: Trinidad
Operator: KLM West-Indisch Bedrijf (the Netherlands)
Aircraft type: Lockheed 14-WF62 Super Electra (PJ-AIP)

The twin-engine transport crashed and burned in a tropical forest about 10 minutes after it had taken off from Piarco Airport, serving Port of Spain, which was an en route stop during a scheduled international service from Willemstad, in Curaçao, to Paramaribo, Dutch Guyana (Suriname). All thirteen persons aboard (ten passengers and a crew of three) were killed.

It was believed that the accident resulted from an encounter with severe, thunderstorm-related turbulence and/or a lightning strike, leading to an uncontrolled descent.

Date: 14 September 1942
Location: Off Western Africa
Operator: British Overseas Airways Corporation (BOAC)
Aircraft type: Short S.30 'Empire' (G-AFCZ)

The four-engine flying boat, carrying eighteen persons (thirteen passengers and a crew of five), crashed in the North Atlantic Ocean during an international service originating at Lagos, Colony and Protectorate of Nigeria, with an ultimate destination of Poole, England. There were no survivors, although the bodies of all but six of the victims were eventually found.

It was believed that G-AFCZ had experienced a catastrophic in-flight fire, possibly related to the design of its fuel-intake system, approximately 90 minutes after its departure from Bathurst, Gambia, bound for Lisbon, Portugal, one segment of the trip.

Date: 27 September 1942
Location: Near Ahmar el Ain, Algeria
Operator: Air France
Aircraft type: Dewoitine D.342 (F-ARIZ)

F-ARIZ was the Dewoitine D.342 operated by Air France that crashed in Algeria after experiencing in-flight structural failure. (Philip Jarrett)

Operating on a scheduled international service from Marseille, France, to Dakar, French West Africa (Senegal), the trimotored airliner crashed and burned some 40 miles (65km) south of Algiers, where it had last stopped, and after the in-flight failure of a wing. All twenty-five persons aboard (twenty-one passengers and a crew of four) were killed.

Date: 28 September 1942 (*c*.09:00)
Location: Near São Paulo, Brazil
Operator: Panair do Brasil SA (Brazil)
Aircraft type: Lockheed 18 Lodestar (PP-PBG)

All fifteen persons aboard (eleven passengers and four crew members) were killed in the crash of the twin-engine aircraft. The Lodestar had been on a scheduled domestic service to São Paulo from Rio de Janeiro but was diverted by bad weather to Santos, in the state of São Paulo. It then proceeded on towards its original destination, but while preparing to land there it slammed into a mountain approximately 5 miles (10km) to the southeast of the state capital, the accident occurring in adverse meteorological conditions.

Date: 3 October 1942 (*c*.19:00)
Location: Near Botwood, Newfoundland
Operator: American Export Airlines (US)
Aircraft type: Vought-Sikorsky VS-44A (NC-41880)

Designated as Trip 71 and on a transatlantic service from New York City to Foynes, Ireland, carrying as passengers American service personnel, the four-engine flying boat crashed in the Bay of Exploits after a scheduled refuelling stop at Botwood, and while taking off for Gander Bay, also in Newfoundland, where an unscheduled stop would be made. Killed in the accident were eleven of the thirty-seven persons aboard the aircraft, including five members of its crew of eleven. Except for one crew member who escaped unscathed, the survivors suffered various injuries; their rescue was carried out by a launch.

Having commenced its departure towards the north, NC-41880 began to porpoise during its take-off run, becoming airborne and ascending to an approximate height of 10ft (3m) before it settled back on to the surface of the bay with a light skip. It then became airborne again, but in a nose-high attitude, and after levelling off at around 30ft (10m) it descended into the water, crashing at an angle estimated at between 15 and 45 degrees about 1 mile (1.5km) north of Killick Island. The accident occurred in twilight, but the local weather, which was not considered a contributing factor, consisted of unlimited ceiling and visibility conditions; the wind was from the north at no more than 5mph (10kmh) and the sea calm, with only light ripples.

Demolished in the impact, the forward section of the aircraft, from the bow to the pilots' compartment, sank in water some 40ft (12m) deep while being towed and was lost, as was the empennage, which got severed during salvage operations. Examination of the wreckage that was recovered revealed that the flaps were fully deflected to 35 degrees, which did not correspond to the proper take-off setting. The exact manner in which the flaps were extended could not be determined by the US Civil Aeronautics Board (CAB). Due to their design, they could not have been moved by any means other than the electric motor that was activated from the cockpit. And the possibility of a short-circuit was considered 'very remote' by the CAB. Nor was there evidence of any other technical failure in the flying boat that could have factored in the crash.

Although the captain apparently intended not to use any flaps during the departure, the navigator later testified that he had seen the flap units being lowered during the start of the take-off run. Based on his testimony, it was also apparent the first officer was not sufficiently familiar with the flap control switch, actually a knob. Significant to the accident sequence was the fact that the captain had given the 'stand by for take off' order before the first officer entered the cockpit and sat down. As a result, the latter had time to only complete part of the cockpit check procedure. With the check being done hurriedly, it was considered entirely possible by the Board that he moved the switch from 'off' to '35 degrees', which was the next position on the knob. Or he may have struck the activating knob when he raised his foot over the instrument panel,

especially considering that the switch rotated in the same direction as the first officer would have moved when taking his seat. It was noted in the CAB report that the flaps would have taken approximately half a minute to reach the 35-degree setting, and this was about the same length of time as the take-off run.

The underlying cause of the crash was therefore the improper flap setting, which would have rendered the aircraft excessively 'nose-heavy' and thus uncontrollable once it became airborne. Considered by the Board as a contributing factor was the absence of a stop spring on the flap control switch, which would have prevented the inadvertent application of full flaps. It was noted in the report that the original switch was modified four months earlier as a safety measure, but that the stop had either been broken off or removed. The requirement of such a stop on Vought-Sikorsky flying boats engaged in passenger operations was recommended by the CAB.

Date: 22 October 1942
Location: Near Bucharest, Romania
Operator: Deutsche Lufthansa AG (Germany)
Aircraft type: Junkers Ju.52/3m (D-AYGX)

The crash of the trimotored airliner claimed the lives of all seventeen persons aboard D-AYGX, including a probable crew of three.

Date: 23 October 1942 (c.17:15)
Location: Near Palm Springs, California, US
First aircraft:
Operator: American Airlines (US)
Type: Douglas DC-3 (NC-16017)
Second aircraft:
Operator: US Army Air Forces
Type: Lockheed B-34 (41-38116)

The airliner and twin-engine bomber collided in mid-air, and the former then crashed and burned on Mount Jacinto. All twelve persons aboard the DC-3 (nine passengers and a crew of three) perished, although the slightly-damaged B-34 landed safely.

At the time of the accident, both aircraft had been flying in the same general direction, NC-16017 on a domestic service from Burbank, California, to Phoenix, Arizona, as Trip 28, and 41-38116 bound for the army air base at Palm Springs from Long Beach, also in California. The collision occurred late in the afternoon and in clear weather conditions at an approximate height of 9,000ft (2,700m).

The pilot of the B-34, who knew the first officer of the DC-3 and had met with him the night before to arrange a rendezvous of their aircraft, was faulted for a 'reckless and irresponsible act' in deliberately manoeuvring his bomber in 'dangerous' proximity to the transport. Although the bomber initiated an evasive manoeuvre just before impact, its starboard propeller took off most of the airliner's vertical tail fin, and during its plunge to earth, the entire tail assembly of NC-16017 was torn from the fuselage. Initially charged with manslaughter, the bomber pilot would subsequently be acquitted by a US military court-martial.

Although it was not considered a factor in this particular accident, the investigation of the collision by US Civil Aeronautics Board (CAB) revealed that the Sixth Ferrying Group of the Air Transport Command based at Long Beach had erroneously interpreted the rules governing contact flight in a civil airway, believing that they pertained to the maximum height of the airway rather than the altitude above the ground. It was noted in the CAB report that the misinterpretation of the rules ought not to have been a factor in this particular case, since the specification of altitude levels should not have been necessary in order to prevent a pilot from bringing his aircraft into such close proximity with another.

One recommendation made in the CAB report was to conduct a study of the air traffic situation in the vicinity of the San Gorgonio Pass, the area wherein this accident occurred, with the intention of eliminating an existing hazard.

Date: 17 November 1942
Location: Near Krasnoyarsk, Russian Soviet Federative Socialist Republic, USSR
Operator: Krasnoyarskie Vozhdushnye Trassy (USSR)
Aircraft type: Grazhdansky Vozdushnyi Flot (GVF) PS-84 (SSSR-L3965)

All twenty persons aboard (sixteen passengers and four crew members) lost their lives when the twin-engine airliner crashed and exploded while taking off from the Krasnoyarsk airport, on a domestic service to Kirensk. The PS-84 had apparently stalled immediately after becoming airborne, with the accident reportedly resulting from ice accretion on its wings.

Date: 12 December 1942
Location: Near Tashkent, Uzbek SSR, USSR
Operator: Aeroflot (USSR)
Aircraft type: Tupolev A.N.T. 20bis (SSSR-L760)

Operating on a scheduled domestic service to Tashkent from Shardzhev, Turkmen SSR, the six-engine airliner crashed approximately 30 miles (50km) from its destination, and all thirty-six persons aboard (thirty passengers and a crew of six) perished.

During its descent in preparation for landing, SSSR-L760 assumed a near-vertical attitude and plummeted to earth, exploding on impact. It was reported by Soviet authorities that the captain had prior to the accident left his seat, and that a passenger then apparently disengaged the autopilot and assumed control of the aircraft. After several abnormal manoeuvres, the A.N.T. 20 descended uncontrollably into the ground from a height of around 1,500ft (500m).

Date: 15 December 1942 (*c*.01:20)
Location: Near Fairfield, Utah, US
Operator: Western Air Lines (US)
Aircraft type: Douglas DC-3A (NC-16060)

Designated as Flight 1 and bound for Las Vegas, Nevada, one segment of a US domestic service with an ultimate destination of Burbank, California, the transport crashed in rolling prairie land approximately 50 miles (80km) south of Salt Lake City, from where it had taken off about 20 minutes earlier. All but two passengers among the nineteen persons aboard the DC-3 lost their lives in the accident, including the four members of its crew; the survivors were seriously injured.

According to its barograph flight recording unit, NC-16060 had been cruising at an altitude of around 10,000ft (3,000m) when it suffered structural failure. Specifically, its port and possibly both wing tips and its horizontal tail surfaces had failed due to excessive aerodynamic loads caused by a severe pull-up manoeuvre. The accident occurred in darkness, but the meteorological conditions in the area at the time were good, with only high, broken clouds.

In its investigation, the US Civil Aeronautics Board (CAB) was unable to draw any conclusion as to whether the manoeuvre resulted from the intentional operation of the controls by the flight crew (which consisted of the first officer and a trainee pilot, with the captain sitting in the jump-seat or standing in the companionway of the cockpit), possibly to avoid a collision with a bird, another aircraft or some object the pilots saw or thought they saw, or was the consequence of other forces that were beyond their control. Subsequently, the US Civil Aeronautics Administration (CAA) modified the Civil Air Regulations to ensure that only someone listed as a pilot in the operations specifications of an air carrier company be allowed to occupy a pilot's seat, since the CAB report noted that the presence of someone more experienced in piloting an aeroplane at the controls of Flight 1 might have prevented this crash.

Date: 19 December 1942 (*c.*16:00)
Location: Near Vienna, Austria
Operator: Det Danske Luftfartselskab A/S (DDL) (Danish Air Lines)
Aircraft type: Junkers Ju.52/3m (OY-DAL)

The trimotored aircraft crashed while approaching to land at the Vienna airport, which was an en route stop during a scheduled international service originating at Copenhagen, Denmark, with an ultimate destination of Budapest, Hungary. All eighteen persons aboard (sixteen passengers and two crew members) were killed in the accident.

Date: 20 December 1942 (*c.*19:00)
Location: Near Chilliwack, British Columbia, Canada
Operator: Canadian Pacific Air Lines
Aircraft type: Lockheed 14-H2 Super Electra (CF-CPD)

The transport crashed in the vicinity of Fraser Valley during a scheduled domestic intraprovincial service from Prince George to Vancouver, killing all thirteen persons aboard (ten passengers and three crew members). Its wreckage and the remains of the victims were located on a slope of Mt Cheam, at an approximate elevation of 7,000ft (2,000m) and some 75 miles (120km) east of its intended destination, in August of the following year.

A ground witness in Fraser Valley had reported an aircraft passing overhead without navigation lights at around the time of the accident, and this combined the absence of radio contact with the flight for nearly an hour beforehand led to speculation that the Super Electra had experienced a complete electrical system failure. This could also explain why it had deviated considerably off course after passing Squamish. In the darkness and cloudy weather conditions, with limited visibility, the pilots could have easily flown into the mountain.

Date: 9 January 1943 (*c.*10:30)
Location: Near Lisbon, Portugal
Operator: British Overseas Airways Corporation (BOAC)
Aircraft type: Short S.26 (G-AFCK)

The four-engine flying boat crashed in the River Tagus approximately 1.5 miles (2.5km) from the Cabo Ruivo Marine Base, and all but two of the fifteen persons aboard the aircraft were killed. Among its four crew members, only the radio officer survived; the rest of the occupants were non-revenue passengers, only one of whom escaped with his life. Nearly two weeks earlier, G-AFCK had during a regular service to England been forced to return to Lisbon by trouble in a power plant, which was subsequently replaced. The installation of a new engine necessitated a test flight, and it was during this operation that the S.26 met with disaster.

The sequence of events began when an unusual vibration was experienced about 20 minutes into the flight, and at a height of around 1,200ft (350m), after which the commander turned back towards the departure point and initiated a descent. As the aircraft continued down, the vibration continued, and fire then erupted in the right inboard power plant. Acrid smoke started entering the cockpit as the fire became more intense, while at the same time the flames swept back towards the empennage. An attempt was made by the commander to alight near a moored ship, but after touching down approximately half a mile (0.8km) off shore, the S.26 porpoised and then slammed back into the water and broke apart, with fire continuing to burn on the surface of the river. The bodies of seven victims were subsequently recovered, as was the main wreckage. The weather in the area at the time consisted of a nearly solid overcast at 15,000ft (c.5,000m), with a visibility of about 5 miles (10km) and a west-south-westerly wind of 5 knots.

Considered as the primary cause of the crash was the dense smoke in the cockpit, which obscured the visibility of the pilot and prevented him from carrying out a successful emergency landing. According to the investigative report, this condition was probably related to the opening by a crewman of a cockpit window, which brought smoke from the rear to the front of the compartment. However, the opening of a window was considered a 'natural' action under the circumstances. It was also noted in the report

that had the wing root hatch cover been replaced immediately after the fire started, the smoke may not have penetrated the cockpit with the intensity that it did. Of course the crew may not have realised at that point that the smoke would increase to such an extent. It was also considered possible that the starboard elevator had been damaged by fire, which would have affected the longitudinal stability of the aircraft.

The precipitating causative factor was believed to have been the failure of the No.4 piston in the engine that caught fire, which led to the failure of the articulated rod system in the power plant and subsequent separation of the No.6 cylinder. The blaze could have started when oil was thrown out of the gap created by the loss of the cylinder and came into contact with the hot exhaust manifold; when oil or fuel vapour was ignited by an ignition spark or by heat or sparks generated during the break-up of the power plant, or by a combination of these factors. The initial blaze may have been fed by gasoline escaping from pipes fractured earlier in the sequence by engine vibration.

It was observed in the report that proper emergency procedures had not been carried out by the crew, and some of the passengers were not fully secured at the time of the attempted emergency landing, which could have cost lives in the crash. Furthermore, the carrying of passengers on an aircraft conducting a test flight infringed upon the safety regulations of the operator, and for this the commander and two members of the ground staff were faulted, although one of the latter was among those killed in the accident. It was also noted that the crash would almost certainly have been prevented had the S.26 been equipped with fully-feathering propellers, as were available on the more widely used sister flying boat, the Short S.25.

Date: 21 January 1943 (c.07:30)
Location: Near Ukiah, California, US
Operator: Pan American Airways System (US)
Aircraft type: Martin M-130 (NC-14715)

Operating as Flight 62100 to San Francisco from Honolulu, US Territory of Hawaii, the four-engine flying boat crashed and burned some 90 miles (145km) north–north–west of its destination and about 20 miles (30km) inland from the Pacific coast. All nineteen persons aboard the aircraft lost their lives in the accident, including the nine members of its crew; the passengers were naval officers, including the commander of the US Pacific Fleet's submarine division. The wreckage of NC-14715 was located nine days later.

In the final radio message from the flight, the crew had requested a navigational fix, and shortly before the crash, the M-130 had been seen at a very low altitude. The aircraft was proceeding in a near-northerly direction when it slammed into a mountain ridge at an approximate elevation of 2,500ft (750m). It was dark at the time, before dawn, and an unusually severe rainstorm was in progress, accompanied by high winds. Specifically, the wind velocity at 3,000ft (c.1,000m) was probably around 65mph (105kmh), and there would also have been considerable turbulence, especially over the mountainous terrain.

Upon coming into the influence of the storm area, NC-14715 would have first encountered winds from the north-west, then from the west, and finally south-westerly winds near the California coast. And in view of the fact that the intensity of the storm must not have been realised, the strength of the winds would not have been anticipated by the crew. In its investigative report on the accident, the US Civil Aeronautics Board (CAB) considered it 'very probable' that due to these wind conditions, the aircraft drifted a considerable distance to the north of where the captain expected to be after reaching the coast. Although the pilot in all probability considered San Diego, in Southern California, as an alternate landing site, he must have intended to hold in the vicinity of San Francisco in the belief that the weather would improve there.

The crash was believed to have resulted from the failure of the captain to determine

his position accurately before descending to a dangerously low altitude in the poor atmospheric conditions. About 15 minutes before the crash, the pilot had advised the Treasure Island facility at San Francisco that the flying boat was in the area and taking a course due west. But on account of the strong south-south-westerly wind, its course would have been deflected to a track closer to 350 degrees. The pilot must have believed that he was at the time over the ocean and thus free to descend, when in fact NC-14715 was considerably farther northward and eastward than he either anticipated or realised.

The CAB concluded that whether the final descent leading to the crash was forced or intentional, the pilot would not have knowingly continued on the course at such a height. There was no evidence of technical failure in the M-130, and although it may have experienced carburettor icing, this almost certainly was not a factor in the accident. Furthermore while power failures had occurred at radio stations that the captain may have been utilising, none of these slight interruptions was considered significant since broadcasting had been resumed before the final transmission from the flight, and the latter contained no hint of difficulty.

It was recommended in the CAB report that a radio marker or facility be installed at some suitable location that could be used as an inner marker for aircraft entering the San Francisco Airway Traffic Control Zone, and also that Pan American establish specific holding procedures for flights in the area when landings were delayed.

Date: 22 January 1943 (c.15:15)
Location: Near Chaparra, Arequipa, Peru
Operator: Pan American–Grace Airways (Panagra) (US)
Aircraft type: Douglas DC-3A (NC-33645)

Designated as Trip 9 and on an international service originating at Santiago, Chile, with an ultimate destination of Lima, Peru, the transport crashed in the Andes Mountains

The Pan American Airways System Boeing 314, serial number NC-18603, the aircraft that crashed in the River Tagus, in Portugal, following a transatlantic service. (Pan Am)

some 100 miles (150km) north-west of the city of Arequipa, where it had last stopped. Its inverted and burned wreckage was found three days later at an approximate elevation of 13,000ft (4,000m), with only one passenger having survived among its fourteen occupants, and he was injured; those killed included the aircraft's four crew members.

It was determined by the US Civil Aeronautics Board (CAB) that NC-33645 had drifted to the right of the prescribed track while on a generally westerly heading due to south-south-westerly winds estimated at around 20mph (30kmh). The pilot had apparently continued on instruments into an overcast, which was contrary to company policy. Considered as contributing factors were the absence of flight dispatch control by the airline and the company's failure to institute and maintain written flight and operating procedures in such a manner as to be constantly available for the guidance of both pilots and dispatchers.

Date: 22 February 1943 (*c*.18:50)
Location: Near Lisbon, Portugal
Operator: Pan American Airways System (US)
Aircraft type: Boeing 314A (NC-18603)

Operating as Flight 9035 and on a service originating at New York City, with an ultimate destination of Foynes, Ireland, the four-engine flying boat crashed in the mouth of the River Tagus, approximately 2 miles (3km) east of Cabo Ruivo Airport, while attempting to land during the second of two en route stops. Killed in the accident were twenty-four of the thirty-nine persons aboard the transport, including five members of its crew of twelve. Among the survivors, all but four passengers suffered injuries.

The aircraft had inadvertently made contact with the surface of the river with its port wing tip during a descending turn as it prepared for alighting. It remained partially submerged for about 10 minutes, then sank completely, although most of the wreckage was subsequently recovered, as were the bodies of about half of the victims. The crash occurred in darkness and cloudy weather conditions, with intermittent rain showers. In its investigation, the US Civil Aeronautics Board (CAB) found no evidence to support the contention of the surviving captain that NC-18603 had assumed a descending attitude or that it failed to respond to the controls. He was also criticised for making a turn at such a low altitude.

The aircraft involved was the famed 'Yankee Clipper,' which had inaugurated the first transatlantic scheduled airline passenger service four years earlier. But amid the tragedy, romance blossomed. One of the surviving passengers was American singer Jane Froman, whom First Officer John Burn helped to save. The two were later married.

Date: 4 April 1943 (c.01:40)
Location: North Sea
Operator: British Overseas Airways Corporation (BOAC)
Aircraft type: Lockheed C-56B Lodestar (G-AGEJ)

All seven occupants (four passengers and a crew of three) were killed when the transport, on a scheduled international service from Stockholm, Sweden, to RAF Leuchars, in Scotland, was shot down in early morning darkness some 30 miles (50km) from Skagen, Denmark, presumably by a German fighter.

Date: 22 April 1943
Location: South Pacific Ocean
Operator: Qantas Empire Airways (Australia)
Aircraft type: Short S.23 'Empire' (VH-ADU)

The four-engine flying boat crashed off Port Moresby, Territory of Papua, and thirteen of the thirty-one persons aboard were killed, including two members of its crew of four. During a charter service being conducted on behalf of Allied military forces, and carrying as passengers Australian and American service personnel, VH-ADU was forced down approximately 5 miles (10km) off shore after bad weather had prevented the crew from locating the designated landing area, and it sank in the heavy seas after alighting in darkness.

Date: 1 June 1943 (c.13:00)
Location: Bay of Biscay
Operator: British Overseas Airways Corporation (BOAC)
Aircraft type: Douglas DC-3 (G-AGBB)

Being operated by BOAC on behalf of KLM Royal Dutch Airlines, due to the occupation of the nation of registry by German forces, and designated as Flight 777A, the transport had been flying on one of the European commercial air routes not disrupted by the Second World War when it became a casualty of the conflict.

The DC-3 had taken off from Lisbon, Portugal, bound for an airfield at Whitchurch, in Somerset, England. It was to follow the coasts of Portugal and Spain, remaining clear of occupied France. Possibly because German intelligence had gained information that British Prime Minister Winston Churchill had been one of the passengers, or perhaps just due to good timing, bad for G-AGBB, during the trip it encountered eight Luftwaffe Junkers Ju.88 twin-engine fighters that had taken off from France. The pilots may have mistaken the DC-3 for a military aircraft.

Soon after visual contact with the airliner had been established, the attack commenced, but not until after the BOAC radio operator was able to transmit a message. Set afire by the gunfire from the fighters, the DC-3 plummeted into the sea some 200 miles (320km) off the northern coast of Spain. All seventeen persons aboard perished, including four crew members. Winston Churchill was not aboard, but one of the passengers killed was British actor and Hollywood star Leslie Howard. The German pilots reported seeing four parachutes, but this could not be explained as the airliner was not known to have been carrying such emergency equipment.

This attack should have come as no surprise, despite the precautions taken, because aircraft had come under attack along the same route twice in the previous six months, although both times they managed to escape.

Date: 28 July 1943 (c.05:20)
Location: Near Brandon, Kerry, Ireland
Operator: British Overseas Airways Corporation (BOAC)
Aircraft type: Short S.25 Sunderland 3 (G-AGES)

A British Overseas Airways Corporation Short Sunderland 3 flying boat, one of which crashed in Ireland, with a loss of ten lives. (Philip Jarrett)

Ten persons lost their lives when the four-engine flying boat crashed on the Dingle Peninsula some 20 miles (30km) south-west of Tralee. The victims included the aircraft's captain; the six other members of its crew and nine passengers survived with various injuries.

Operating on the service 20W223, which had originated at Lagos, Nigeria, and last stopped at Lisbon, Portugal, with an ultimate destination of Foynes, Ireland, the Sunderland arrived over the Shannon Estuary at 6,000ft (*c.*1,800m), which was above the overcast. The captain first reported that he would land after about 45 minutes, presumably waiting for daybreak, but after only about half that amount of time, he disengaged the autopilot and started to descend.

During the descent through the clouds, the ground was observed, whereupon the crew initiated an evasive manoeuvre. However, G-AGES hit Slieveglass while on a near-westerly heading, initially striking the mountain with its starboard wing, then slid to a stop and caught fire. The accident occurred in twilight conditions, and the weather in the area was characterised by a low overcast accompanied by generally light rain or drizzle, with the visibility under the cloud base ranging from 2 to around 5 miles (3–10km). The wind at the surface level was blowing at 15 knots from a north-westerly direction, and nearly twice that velocity at 5,000ft (*c.*1,500m). In a related matter, it was noted in the investigative report that whereas the forecast wind during the trip from Lisbon would have resulted in a drift of more than 10 degrees to the right, the actual conditions deduced by the meteorological office at Foynes after the crash indicated a drift of about the same amount, but to the left.

It was determined that the captain had decided to land without obtaining bearings from the ground (QTE) to determine his position accurately, and decided to descend when he apparently thought he was over or near Loop Head (Cape Leon). This error in judgement was considered to be the direct cause of the accident. For reasons that could not be determined, the captain had not been issued an instrument approach procedure for Foynes, although this was not considered to have been a contributing factor. Pertaining to the issue of survival and the post-crash rescue effort, the report lauded the medical and general assistance provided by Irish military authorities.

Date: 28 July 1943 (*c.*22:45)
Location: Near Trammel, Kentucky, US
Operator: American Airlines (US)
Aircraft type: Douglas DC-3 (NC-16014)

Designated as Flight 63 and on a US domestic service that had originated at Cleveland, Ohio, with an ultimate destination of Memphis, Tennessee, the transport crashed and burned around 15 miles (25km) south-east of Bowling Green, and twenty persons aboard were killed, including its entire crew of four. Two passengers survived with injuries.

Having taken off earlier from Louisville, Kentucky, bound for Nashville, Tennessee, one segment of the trip, NC-16014 had been flying at an approximate height of 2,000ft (600m), or some 1,300ft (400m) above ground level, in darkness and in an area of severe thunderstorm activity, accompanied by heavy rain and high winds, before it slammed to earth. The impact was in a wooded area and on practically level terrain. The loss of altitude leading to the accident was attributed to the encounter with heavy turbulence and a strong down draught.

A significant change to the Civil Air Regulations came about as a result of this crash, and which would later become effective, requiring that all emergency exits in passenger-carrying aircraft be clearly marked with luminous paint. This could have been an issue in this accident as most of the fatalities on NC-16014 were attributed to the effects of the post-crash fire, with the victims apparently unable to open the cabin door.

Date: 26 August 1943 (*c.*09:00)
Location: Near Rio de Janeiro, Brazil
Operator: Viação Aérea São Paulo SA (VASP) (Brazil)
Aircraft type: Junkers Ju.52/3mg3e (PP-SPD)

Operating on a scheduled domestic service from São Paulo, the trimotored airliner struck a building while attempting to land during a heavy fog at Santos-Dumont Airport, serving Rio de Janeiro, then plunged into Guanabara Bay. Killed in the accident were eighteen of the twenty-one persons aboard the Ju.52, including the three members of its crew, while the surviving passengers suffered injuries.

Date: 15 October 1943 (*c.*23:15)
Location: Near Centerville, Tennessee, US
Operator: American Airlines (US)
Aircraft type: Douglas DC-3 (NC-16008)

For the second time in less than three months, the same airline and flight number met with tragedy, and again, the weather was an underlying factor. Ten persons lost their lives in this accident, including three crew members; one of the passengers was an off-duty airline captain. There were no survivors. Flight 63 crashed some 50 miles (80km) south-west of Nashville, where it had last stopped, bound for Memphis, the intra-state segment of a US domestic service originating at Cleveland, Ohio. There was no fire. It was dark at the time, and the weather conditions along the route consisted of clouds and intermittent light rain.

Less than 10 minutes before the accident, the crew had requested authorisation to ascend from 6,000ft (*c.*1,800m), the height in its flight plan, to 8,000ft (*c.*2,500m). It could not be determined whether NC-16008 had ascended to a higher altitude, but the US Civil Aeronautics Board (CAB) nevertheless concluded that the transport had apparently encountered icing conditions. Its pilot must then have found it necessary to make a rapid descent to a height where the air was warmer. But after descending, the DC-3 had apparently been unable to either climb or maintain altitude, possibly due to a loss of power induced by carburettor icing, coupled with any wing or propeller ice that might have remained.

The CAB theorised that the pilot had used his landing lights to assist him in avoiding obstructions or to make a forced landing, if necessary. But he apparently had to pull up in order to avoid some trees, and in doing so stalled the aircraft. The DC-3 then plummeted almost vertically into a wooded area on the southern slope of a hill. That an aircraft had been dispatched without wing or propeller de-icing equipment was considered a contributing factor.

Date: 22 October 1943
Location: Near Uddevalla, Bohuslan, Sweden
Operator: Aktiebolaget Aerotransport (ABA) (Sweden)
Aircraft type: Douglas DC-3 (SE-BAG)

The transport had been on a scheduled international service when shot down by German aircraft over Hallo Island, located north of Gothenburg. All but two of the fifteen persons aboard the DC-3 were killed.

Date: 5 November 1943 (c.22:45)
Location: Eastern Libya
Operator: British Overseas Airways Corporation (BOAC)
Aircraft type: Short Sunderland 3 (G-AGIB)

The flying boat crashed and burned in the desert approximately 100 miles (150km) south-south-east of the seaport of Tobruk and some 25 miles (40km) west of the Egyptian border. All nineteen persons aboard perished in the accident; the passengers and two of the aircraft's nine crewmen were British service personnel.

Having taken off earlier from Raud Al-Farang, Egypt, located near Cairo, bound for the island of Djerba, Tunisia, with an ultimate destination of Poole, England, G-AGIB was believed to have experienced an in-flight fire that must have erupted behind its right

outboard power plant. Ultimately, the starboard wing outboard of the engine apparently failed, probably after the pilot had placed the aircraft in a steep dive in an attempt to extinguish the blaze with the rushing airstream. The crash occurred in darkness, but the weather conditions in the area were good.

A number of structural changes in the Sunderland, designed to reduce the threat of an in-flight fire, were recommended by the Accident Investigation Section in the wake of this accident.

Date: 26 November 1943 (c.04:15)
Location: Territory of Papua
Operator: Qantas Empire Airways (Australia)
Aircraft type: Lockheed C-56B Lodestar (VH-CAB)

The twin-engine airliner, which was being operated under military contract and bound for Townsville, Queensland, Australia, crashed into a hill shortly after its departure from the airfield serving Port Moresby, the accident occurring in pre-dawn darkness. Including the four members of its crew, all fifteen persons aboard the Lodestar lost their lives in the accident; the passengers consisted of Australian service personnel.

Date: 17 December 1943 (c.22:45)
Location: North Sea
Operator: British Overseas Airways Corporation (BOAC)
Aircraft type: Lockheed 18-56 Lodestar (G-AGDE)

Operating on a scheduled international service from Stockholm, Sweden, the transport crashed some 10 to 15 miles (c.15–25km) south-east of Montrose, Scotland, shortly before it was to have landed at RAF Leuchars, in Scotland. Among its ten occupants (seven passengers and three crew members), no survivors or bodies were found. Nor was any wreckage recovered, although an oil patch was seen in the water in the area where the aircraft had gone down.

A Lockheed Lodestar, two of which were involved in accidents in opposite parts of the world in late 1943. (Smithsonian Institution)

The Lodestar had last been observed on radar at a height of 6,000ft (*c.*1,800m), and the captain of a trawler reported seeing a flash less than 50ft (15m) above the ocean surface, which was associated with the loss of the aircraft. It was dark at the time of the disappearance, and the pilot of an aircraft flying about 15 minutes behind G-AGDE reported a solid overcast along the route.

Investigation revealed no indication of sabotage or hostile action, and double power plant failure was considered 'most unlikely'. And although there was no evidence of such, physical incapacitation of the pilot could not be completely ruled out as the cause. Nor was there evidence of a collision with another aeroplane, but the possibility that the Lodestar had collided with a drifting balloon, perhaps one launched from a ship, could not be entirely disregarded, especially

when considering the aforementioned flash that was observed.

One possibility was that G-AGDE, which would have been cold, had encountered icing conditions while descending through the clouds between 6,000 and 5,000ft (1,800–1,500m), leading to the build-up of ice, then went into an uncontrollable spin and plummeted into the sea. However, the Chief Inspector of Accidents for the RAF expressed the belief that the pilot of the Lodestar had deliberately let down with the intention of approaching the base at a low altitude, and during this time either allowed the aircraft to descend into the water, or lost control at a height that did not allow for a successful recovery. A possibly significant factor was the lack of experience along the route taken on the part of the captain, who had only once before made the trip to Sweden, and only as a first officer.

Date: 10 February 1944 (*c*.23:35)
Location: Near Memphis, Tennessee, US
Operator: American Airlines (US)
Aircraft type: Douglas DC-3 (NC-21767)

Designated as Trip 2, the transport crashed in the Mississippi River some 20 miles (30km) south-west of the Memphis airport, where it was scheduled to land, having last stopped at Little Rock, Arkansas, during a transcontinental US domestic service originating at Los Angeles, California, with an ultimate destination of New York, New York. All twenty-four persons aboard (twenty-one passengers and a crew of three) were killed.

The DC-3 was observed flying at a low altitude before it slammed into the water at a high rate of speed, exploding and disintegrating on impact. At the time of the crash, it was descending at an angle of approximately 20 degrees with its starboard wing down and undercarriage still retracted. It was dark at the time of the accident, but the weather conditions were not considered to have been a factor. The bodies of at least five victims and about 75 per cent of the aircraft's wreckage would later be recovered. Examination of the latter revealed no evidence of sabotage or malfunction in its engines or flight control system.

Although no determination as to the cause of the accident could be made by the US Civil Aeronautics Board (CAB), one possible explanation was an in-flight bird collision that had incapacitated both pilots. In view of this possibility, the Civil Aeronautics Administration (CAA) subsequently launched a project towards the development of an aircraft windscreen capable of sustaining such an impact.

Date: 23 February 1944
Location: Near Quelimane, Portuguese East Africa (Mozambique)
Operator: Divisão de Exporação des Transportes Aéreos (DETA) (Portuguese Mozambique)
Aircraft type: Lockheed 14-H2 Super Electra (CR-AAV)

The twin-engine transport crashed and burned while taking off from the Quelimane airport, which was an en route stop during a scheduled international service originating at Lisbon, Portugal, with an ultimate destination of Lourence Marques, also in Portuguese East Africa. All fourteen persons aboard (ten passengers and a crew of four) were killed in the accident.

Date: 21 April 1944
Location: Near Fredrickstad, Ostfold, Norway
Operator: Deutsche Lufthansa AG (Germany)
Aircraft type: Douglas DC-3 (D-AAIG)

One of the aircraft taken over from Czechoslovakia by their German occupiers, D-AAIG had been on a scheduled international service from Copenhagen, Denmark, to Oslo, Norway when ditched in Oslofjord, some 50 miles (80km) south of its destination. Including the three members of its crew, nine persons aboard the DC-3 were killed in the accident. Eleven others survived the water landing, which was necessitated by smoke and flames in the aircraft's cockpit attributed to the ignition of a signal flare.

Date: 26 May 1944
Location: Southern China
Operator: China National Aviation Corporation
Aircraft type: Douglas DC-3C (82)

Its passengers comprised of airline mechanics, the airliner had been on a non-scheduled service within India, from Calcutta to Dinjan Airfield, near Chabua, Assam, before it crashed in the Himalayas of Tibet, north of Burma (Myanmar). Including its two pilots, all twelve persons aboard were killed.

The DC-3 had encountered extremely bad weather conditions, with a strong tailwind and static so severe that the crew could not obtain bearings using any radio station. As a result, it flew past its intended destination until impact.

A Pan American Airways System Sikorsky S-42 of the type that crashed while taking off from Nipe Bay, in Cuba. (Pan Am)

The aft end of NC-823M remained above the surface of the water after the accident that claimed seventeen lives. (Civil Aeronautics Board)

Date: 20 June 1944
Location: Near Porto Alegre, Rio Grande do Sul, Brazil
Operator: Viação Aérea Rio Grandense (VARIG) (Brazil)
Aircraft type: Lockheed 10C Electra (PP-VAQ)

The twin-engine transport crashed in the River Guiaba during a scheduled domestic service with a destination of Porto Alegre, and all ten persons aboard (eight passengers and two pilots) were killed.

Date: 8 August 1944 (*c*.13:20)
Location: Near Antilla, Oriente, Cuba
Operator: Pan American Airways System (US)
Aircraft type: Sikorsky S-42 (NC-823M)

Designated as Flight 218 and on an international service originating at San Juan, Puerto Rico, with an ultimate destination of Miami, Florida, the four-engine flying boat crashed in Nipe Bay approximately half a mile (0.8km) off shore from Antilla, which was one of two scheduled en route stops. Killed in the accident were seventeen of the thirty-one persons aboard the aircraft. Among the survivors were all five crew members, one of whom, the steward, a former Red Cross life-saving examiner, was credited with rescuing passengers from the partially sunken rearmost portion of the cabin. The bodies of the victims were subsequently recovered.

The S-42 had just taken off when it settled back on to the water, and after two bounces, control was lost. It then climbed to a height of around 25ft (7.5m) before plunging steeply into the sea, breaking apart on impact. The local weather conditions at the time were good, and the ocean was described as 'choppy', but with no ground swells. The failure of the pilot to keep the aircraft airborne and also to effect a safe recovery after it first touched the water was attributed largely to his limited experience in the Sikorsky-type flying boat.

Date: 28/29 August 1944 (*c*.00:00)
Location: Near Lidkoping, Västergötland, Sweden
Operator: British Overseas Airways Corporation (BOAC)
Aircraft type: Lockheed 18-56 Lodestar (G-AGIH)

Operating on a scheduled international service to RAF Leuchars, in Scotland, the transport struck Kinnekulle Hill some 180 miles (290km) south-west of Stockholm, from where it had taken off earlier. Killed in the crash were eleven persons aboard the Lodestar, including the three members of its crew, while four passengers survived with injuries. The accident occurred in darkness, at or shortly before midnight, after G-AGIH had diverted towards Gothenburg due to radio trouble.

Date: 30/31 August 1944 (*c*.00:00)
Location: Near São Paulo, Brazil
Operator: Panair do Brasil SA (Brazil)
Aircraft type: Lockheed 18 Lodestar (PP-PBI)

The twin-engine transport crashed in darkness, around midnight, while approaching to land at Congonhas Airport, serving São Paulo. All eighteen persons aboard (fourteen passengers and a crew of four) were killed in the accident, which apparently occurred during a scheduled domestic service.

Date: 21 September 1944
Location: Near Rio Espera, Minas Gerais, Brazil
Operator: Panair do Brasil SA (Brazil)
Aircraft type: Lockheed 18 Lodestar (PP-PBH)

The twin-engine transport crashed some 175 miles (280km) north of Rio de Janeiro, presumably during a scheduled domestic service, and all seventeen persons aboard (thirteen passengers and four crew members) were killed.

Date: 27 September 1944 (*c*.20:30)
Location: Near Dijon, Burgundy, France
Operator: Deutsche Lufthansa AG (Germany)
Aircraft type: Focke Wulf Fw.200A Condor
(D-AMHL)

All nine occupants (five passengers and a crew of four) were killed when the four-engine airliner, on a scheduled international service from Stuttgart, Germany, to Barcelona, Spain, was shot down in darkness by a British fighter.

Date: 16 October 1944 (*c*.20:25)
Location: Near Seljord, Telemark, Norway
Operator: Deutsche Lufthansa AG (Germany)
Aircraft type: Junkers Ju.52/3mg8e
(D-ADQV)

Operating on a scheduled international service from Berlin, Germany, to Oslo, Norway, the trimotored airliner crashed in hilly terrain near the Seljordsvatnet inlet some 80 miles (130km) south-west of its destination. All fifteen persons aboard (twelve passengers and three crew members) were killed.

Having last stopped at Copenhagen, Denmark, the aircraft was considerably off the direct course when the accident occurred in darkness and, apparently, adverse meteorological conditions. Also significant was the low overcast, with a ceiling of approximately 1,000 to 1,500ft (*c*.300–500m), and the north-north-easterly wind of 5 to 10mph (*c*.10–15kmh) that the Ju.52 had encountered along the route.

Date: 4 November 1944 (*c*.17:15)
Location: Near Hanford, California, US
Operator: Transcontinental and Western Air, Inc. (TWA) (US)
Aircraft type: Douglas DC-3 (NC-28310)

Designated as Flight 8, the airliner crashed approximately 175 miles (280km) south-east of San Francisco, from where it had taken off earlier, bound for Los Angeles, the initial, intra-state segment of a US domestic transcontinental service with an ultimate destination of New York, New York. All twenty-four persons

aboard perished, including a crew of three; except for one, the passengers were American service personnel.

The DC-3 had been cruising at 10,000ft (*c*.3,000m) when it entered an area of thunderstorm activity, and shortly thereafter was seen plummeting earthward in pieces, falling into open terrain. Its main portion, consisting of its centre section, cockpit, starboard outer wing panel, engines and undercarriage, struck the ground in an attitude slightly past the vertical and burned.

Severe turbulence associated with the thunderstorm had apparently resulted in the structural failure of the aircraft. After its port wing initially broke in a downward direction just outboard of the landing light, its horizontal tail surfaces separated. Significant to the break-up sequence was that NC-17322 had been inverted at the time, although how it got into that attitude could not be determined. The crew of Flight 8 probably did not see the cumulonimbus build-up they would enter because it must have been obscured by other clouds.

Date: 10 November 1944
Location: Near Kunming, Yunnan, China
Operator: Central Air Transport Corporation (China)
Aircraft type: Lockheed Hudson

The twin-engine airliner crashed near the Kunming airfield while on a domestic charter service, and all twenty persons aboard (seventeen passengers and a crew of three) were killed.

Date: 28 November 1944 (*c*.15:00)
Location: Near Tegucigalpa, Honduras
Operator: Compañía de Transportes Aéreos Centro-Americanos (TACA) (Honduras)
Aircraft type: Ford Tri-Motor (XH-TAN)

All sixteen persons aboard (fourteen passengers and two crew members) perished when the trimotored airliner crashed shortly after its departure from the capital city, on a domestic scheduled service to San Pedro Sula.

The accident had resulted from the in-flight failure of a wing, the structure probably having been weakened by vibration, turbulence and constant operation of the Tri-Motor from rough airfields.

Date: 29 November 1944 (*c.*10:30)
Location: Near Falsterbo, Malmohus, Sweden
Operator: Deutsche Lufthansa AG (Germany)
Aircraft type: Focke Wulf Fw.200A Condor (D-ARHW)

During a scheduled international service to Stockholm from Berlin, Germany, the four-engine airliner crashed was shot down, apparently accidentally by a German patrol boat, falling into the Baltic Sea some 25 miles (40km) west of Trelleborg. All ten persons aboard the Condor (six passengers and a crew of four) were killed.

Date: 29 November 1944
Location: Near Nairobi, Kenya
Operator: British Overseas Airways Corporation (BOAC)
Aircraft type: Lockheed 18-56 Lodestar (G-AGBW)

Operating on a scheduled international service to Nairobi from Juba, Sudan, the twin-engine transport crashed in the Aberdare Mountains approximately 50 miles (80km) from its destination. All eleven persons aboard were killed, including the four members of its crew; the passengers were British servicemen.

The accident occurred during an afternoon thunderstorm after G-AGBW had begun its descent to land, although the wreckage of the aircraft would not be located for more than a month.

Date: 1 December 1944 (*c.*03:00)
Location: Near Van Nuys, California, US
Operator: Transcontinental and Western Air, Inc. (TWA) (US)
Aircraft type: Douglas DC-3 (NC-17322)

Flight 18 was scheduled to land at Lockheed Air Terminal, in Burbank, its first en route stop while on a US domestic transcontinental service originating at San Francisco, California, and ultimately bound for New York, New York. But during the instrument approach the transport crashed in a walnut grove some 7 miles (11km) north-west of the airport. Eight persons aboard lost their lives in the accident, including both pilots; among the fifteen survivors, who suffered various injuries, was the hostess.

Its undercarriage down, the DC-3 had initially clipped trees and broken an electric power line and pole before it slammed to earth, although there was no post-impact fire. The crash occurred in early morning darkness and during a heavy fog, which had reduced the visibility to practically zero.

It was concluded by the US Civil Aeronautics Board (CAB) that the pilot of NC-17322 had deviated from the standard instrument approach procedure in descending below the minimum safe altitude. A contributing factor was considered to have been the failure of the carrier to enforce adherence to company procedures.

Date: 8 January 1945 (*c.*21:15)
Location: Near Port of Spain, Trinidad, West Indies
Operator: Pan American Airways System (US)
Aircraft type: Martin M-130 (NC-14716)

The famed 'China Clipper,' which had inaugurated the first scheduled passenger service across the Pacific Ocean ten years earlier, suffered a catastrophic demise while operating as Flight 161, which on this date had been on a transatlantic service originating at Miami, Florida, US, with an ultimate destination of Leopoldville (Kinshasa), in the Belgian Congo. As it was landing at sea off Port of Spain, an en route stop, the four-engine flying boat crashed, killing twenty-three persons aboard. Four passengers and three of its twelve crew members survived, including one of the two qualified captains serving as pilots of the aircraft.

Contacting the water at a higher-than-normal speed and in an excessively nose-down attitude a little more than 1 mile (1.5km) from the correct landing area, NC-14716 was destroyed by impact forces, which broke its hull in two and tore off both wings. A major portion of the aircraft then sank immediately. However, the bodies of at least seventeen of the victims were recovered, as was the main wreckage. The accident occurred in darkness, although the visibility was unlimited and the correct landing area had been lighted.

The captain serving as first officer, who was at the controls of the aircraft and among those killed in the crash, and who possessed limited experience in the Martin M-130, had apparently misjudged his altitude over the water and also failed to properly flare the aircraft before touching down. It was further determined by the US Civil Aeronautics Board (CAB) that the first officer had not been ade-

quately supervised by the acting captain, who himself was apparently preoccupied monitoring his instruments. Considered by the CAB as contributing factors were the smooth, glassy water, over which it would have been difficult to determine one's height, and, possibly, the failure of the co-pilot to wear his eye glasses, as required by his pilot's certificate.

Date: 10 January 1945 (*c.*04:10)
Location: Near Burbank, California, US
Operator: American Airlines (US)
Aircraft type: Douglas DC-3 (NC-25684)

Designated as Flight 6001 and on a US domestic transcontinental service from New York, New York, the transport crashed and burned in the Verdugo Mountains north of Los Angeles and approximately 3 miles (5km) north-east of Lockheed Air Terminal, where it was scheduled to land. All twenty-four persons

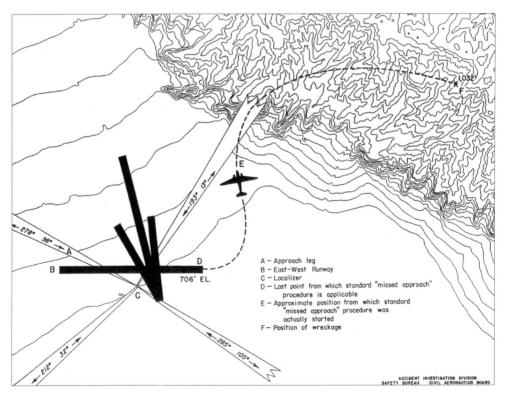

The flight path of the American Airlines Douglas DC-3 after an abandoned landing at Lockheed Air Terminal, which ended in a crash. (Civil Aeronautics Board)

aboard (twenty-one passengers and a crew of three) were killed.

After initiating an overshoot procedure, NC-25684 flew west-to-east over the airport, and was seen to make a left turn before it disappeared from view. Shortly afterwards, the pilot radioed that he was unable to maintain visual contact with the ground, and was diverting to Palmdale, located in the Mojave Desert. Its undercarriage having been retracted, the DC-3 was on an approximate heading of 110 degrees and in a right climbing turn when it slammed into a cloud-obscured ridge at an elevation of about 1,000ft (300m). It was dark at the time, being before dawn, and the Burbank weather consisted of a low overcast, with a ceiling of around 500ft (*c*.150m) and a visibility of approximately 2 miles (3km) in light fog.

It was concluded by the US Civil Aeronautics Board (CAB) that the pilot had apparently tried to execute the standard missed approach procedure, which involved a right turn, after first initiating the left turn. This error prevented a safe application of the procedure, and as a result the aircraft was placed on a course that took it into the rising terrain. Additionally, airline personnel on the ground were deemed 'negligent' by the CAB for failing to obtain and transmit to the flight important meteorological information, specifically the fact that the conditions at the airport were below the prescribed minimum authorised for landing.

Date: 31 January 1945 (*c*.08:25)
Location: Near Spring Plains, Victoria, Australia
Operator: Australian National Airways
Aircraft type: Stinson A2W (VH-UYY)

Ten persons aboard (eight passengers and two pilots) lost their lives when the trimotored transport crashed and burned some 60 miles (100km) north of Melbourne, from where it had taken off earlier, on a scheduled domestic service with an ultimate destination of Broken Hill. There were no survivors.

The Stinson had been cruising at 1,000ft (*c*.300m) when its port outer wing failed, after which there was a more complete break-up of the aircraft, including the loss of its starboard wing and tail assembly. The accident was attributed to the tension failure of the port wing lower main front spar boom under exceptionally heavy flight loads, and which resulted from the presence of a fatigue crack extending around some 40 per cent of the perimeter of the corresponding attachment fitting. Considered as contributory were the local weather conditions, with an overcast accompanied by strong, gusty winds. One of the recommendations of the investigative panel was for joints of all heat-treated, welded steel tube airframes to be subject to magnaflux examination at every annual overhaul.

Date: 15 February 1945
Location: Near Lagoa Santa, Goias, Brazil
Operator: Navegação Aérea Brasiliera (Brazil)
Aircraft type: Lockheed 18 Lodestar (PP-NAE)

The twin-engine transport crashed approximately 220 miles (350km) south-west of the town of Goiana, presumably during a scheduled domestic service, and all eleven persons aboard (seven passengers and a crew of four) were killed.

Date: 23 February 1945 (*c*.02:25)
Location: Near Rural Retreat, Virginia, US
Operator: American Airlines (US)
Aircraft type: Douglas DC-3 (NC-18142)

The aircraft struck Glade Mountain, in the Appalachian range, approximately 5 miles (10km) east of Marion, killing seventeen persons, including both pilots. Four passengers and the hostess survived the accident with serious injuries.

Operating as Flight 9 and on a US domestic transcontinental service originating at New York, New York, with an ultimate destination of Los Angeles, California, NC-18142 had last stopped at Washington, DC, and was proceeding on a south-westerly course when it crashed on the wooded summit of the mountain some 65 miles (105km) north-east of Tri-City Airport, serving Nashville, Tennessee, where it was scheduled to land. The accident occurred in darkness, and the local weather consisted of a broken overcast, with the cloud base down to 3,500ft (c.1,050m). Light to moderate turbulence prior to the crash had been reported by the survivors.

The pilot of Flight 9 had apparently failed to remain at a safe instrument altitude under the prevailing conditions, which violated Civil Air Regulations (CAR). Considering that the mountain struck by the DC-3 rose to nearly 4,000ft (c.1,200m), the company's minimum instrument cruising height in the area was 7,000ft (c.2,000m), and CAR specified a minimum cruising altitude of at least 1,000ft (300m) above the terrain. His actions may have been due to poor judgement, or to some mechanical or operational difficulty, such as wing icing. A contributing factor was what the US Civil Aeronautics Board (CAB) referred to as 'laxity' by the carrier in dispatching and supervising this and other flights along the route without requiring them to maintain the specified minimum height.

Date: 14 April 1945 (c.17:00)
Location: Near Morgantown, West Virginia, US
Operator: Pennsylvania Central Airlines (US)
Aircraft type: Douglas DC-3 (NC-25692)

Designated as Flight 142 and on a US domestic service from Pittsburgh, Pennsylvania, to Birmingham, Alabama, the transport crashed on the west slope of Cheat Mountain, in the vicinity of Morgantown Airport, which was a scheduled en route stop. All twenty persons aboard (seventeen passengers and a crew of three) were killed.

The aircraft was in a slight right-banking attitude when it cut through trees and underbrush and then slammed into the ground near the top of a ridge at an approximate elevation of 2,000ft (600m). The late afternoon accident occurred during a fog and low overcast, with a ceiling of around 1,200ft (350m).

At the time of the crash, NC-25692 had been some 7 miles (11km) off course and about 2 miles (3km) from the prescribed airway, and considerably below the minimum height of 3,300ft (1,005m) authorised by the carrier when flying in the area in instrument weather conditions. It was believed that the pilot had continued under contact procedures over the mountainous terrain, and may have been off

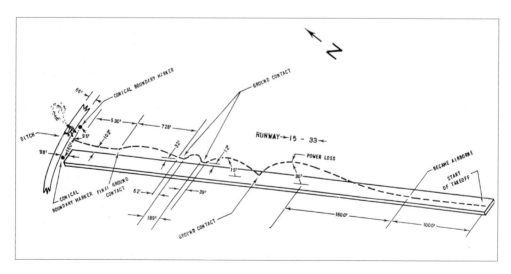

Chart showing the unstabilised forced landing of the Page Airways Lockheed Lodestar after abandoned take-off at Washington National Airport. (Civil Aeronautics Board)

course because he confused two rivers, mistaking the Cheat for the Monongahela.

Date: 20 April 1945
Location: Near Steinreich, Germany
Operator: Deutsche Lufthansa AG (Germany)
Aircraft type: Junkers Ju.52/3m (D-ANAJ)

In the closing days of the Second World War, the trimotored airliner was shot down in evening darkness by Soviet forces south of Berlin, from where it had taken off earlier, on an evacuation flight with an ultimate destination of Munich, Germany, and planned en route stops at Prague, Czechoslovakia, and Vienna, Austria. All but two passengers among the twenty persons aboard the Ju.52 lost their lives, including the three members of its crew.

Date: 21 April 1945
Location: Near Piesenkofen, Bavaria, Germany
Operator: Deutsche Lufthansa AG (Germany)
Aircraft type: Focke Wulf Fw.200KB-1 Condor (D-ASHH)

In this wartime incident, the four-engine airliner, on a scheduled domestic service from Berlin to Munich, was shot down by Allied forces approximately 50 miles (80km) north-north-west of its destination. All twenty-one persons aboard the Condor (sixteen passengers and five crew members) were killed.

Date: 27 April 1945 (*c.*12:40)
Location: Near Alexandria, Virginia, US
Operator: Page Airways (US)
Aircraft type: Lockheed 18-56 Lodestar (NC-33328)

The twin-engine transport crashed at Washington National Airport, serving the nation's capital city and an en route stop during a non-scheduled US domestic service that had originated at Miami, Florida, and was ultimately bound for New York, New York. Six passengers lost their lives in the accident; the two pilots were among the seven survivors, all of whom suffered injuries.

Taking off from Runway 33, NC-33328 had just become airborne when its starboard power plant failed, necessitating a forced landing. Its undercarriage was lowered, and the aircraft touched down, bouncing three times as it went off the right side of the runway. The Lodestar then caught fire after rolling into a concrete-lined drainage ditch.

The cause of the power plant malfunction was determined by the US Civil Aeronautics Board (CAB) to have been a cracked valve spring washer, the type of which that had been condemned by Wright, the engine manufacturer. During the failure sequence, the valve had entered the corresponding cylinder. Strong gusts and ground-level turbulence, coupled with the captain's application of flaps, probably contributed to the crash by making the aircraft 'float' during the attempted landing. Contributing to the seriousness of the accident was the presence of the deep drainage ditch, which had not been indicated by markers.

Date: 1 August 1945 (*c.*09:50)
Location: Near San Luis Potosi, Mexico
Operator: Líneas Aéreas Mineras SA (Mexico)
Aircraft type: Boeing 247D (XA-DUY)

Operating on a scheduled domestic service with an ultimate destination of Nogales, Sonora, the twin-engine airliner crashed in mountainous terrain some 220 miles (350km) north-west of Mexico City, from where it had taken off earlier, and shortly before it was to have landed at the airport serving San Luis Potosi, an en route stop. All twelve persons aboard (nine passengers and a crew of three) were killed. A press report that was not officially confirmed indicated that the accident had resulted from power plant failure.

Date: 11 August 1945 (*c.*16:00)
Location: Near San Salvador de Verde, Puebla, Mexico
Operator: Compañía Mexicana de Aviación SA (Mexico)
Aircraft type: Douglas DC-2 (XA-DOT)

The airliner struck Ixtaccihuatl mountain some 40 miles (65km) east-south-east of Mexico City, which was its destination during a scheduled domestic service from Tapachula, Chiapas. All sixteen persons aboard (twelve passengers and four crew members) were killed in the accident.

In its last message, XA-DOT was reported in instrument flight conditions over the city of Puebla. Its wreckage was subsequently located on the side of the inactive volcano at an elevation of nearly 15,000ft (*c.*5,000m), and the site of the crash indicated a significant error from its reported position.

Date: 7 September 1945 (*c.*02:15)
Location: Near Florence, South Carolina, US
Operator: Eastern Air Lines (US)
Aircraft type: Douglas DC-3 (NC-33631)

Designated as Flight 42 and on a US domestic service originating at Miami, Florida, with an ultimate destination of New York, New York, the transport crashed and burned in a swampy area, killing all twenty-two persons aboard (nineteen passengers and three crew members).

Having last stopped at Savannah, Georgia, NC-33631 had flown over Florence and then turned back in an attempt to reach the city's airport before the accident occurred, in early morning darkness. It was determined by the US Civil Aeronautics Board (CAB) that a fire of an unknown origin had erupted in the aircraft's rear cargo compartment, and futile attempts then must have been made to put out the blaze, using two hand-held fire extinguishers. The flames must have burned through structural sheet aluminium between the cabin compartments and ultimately through the rear spar web fabric, and spread to the right rear elevator. The fire would have been fed by such items as mail, baggage, lavatory and buffet facilities and insulation material.

Unable to reach Florence, the pilot apparently tried to make a forced landing in an open field but must have been unable to maintain altitude, and the DC-3 was flying at a low altitude with its undercarriage retracted when it struck two tall pine trees. The aircraft then rolled over until its port wing was almost vertical and slammed into the ground. There was evidence that the occupants had moved forward towards the flight deck to escape the flames, which would have rendered longitudinal control particularly difficult. Among other conclusions made by the CAB in its report on the crash of Flight 42 was that maximum flight safety necessitated the installation of fire-detection systems in the cargo compartments of commercial aircraft; such equipment and the use of fire-resistant materials in certain vital areas would in fact be mandated by the US government the following year.

Date: 20 October 1945
Location: South-western China
Operator: China National Aviation Corporation
Aircraft type: Douglas C-47

All thirty-one persons aboard (twenty-eight passengers and a crew of three) were killed when the airliner crashed during a regular service from Shanghai to Canton (Guangzhou). Reportedly, the DC-3 had been flying at a low altitude in adverse meteorological conditions when it slammed into a mountain.

Date: 13 November 1945 (*c.*20:15)
Location: Near Tacloban, the Philippines
Operator: Australian National Airways
Aircraft type: Douglas C-48 (VH-CDC)

Belonging to the US Army Air Forces, the twin-engine transport was being operated by the Australian carrier when it crashed in the sea off the island of Leyte after an aborted landing. All but one passenger among the seventeen persons aboard were killed in the accident, including the three members of its crew; the survivor was rescued after more than 5 hours in the water. Most of the victims were believed to have been American service personnel.

Having nearly completed an inter-island charter service from Manila, the aircraft had touched down hard at the airstrip, then pulled up and circled the control tower at a height of around 200ft (60m) before plunging into the water. The crash occurred in darkness, high winds and heavy rain, which had reduced the visibility to only about half a mile (0.8km).

The underlying cause of the accident was a judgement error by the pilot in attempting to land in the unfavourable weather conditions, especially considering that he had sufficient fuel to divert to an alternate airport. Subsequent to the crash, military air transport operations conducted at night in the Philippines were discontinued.

Date: 25 December 1945
Location: Near Dudinka, Russian Soviet Federative Socialist Republic, USSR
Operator: Polyarnya Aviatsiya (USSR)
Aircraft type: Douglas DC-3

Ten persons aboard (six passengers and a crew of four) were killed when the airliner crashed and burned some 50 miles (80km) north-west of Norilsk. There were no survivors from the accident. Reportedly, the DC-3 caught fire at an approximate height of 1,000ft (300m) soon after it had taken off from Dudinka airport, presumably on a non-scheduled or special service to a location in the Arctic region.

AFTER THE WAR
(1946–1949)

Peace and rising prosperity helped fuel the air travel boom of the second half of the 1940s. This also marked the period of modern aircraft – four-engine transports with higher speeds, greater range and more passenger comfort. Famous aircraft entering service during this period included the American Douglas DC-4 and DC-6, the Lockheed Constellation, and the British Avro Tudor and Vickers Viking. Expanding air routes would also bring air transportation to virtually everywhere in the world.

Every advancement has drawbacks, and with commercial aviation this would come with more accidents and fatalities. One reason for this would be the appearance of supplemental carriers, offering passenger services on routes and at times not available to those using regularly scheduled airlines. The operating practices of these carriers would come into serious question after a number of crashes involving loss of life.

Due to the relative size of transport aircraft, commercial aviation crashes prior to the end of the war were generally not major disasters. After the war, accidents involving dozens or even scores of fatalities became far more common. This was reflected during one 24-hour period, with two crashes in the US taking ninety-six lives, and the second accident eclipsing the first in the category of the 'worst airline disaster in American history'. Of course, by today's standards, fifty fatalities in a single air crash would not be considered a catastrophic disaster. Furthermore, the slower speeds of piston-engine aircraft would assure a higher chance of survival. But survivability in any air crash is always a matter of chance, and indeed readers of the accounts in this chapter will note the frighteningly common phase: 'All aboard were killed'.

This section takes the record up to the end of the first half of the twentieth century. For information on crashes occurring beyond this, readers can refer to my other work, *Aviation Disasters: The World's Major Airliner Crashes Since 1950*, also available from The History Press.

Date: 14 January 1946
Location: Near Netrubezh, Russian Soviet Federative Socialist Republic, USSR
Operator: Aeroflot (USSR)
Aircraft type: Lisunov Li-2 (SSSR-L4150)

All twenty-two persons aboard (seventeen passengers and five crew members) were killed when the twin-engine airliner, which had been on a scheduled domestic service to Moscow from Kharkov, Ukrainian SSR, crashed some 250 miles (400km) south of its destination. The Li-2 had apparently experienced severe icing, resulting in buffeting and consequent structural failure.

Date: 18 January 1946 (*c.*11:00)
Location: Near Cheshire, Connecticut, US
Operator: Eastern Air Lines (US)
Aircraft type: Douglas DC-3 (NC-19970)

Designated as Flight 16B and en route from New York, New York, to Boston, Massachusetts, the final segment of a US domestic service originating at Miami, Florida, the transport crashed and burned some 5 miles (10km) south-east of Waterbury. All seventeen persons aboard (fourteen passengers and a crew of three) were killed.

The aircraft was observed flying at an approximate height of 1,500ft (500m) when it caught fire. Shortly thereafter, its port wing failed upwards and the DC-3 plummeted into a wooded ravine in an attitude slightly past vertical, and with a slow rolling motion to the left.

In its investigation, the US Civil Aeronautics Board (CAB) determined that gasoline leaking in the port power plant nacelle, which resulted from either the failure of a fuel line or a related connection, was apparently ignited by either a generator or the exhaust manifold. The flames then spread through the wheel well and all the way back to the aircraft's empennage, apparently with such rapidity (perhaps as little as two minutes) that the crew was probably not aware of the situation. During the sequence, a dural line at a fuel pump fitting, as well as hydraulic and oil lines, were successively consumed and their contents ignited, and the blaze also burned through the aforementioned engine nacelle inboard of the wheel well. The structural break-up finally occurred when the heat weakened the wing structure, and the lower surface and rear spar flange failed in tension.

As a result of this and other US air carrier accidents, US Civil Air Regulations were amended, requiring in certain power plants fire-resistant flexible lines that carry combustible fluids, and also fire walls, engine fire-extinguishing systems and the use of the most flame-resistant materials available in such furnishings as upholstery and carpets in pas-senger and crew compartments, as well as fire detection and extinguishing systems in cargo compartments.

Date: 31 January 1946 (02:47)
Location: Near Walcott, Wyoming, US
Operator: United Air Lines (US)
Aircraft type: Douglas DC-3 (NC-25675)

Operating as Flight 14, the aircraft crashed on Elk Mountain around 90 miles (145km) north-west of Cheyenne while en route from Boise, Idaho, to Denver, Colorado, one segment of a transcontinental US domestic service originating at Seattle, Washington, with an ultimate destination of New York, New York. All twenty-one persons aboard (eighteen passengers and three crew members) perished.

The aircraft had been cruising in darkness on a heading of 80 degrees when it struck the cloud-obscured peak at an approximate elevation of 10,800ft (3,300m), or about 350ft (105m) from its summit, disintegrated and burned. The low overcast in the area was accompanied by high winds, which were blowing at a velocity of between 50 and 55mph (*c.*80–90kmh).

At the moment of impact, NC-25675 had been some 5 miles (10km) south of the pre-scribed airway, and was nearly 200ft (60m) below its assigned altitude. The height deviation was attributed to a decrease in the barometric pressure and the unusually low temperature encountered in the area. The cause of the deviation from the proper route, which was the primary cause of the accident, probably resulted from an attempt by the pilot to fly on a direct line between the Sinclair and Laramie radio range stations.

Date: 3 March 1946 (08:12)
Location: Near Pine Valley, California, US
Operator: American Airlines (US)
Aircraft type: Douglas DC-3 (NC-21799)

Designated as Flight 6-103 and on a transcontinental US domestic service originating at

New York, New York, the transport crashed and burned in the Laguna Mountains some 40 miles (65km) east-north-east of San Diego, which was its ultimate destination, having last stopped at Tucson, Arizona. All twenty-five persons aboard (twenty-two passengers and a crew of three) were killed.

The DC-3 was in a slight descent when its port wing tip initially hit the sloping terrain, causing the aircraft to 'whip' to the left and then slam into Thing Mountain at an elevation of just under 5,000ft (1,500m). At the time of the accident, the mountain was obscured by clouds.

It was concluded by the US Civil Aeronautics Board (CAB) that the pilot-in-command had apparently descended or permitted the first officer to descend into the instrument meteorological conditions to a height below that required to maintain terrain clearance. However, the Board was unable to determine the reason for the premature descent that led to the crash.

Date: 5 March 1946 (*c.*17:00)
Location: Near Prague, Czechoslovakia
Operator: Ceskoslovenske Aerolinie (CSA) (Czechoslovakia)
Aircraft type: Junkers Ju.52/3m (OK-ZDN)

The trimotored airliner crashed and burned while approaching to land at Ruzyne Airport, serving the nation's capital, killing twelve persons aboard. The three survivors, who included two members of the aircraft's four-person crew suffered various injuries. Having nearly completed a scheduled international service that had originated at Paris, France, OK-ZDN was on its approach to Runway 22 when the accident occurred, reportedly after the aircraft had experienced engine trouble.

Date: 10 March 1946 (*c.*21:00)
Location: Near Hobart, Tasmania, Australia
Operator: Australian National Airways
Aircraft type: Douglas DC-3C (VH-AET)

The airliner crashed in Frederick Henry Bay approximately 3 miles (5km) east-south-east of Cambridge Airport, serving Hobart, from where it had taken off moments earlier, on a scheduled domestic service to Melbourne, Victoria. All twenty-five persons aboard were killed in the accident; the four crew members included one cabin attendant and a supernumerary pilot who was riding on the flight deck while receiving instruction.

After what appeared to be a normal departure, VH-AET proceeded in a south-easterly direction as it climbed to a height of around 400ft (120m). According to witness accounts, the aircraft initiated a slight turn to the left before its nose dropped. The DC-3 then plunged into the sea some 600ft (180m) off shore from the high water mark on Seven Mile Beach. It was dark at the time of the crash, and the local weather consisted of a low overcast, with a ceiling of about 3,000ft (1,000m) and a visibility of around 10 miles (15km).

Considerable wreckage and the bodies of more than half of the victims were subsequently recovered, and the investigation, which included a detailed examination of the former, found no evidence that the accident had been precipitated by a bird strike or the failure of the aircraft's power plants or flight controls. Significantly, the thirty-year-old captain of VH-AET suffered from diabetes, which he was able to manage through diet and insulin treatment. In view of this fact, a court of inquiry concluded that the most probable cause of the crash was the physical incapacitation of the pilot resulting from insulin shock, related to insufficient sugar in the blood system. His condition could have led to his improper manipulation of the control wheel and, in turn, to the unwanted descent into the water. In the darkened flight deck, the other two members of the flight crew might not have detected the mental and muscular un-coordination affecting the captain.

It was also determined that at the moment of impact, the bank and climb gyroscope of the aircraft's autopilot had been 'caged,' or

A Railway Air Services de Havilland 89, one of which crashed in Northern Ireland during an air-taxi service from Liverpool, England. (Philip Jarrett)

locked in position. This finding led to speculation that the autopilot, set in a descent, could have been inadvertently activated by the first officer while trying to engage the fuel cross-feed system. The investigative report noted that both the autopilot and the cross-feed in the DC-3 were activated in the same manner, i.e. by turning a small lever in a clockwise direction, and that the levers are about 1ft (30cm) apart; however, the former also had a spring-tension mechanism. Although there was sufficient evidence to support the theory, the court did not consider the inadvertent engagement of the autopilot as a causative factor. Nevertheless, one recommendation made in the report was for a physical change in them, in terms of their appearance and shape, to prevent confusion between its activating lever and that of the cross-feed system.

Date: 23 March 1946
Location: Indian Ocean
Operator: British Overseas Airways Corporation (BOAC)
Aircraft type: Avro Lancastrian 1 (G-AGLX)

Flown by employees of Australia's Qantas Empire Airways and on a scheduled international service from Karachi, India (Pakistan), to Perth, Western Australia, the four-engine airliner disappeared with ten persons aboard (five passengers and five crew members). The aircraft was to have reached Cocos Island, an intermediate stop, at 19:50 local time.

Date: 1 April 1946 (*c.*10:00)
Location: Near Craigavad, Northern Ireland
Operator: Railway Air Services Ltd (UK)
Aircraft type: de Havilland 89A Dragon Rapide (G-AERZ)

All six occupants (four passengers and two crew members) lost their lives when the twin-engine aeroplane crashed and burned near the shore of Belfast Lough some 5 miles (10km) north-east of Belfast, where it was to have landed.

Having nearly completed a scheduled domestic air-taxi flight from Liverpool, England, G-AERZ had struck trees and then slammed to the ground during the landing approach, the accident occurring in adverse weather conditions, with fog and a visibility no more than 600ft (180m). The crash was attributed by the UK Ministry of Aviation to an error in navigation by the pilot, who failed to maintain a course necessary to avoid the higher terrain.

Date: 22 April 1946
Location: Near La Libertad, Nicaragua
Operator: TACA de Nicaragua SA
Aircraft type: Lockheed 14 Super Electra (AN-ACC)

The twin-engine transport crashed and burned while taking off from the La Libertad airport, on a scheduled domestic service to the Nicaraguan capital of Managua, located some 80 miles (130km) to the west. Killed in the evening accident were twenty persons aboard the Super Electra, including the three members of its crew; according to press reports, the sole surviving passenger was a child who escaped serious injury.

Date: 16 May 1946 (01:04)
Location: Near Richmond, Virginia, US
Operator: Viking Air Transport Company (US)
Aircraft type: Douglas DC-3C (NC-53218)

The transport crashed and burned in the vicinity of Byrd Field, from where it had taken off earlier, an en route stop during a non-scheduled US domestic service originating at Newark, New Jersey, with an ultimate destination of Norfolk, Virginia. All twenty-seven persons aboard lost their lives in the accident, including the two-member flight crew; most of the passengers were recently discharged members of the US Merchant Marine.

Initially reporting that one power plant was 'running rough', the pilot elected to return to the airport at Richmond. However, an attempted instrument approach had to be abandoned because the aircraft was not properly aligned with the runway. After it passed over Byrd, the crew reported losing sight of the airport and that they were returning to the radio range. Subsequently, the DC-3

plummeted into a densely wooded area in a steep nose-down attitude, the crash occurring in darkness and 'zero-zero' visibility and ceiling conditions.

It was determined by the US Civil Aeronautics Board (CAB) that after the overshoot procedure had been initiated, the aircraft's starboard engine, which had apparently been misidentified as malfunctioning, was shut down, but the crew failed to feather the corresponding propeller. Additionally, the undercarriage remained extended, and the port engine was unable to develop enough power due to a defective cylinder. These factors prevented the crew from maintaining air speed and altitude, and thus control of the aircraft in order to effect an emergency landing, especially considering the adverse weather. Ultimately, the DC-3 stalled.

In addition to the improper emergency actions on the part of the pilot, factors contributing to the accident were his decision to continue the flight into meteorological conditions he previously had considered unsafe, and his negligence in not having an inspection of the power plants even though he had reported the engine oil pressure gauge to be fluctuating before the flight that ended in a crash. The captain, who himself lacked experience as a pilot-in-command, had apparently been persuaded into making the flight by his even-less-experienced first officer.

Date: 22 May 1946 (c.13:00)
Location: Near Oslo, Norway
Operator: Det Norske Luftfartselskap A/S (DNL) (Norwegian Air Lines)
Aircraft type: Junkers Ju.52/3m (LN-LAB)

The trimotored airliner crashed and burned in a residential area on Snaroya Peninsula, and in the vicinity of Fornebu Airport, serving Oslo, from where it had taken off shortly before, on a scheduled international service to Stockholm, Sweden. All but one passenger among the fourteen persons aboard the Ju.52 were killed in the accident, including the three members of its crew. After suffering a power plant malfunction, LN-LAB was proceeding back to the airport at a low altitude when it apparently stalled, then struck some trees and slammed into a house.

Date: 11 July 1946 (*c*.11:40)
Location: Near Reading, Pennsylvania, US
Operator: Transcontinental and Western Air, Inc. (TWA) (US)
Aircraft type: Lockheed 049 Constellation (NC-86513)

Five crewmen lost their lives in the crash of the four-engine airliner, while the sole survivor of the accident, an instructor pilot, was seriously injured. Having been delivered to the carrier only six months earlier, NC-86513 was on a pilot training flight when fire erupted in its fuselage. Fire-fighting efforts by the crew were unsuccessful, and an emergency descent was initiated. During this manoeuvre, a hatch was opened in an attempt to reduce the smoke within the flight deck, but this only aggravated the situation, and the instructor pilot then opened the window on the port side of the cockpit and tried to fly with his head out the window. Blinded by the intense smoke and unable to maintain control, he attempted to set down the aircraft without visual reference. The Constellation initially struck two electric power lines before slamming to earth, coming to rest in a field; it was destroyed by both impact forces and by flames.

In its investigation of the accident, the US Civil Aeronautics Board (CAB) determined that the failure of at least one of the generator lead through-stud installations in the fuselage skin of the aircraft's forward baggage compartment had resulted in intense local heating due to electrical arcing, which in turn ignited fuselage insulation. A contributing factor was considered to have been a deficiency in the inspection methods being used, which permitted defects in the aircraft to persist over a long period of time, reaching such proportions as to create a 'hazardous' condition.

The aforementioned defects led to the grounding for six weeks of the entire Constellation fleet to allow for modifications, which included insulation of certain wiring; improved fire-extinguishing capability for the accessory section of the engine nacelles; provisions made for increased drainage and ventilation of the nacelles aft of the fire wall in order to prevent the accumulation of combustible fluids or vapours, and modification of the cabin supercharger drive shafts. Also out of this accident came specially designed bolts used in various parts of aircraft in order to provide relatively airtight electrical conductors through the skin of pressurised fuselage through-studs.

Date: 13 July 1946
Location: Near Tsinan (Jinan), Shandong, China
Operator: Central Air Transport Corporation (China)
Aircraft type: Curtiss-Wright C-46

The twin-engine airliner crashed less than 1 mile (1.5km) from the city's airport, from where it had just taken off, presumably on a scheduled domestic service. Killed in the accident were thirteen of the forty-nine persons aboard, including two members of its crew of three; among the survivors, all but three suffered injuries. Reportedly related to a power plant malfunction, the crash led to the grounding of the carrier's fleet of C-46 aircraft.

Date: 17 July 1946 (*c*.11:30)
Location: Near Cuenca, Azway, Ecuador
Operator: Aerovias Nacionales del Ecuador SA (ANDESA) (Ecuador)
Aircraft type: Curtiss-Wright C-46D (HC-SCA)

Operating on a scheduled domestic service from Guayaquil, the airliner crashed and burned on a ridge in the vicinity of the city's airport, where it was to have landed. All thirty persons aboard (twenty-seven passengers and a crew of three) were killed.

The accident apparently occurred as HC-SCA was executing an overshoot manoeuvre from a missed landing approach. Its failure to gain sufficient height during the 'go-around' may have resulted from an engine malfunction.

Date: 26 July 1946 (*c*.08:30)
Location: Near Huatesco, Veracruz, Mexico
Operator: Comunicaciones Aéreos de Veracruz (Mexico)
Aircraft type: Fairchild Pilgrim 100A (XA-DEJ)

Nine persons lost their lives when the single-engine aeroplane crashed some 40 miles (65km) south-east of Jalapa, from where it had taken off earlier, on a scheduled domestic intra-state service to Cordoba. There were no survivors.

Reportedly, XA-DEJ had turned back towards its departure point due to a power plant malfunction before the accident occurred, in adverse weather conditions. Trouble had in fact been reported in the aircraft's engine even before its departure from Jalapa.

Date: 20 August 1946 (*c*.06:15)
Location: Near Brogile, Normandy, France
Operator: British Overseas Airways Corporation (BOAC)
Aircraft type: Avro Lancastrian 1 (G-AGMF)

All but one of its nine occupants were killed when the four-engine airliner crashed some 20 miles (30km) south-east of Lisieux while on a long-distance training flight from Palestine to London. The sole survivor of the accident escaped serious injury.

It was believed that the crew had incorrectly assessed their position while letting down in twilight and adverse meteorological conditions, which according to eyewitnesses consisted of a 'very' low cloud base and poor visibility due to a fine but dense rain, resulting in the impact with the terrain.

Date: 31 August 1946
Location: Near Prince Rupert, British Columbia, Canada
Operator: Queen Charlotte Airlines (Canada)
Aircraft type: Supermarine Stranraer (CF-BYL)

The twin-engine flying boat, which was on a domestic intra-provincial 'mercy' flight from Stewart to Prince Rupert, went down in Chatham Sound, presumably while preparing to land. Including four designated crew members, all seven persons aboard the aircraft were killed in the crash, which occurred in evening darkness and during a heavy fog.

Date: 3 September 1946 (*c*.17:00)
Location: Near Køge, Sjælland, Denmark
Operator: Air France
Aircraft type: Douglas DC-3C (F-BAOB)

The airliner crashed and burned in a field on the island some 40 miles (65km) south of Copenhagen, from where it had taken off earlier, on a scheduled international service to Paris. All twenty-two persons aboard (seventeen passengers and a crew of five) were killed in the accident. One engine of the DC-3 had caught fire in the air prior to the crash, the blaze resulting from a fuel leak.

Date: 4 September 1946 (*c*.09:15)
Location: Near Gonesse, Ile-de-France, France
Operator: Air France
Aircraft type: Douglas DC-3D (F-BAXD)

Operating on a scheduled international service to London, the airliner crashed and burned shortly after its departure from Le Bourget Airport, serving Paris. Killed in the accident were twenty persons aboard the DC-3, including all but one of its five crew members, plus one person on the ground; the five survivors from the flight, who included a stewardess, suffered various injuries.

The aircraft had inexplicably lost height before it slammed into a factory, the accident occurring in cloudy weather and conditions of variable wind.

Date: 5 September 1946 (*c*.01:30)
Location: Near Elko, Nevada, US
Operator: Trans-Luxury Airlines (US)
Aircraft type: Douglas DC-3C (NC-57850)

The transport crashed and burned while attempting to land at Elko Airport, to where it had diverted for refuelling during a non-scheduled US domestic service that had originated at New York, New York, and last stopped at Cheyenne, Wyoming, and was ultimately bound for San Francisco, California. All but one of the twenty-two persons aboard the aircraft lost their lives in the accident, including the three members of its crew; the surviving passenger, a two-year-old boy whose parents and baby sister were among those killed, escaped serious injury.

Its undercarriage extended, the DC-3 had slammed into a ridge, just below its crest, some 100ft (30m) above the level of the airport and about 2.5 miles (4km) west of the threshold of Runway 05, which was being used. The crash occurred in darkness, and the local weather consisted of a dense ground fog.

The pilot of NC-57850 had continued the approach after apparently losing visual contact with the airport due to the fog. Considered as contributory to the accident was the unfamiliarity of the pilot with the terrain in the immediate area of the airport. Also, the original flight plan was found to be deficient in that the fuel carried aboard the aircraft did not provide a sufficient margin of safety needed to proceed to the alternate landing site. And for reasons that could not be determined, the flight had taken approximately half an hour longer than anticipated, making the fuel situation even more critical.

A review of supplemental air carrier operations made in light of this and other accidents led to the proposal of new safety requirements for such companies. Previously, discretion had been allowed in the enforcement of Civil Air Regulations to prevent restrictive regulations that could have threatened the economic survival of these operators. These and other factors apparently led to the demise of Trans-Luxury Airlines, which ceased operations in early 1948.

Date: 7 September 1946 (*c*.04:10)
Location: Near Bathurst, Gambia
Operator: British South American Airways
Aircraft type: Avro York (G-AHEW)

This was the British South American Airways Avro York 'Star Leader' that crashed shortly after take-off from Bathurst airport, in Gambia. (British Airways)

Operating on a scheduled international service originating at London, with an ultimate destination of Buenos Aires, Argentina, the four-engine transport crashed and burned approximately 3 miles (5km) from Yundum Airport, serving Bathurst, from where it had just taken off and which was an en route stop. All twenty-four persons aboard (twenty passengers and a crew of four) were killed.

Occurring in pre-dawn darkness, the accident apparently resulted from a loss of control. The reason for this could not be determined with certainty, although the mishandling of the flight controls by the captain was considered the most likely explanation.

Date: 18 September 1946 (c.05:10)
Location: Near Gander, Newfoundland
Operator: Société Anonyme Belge d'Exploitation de la Navigation Aérienne (SABENA) (Belgium)
Aircraft type: Douglas DC-4 (OO-CBG)

The four-engine transport crashed and burned in a wooded area some 25 miles (40km) southwest of the Gander airport, where it was to have landed during a scheduled transatlantic flight originating at Brussels, Belgium, with an ultimate destination of New York City. Killed in the accident were twenty-seven of the forty-four persons aboard the DC-4, including all but one member of its crew of seven; the survivors suffered various injuries.

Occurring in darkness and heavy fog, the crash was attributed to the failure of the pilot to execute the approach procedure to be used in adverse meteorological conditions. Considered as a possible contributing factor were magnetic perturbations of the aircraft's radio compass.

Date: 20 September 1946
Location: Near Xichang, Sichuan, China
Operator: China National Aviation Corporation
Aircraft type: Curtiss-Wright C-46

The airliner crashed into a mountain that rose to about 15,000ft (5,000m), the accident occurring shortly after its departure from Sichang, on a scheduled domestic service to Kunming, Yunnan. All twenty-eight persons aboard (twenty-five passengers and three crew members) were killed in the accident.

Date: 27 September 1946 (c.13:30)
Location: Near Milngavie, Stirlingshire, Scotland
Operator: Railway Air Services Ltd (UK)
Aircraft type: de Havilland 89A Dragon Rapide (G-AFFF)

All seven persons aboard (five passengers and two crew members) lost their lives when the twin-engine aeroplane crashed on a hillside approximately 5 miles (10km) north of Renfrew Airport, serving Glasgow, where it was to have landed at the end of a scheduled domestic air-taxi service from the Island of Islay.

The accident occurred during a low overcast, with solid cloud coverage at 1,200ft (c.350m) and a visibility of around 2 miles (3km) in drizzle, after the Dragon Rapide had flown over, and assumed a north-westerly course away from, the airport. The navigational error that led to the crash may have been related to a misunderstanding between the pilot and the radio operator and their confusion of bearing information from the ground controller that was intended for another aircraft. Factors considered as contributory included a message from the second aircraft requesting priority to land due to a low fuel situation, which initially interrupted communications with G-AFFF, and a lack of experience by the radio operator of the former and the captain of the latter.

Date: 27 September 1946 (c.17:30)
Location: Near Alto Rio Doce, Minas Gerais, Brazil
Operator: Panair do Brasil SA (Brazil)
Aircraft type: Douglas DC-3A (PP-PCH)

Operating on a scheduled domestic service to Rio de Janeiro, the aircraft crashed and burned on a mountain some 75 miles (120km) south-south-east of Belo Horizonte, from where it had taken off earlier, killing all twenty-five persons aboard (twenty-two passengers and a crew of three).

According to press reports that were not verified, PP-PCH had caught fire in the air after being struck by lightning; in some way, poor meteorological conditions probably factored in the accident.

Date: 3 October 1946 (05:03)
Location: Near Stephenville, Newfoundland
Operator: American Overseas Airlines (US)
Aircraft type: Douglas DC-4 (NC-90904)

The second major airline disaster occurring in Newfoundland in only about two weeks involved Flight 904, which had been on a transatlantic service originating at New York City, with an ultimate destination of Berlin, Germany.

All thirty-nine persons aboard (thirty-one passengers and eight crew members) perished when the four-engine transport crashed 2½ minutes after its departure from Harmon Field, serving Stephenville, where it had landed due to bad weather at Gander, which was its intended en route stop. The accident occurred in pre-dawn darkness and cloudy weather conditions, with an overcast at 5,000ft (c.1,500m). Although the visibility under the clouds was 10 miles (c.15km), the terrain in the area of the crash was unlighted, and the moon and stars were obscured by the overcast.

Initially cleared to take-off on Runway 30, the aircraft was switched to Runway 07 due to a wind shift. However, a subsequent investigation by the US Civil Aeronautics Board (CAB) concluded that a departure from the latter under the existing conditions was hazardous unless the crew initiated a turn shortly after becoming airborne and climbed to a safe altitude away from the rising terrain. The pilot of NC-90904 did not take such action and maintained a north-easterly heading until

the DC-4 struck a ridge some 7 miles (11km) from the airport and at an approximate elevation of 1,200ft (350m), bursting into flames on impact.

No restrictions had been placed on the runways used for take-off from Harmon Field, and no special procedures had been established for climbing to a cruising altitude. It was nevertheless noted in the CAB report that the pilot of Flight 904 had flown out of the airport previously, and had been furnished with sufficient data for him to determine the proper climb-out procedure. Subsequently, the CAB circulated proposed regulations requiring US carriers to clearly define the departure procedures at every airport in which the terrain or other obstacles present a hazard to aircraft at night or in instrument meteorological conditions.

Date: 8 October 1946
Location: Near Taiyuan, Shanxi, China
Operator: China National Aviation Corporation
Aircraft type: Unknown

The aircraft, probably a Douglas C-47 or Curtiss-Wright C-46 that had presumably been on a domestic service, struck a mountain, and all thirty-one persons aboard were killed, including an estimated crew of three.

Date: 10 October 1946 (c.20:00)
Location: Near Sefrou, Morocco
Operator: Air Ocean (France)
Aircraft type: Amiot AAC.1 Toucan (F-BCAA)

The trimotored airliner crashed and burned about 20 miles (30km) south-south-east of Fez during a scheduled international service originating at Paris, with an ultimate destination of Casablanca, Morocco. All sixteen persons aboard (eleven passengers and a crew of five) were killed.

Due to an apparent navigational error, F-BCAA slammed into a mountain at an approximate elevation of 3,600ft (1,100m), the accident occurring in darkness.

Date: 17 October 1946 (00:57)
Location: Near Laramie, Wyoming, US
Operator: NATS Air Transportation Service
(US)
Aircraft type: Douglas DC-3C (NC-38942)

All thirteen persons aboard (ten passengers
and three crew members) were killed when
the airliner crashed in the vicinity of the
Laramie airport, where it was to have landed,
its first en route stop during a non-scheduled
US domestic service that had originated
at Oakland, California, and was ultimately
bound for Newark, New Jersey. The accident
occurred in darkness and cloudy weather
conditions, with an overcast of 400ft (120m)
and light rain.

Prior to the crash, NC-38942 had flown
over the airport at least three times, indicating that the pilot was having considerable
difficulty in effecting alignment with the
runway. While manoeuvring under the
clouds at a dangerously low altitude, and
in an apparent attempt to keep the airport
in sight, the pilot must have momentarily
lost control, permitting the aircraft to bank
excessively until its port wing tip struck
the ground. Its undercarriage extended, the
DC-3 then slammed to earth, although there
was no post-impact fire.

Considered as a contributing factor was the
negligence of the pilot in planning a flight
into an area of adverse meteorological conditions without making adequate provisions
for a suitable alternate airport. The Denver
air-traffic control centre had in fact tried to
provide the aircraft with such information,
but it was not done in sufficient time to have
been any assistance to the crew.

Date: 1 November 1946 (c.11:20)
Location: Near St Leger-La Montagne, Haute-
Vienne, France
Operator: Compagnie de Transports Aerien
Languedoc-Roussillon (France)
Aircraft type: Amiot AAC.1 Toucan
(F-BCAD)

The trimotored airliner crashed and burned
approximately 20 miles (30km) north-north-
east of Limoges while en route from Paris
to Perpignan, the initial, domestic segment
of a service with an ultimate destination of
Casablanca, Morocco. Killed in the accident were all but four passengers among the
twenty-seven persons aboard the Toucan,
including the three members of its crew; only
one of the survivors escaped serious injury.

Occurring in conditions of poor visibility
due to fog, the crash probably resulted from
a loss of control due to the icing of its wings
and tail surfaces.

Date: 5 November 1946 (c.18:30)
Location: Near Moscow, Russian Soviet
Federative Socialist Republic, USSR
Operator: Aeroflot (USSR)
Aircraft type: Douglas C-47 (SSSR-L946)

Operating on a scheduled domestic service
from Riga, Latvian SSR, the transport crashed
in the vicinity of Vnukuvo Airport, serving
Moscow, where it was to have landed, and
thirteen of the twenty-six persons aboard were
killed. The accident occurred in darkness and
conditions of poor visibility due to heavy fog.

The C-47 had circled in a holding pattern
for two hours due to the weather and the
high volume of traffic, but during the landing approach the crew initiated an overshoot
manoeuvre, at which time the aircraft apparently stalled, then plummeted to the ground.

Date: 13 November 1946 (c.03:40)
Location: Near Lebec, California, US
Operator: Western Air Lines (US)
Aircraft type: Douglas DC-3C (NC-18645)

Designated as Flight 23 and on a US domestic
service to Burbank, California, from Las Vegas,
Nevada, the transport crashed some 25 miles
(40km) north-west of Newhall, killing all
eleven persons aboard (eight passengers and
three crew members).

The DC-3 had been on a heading of 155
degrees when it struck White Mountain, just

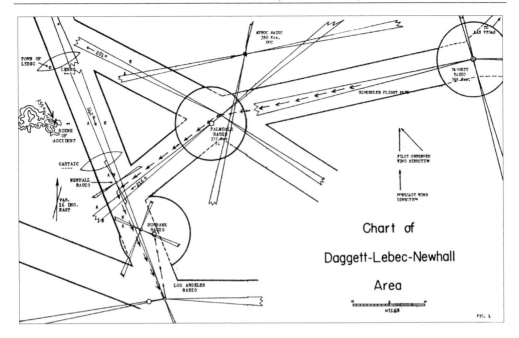

Chart of

Daggett-Lebec-Newhall

Area

This chart indicates the correct path and site where Western Air Lines Douglas DC-3 crashed after deviating from the airway system. (Civil Aeronautics Board)

below its crest and at an approximate elevation of 6,000ft (1,800m), bursting into flames on impact. Its wreckage was located two days later. It was dark at the time of the accident, and the weather conditions in the area were cloudy. The scene of the crash was 27 miles (43km) north-west of the airway intersection where the flight should have turned towards the south-east and 10 miles (c.15km) to the right of the radio range course that would have been used in the initial approach to Lockheed Air Terminal, where NC-18645 was scheduled to land.

It was concluded by the US Civil Aeronautics Board (CAB) that the pilot may have tuned his automatic direction finder (ADF) to the wrong radio station, and apparently then commenced an instrument letdown without establishing a positive fix. His actions must have been aggravated by conditions of severe static; a wind in excess of the anticipated velocity; preoccupation with an unusual amount of radio conversation; and an inoperative radio range station on which a fix could be established. Subsequently, the

south-west leg of the Palmdale range was moved nine degrees to the north so to pass directly over the Newhall range station, and the latter was also designated as a compulsory reporting point.

Date: 13 November 1946 (c.08:20)
Location: Near Perote, Veracruz, Mexico
Operator: Comunicaciones Aéreas de Veracruz SA (Mexico)
Aircraft type: Douglas DC-3 (XA-FOZ)

All sixteen persons aboard (thirteen passengers and three crew members) were killed when the airliner crashed and burned some 30 miles (50km) west of Jalapa. The DC-3 had been on a scheduled domestic service from Mexico City to the city of Veracruz and was cruising at 11,000ft (c.3,400m) when it slammed into a cloud-obscured mountain. Just prior to impact, the crew had issued a position report indicating that XA-FOZ was flying off the normal route, but an attempt by those on the ground to put the aircraft back on to the correct course came too late to prevent the accident. Had the DC-3 been only about 700ft (200m) higher, the crash would have been prevented even when considering its erroneous position.

Date: 14 November 1946 (*c.*19:15)
Location: Near Amsterdam, the Netherlands
Operator: Koninklijke Luchtvaart Maatschappij voor Nederland en Kalonien (KLM) (the Netherlands)
Aircraft type: Douglas DC-3C (PH-TBW)

Operating on a scheduled international service from London, the transport crashed and burned while attempting to land at Schiphol Airport, serving Amsterdam. All twenty-six persons aboard (twenty-one passengers and five crew members) were killed.

The accident occurred during the final phase of the approach, and in darkness and weather conditions consisting of a low overcast, with a ceiling of around 500ft (150m) but good visibility under the clouds. It was believed that the crash resulted from the disorientation of the pilot, which was followed by an excessively sharp corrective turn that led to a loss of control. The DC-3 then slammed to earth, its undercarriage extended at the moment of impact.

Date: 26 November 1946 (*c.*10:30)
Location: Near San José, Costa Rica
Operator: Líneas Aéreas Costaricenses (LASCA) (Costa Rica)
Aircraft type: Douglas DC-3C (RX-76)

The airliner struck a mountain while approaching to land at the San José airport, at the end of a scheduled domestic service from Parrita. All twenty-three persons aboard (twenty passengers and a crew of three) were killed in the accident, which occurred in a dense fog.

Date: 4 December 1946
Location: Near Meshed, Khorasan, Iran
Operator: Aeroflot (USSR)
Aircraft type: Lisunov Li-2

The twin-engine airliner crashed, presumably while on a scheduled international service either to or from the USSR. All twenty-four persons aboard the Li-2 were killed.

Date: 14 December 1946
Location: Near San Pablo, Laguna, the Philippines
Operator: Far East Air Transport (the Philippines)
Aircraft type: Douglas DC-3C (PI-C-1)

The airliner crashed at an approximate elevation of 3,600ft (1,100m) on cloud-obscured Mt Banahaur on the island of Luzon, some 50 miles (80km) south-east of Manila, from where it had taken off earlier, on a scheduled domestic service to Lucena. Killed in the accident were twelve persons aboard the DC-3, including all but one member of its crew of four; the pilot and one passenger survived with serious injuries.

Date: 23 December 1946 (*c.*14:30)
Location: Near Tijuca, Rio de Janeiro, Brazil
Operator: Flota Aérea Mercante Argentina (FAMA)
Aircraft type: Avro York (LV-XIG)

Operating on a scheduled international service originating at London, with an ultimate destination of Buenos Aires, Argentina, the four-engine airliner crashed some 10 miles (15km) west of the city of Rio de Janeiro, which was an en route stop. All twenty-one persons aboard (fifteen passengers and a crew of six) were killed. The York had been approaching to land at the Rio de Janeiro airport when it slammed into a mountainside, the accident occurring in adverse meteorological conditions, with fog and rain in the area.

Date: 24 December 1946 (*c.*19:20)
Location: Near Pine Valley, California, US
Operator: Western Air Lines (US)
Aircraft type: Douglas DC-3C (NC-45395)

Designated as Flight 44 and en route from Holtville to San Diego, one segment of a US domestic intra-state service originating at Los Angeles, the transport crashed and burned about 45 miles (70km) east-north-east of its destination. Its wreckage was located on Cuyapaipe Mountain three days later, with no survivors among the twelve persons who had been aboard the DC-3 (nine passengers and a crew of three).

The aircraft had struck the mountain at an approximate elevation of 6,000ft (1,800m), or less than 100ft (30m) below its crest, while flying in darkness and during a low overcast. It was also determined that at the moment of impact, NC-45395 had been in a left turn, indicating that the pilot had initiated an evasive manoeuvre in an attempt to avoid the terrain.

At the time of the crash, the aircraft had been proceeding below a safe height and was also some 20 miles (30km) east of where it reported being, apparently due to an error by the pilot in determining his position with respect to the nearby Mount Laguna. A contributing factor was that the pilot must not have made use of the local radio beacon in order to establish his position.

Date: 25 December 1946 (*c*.17:00)
Location: Near Wusong, Jiangsu, China
Operator: Central Air Transport Corporation (China)
Aircraft type: Douglas C-47 (48)

Operating on a scheduled domestic service from Hankou, Hubei, the airliner crashed after a failed landing attempt to Kiangwan Airport, serving Shanghai, the accident occurring in twilight and adverse weather conditions, with rain, fog and a low overcast. All thirteen persons aboard the C-47 (ten passengers and a crew of three) and three others on the ground, the latter victims believed to have been a woman and two of her children, lost their lives in the crash. Reportedly, the aircraft had overshot the airport before it plunged into a residential section.

Date: 25 December 1946 (*c*.19:00)
Location: Near Shanghai, China
Operator: China National Aviation Corporation
Aircraft type: Curtiss-Wright C-46 (115)

As with the previous one, this accident also involved a transport on a scheduled domestic service from Hankou, Hubei. During its attempted landing at Kiangwan Airfield, the C-46 struck the roof of a school building and slammed to earth approximately 1 mile (1.5km) from the threshold of the runway, the accident occurring in darkness and overcast weather conditions, with accompanying rain and fog having reduced the visibility. Killed were twenty-one persons aboard the aircraft, including its co-pilot; two other crew members and six passengers survived with injuries.

Date: 25 December 1946 (*c*.20:00)
Location: Shanghai, China
Operator: China National Aviation Corporation
Aircraft type: Douglas DC-3C (140)

The third crash on this night of disaster involved an aircraft on a scheduled domestic service from Nanking, and occurred at Lunghwa Airfield in darkness and conditions of poor visibility, due to fog and rain, and reportedly after the DC-3 had experienced fuel exhaustion while attempting to land. This accident killed thirty-seven persons aboard the transport, including the three members of its crew, while three passengers survived.

Date: 28 December 1946 (*c*.02:10)
Location: Near Limerick, Ireland
Operator: Transcontinental and Western Air, Inc. (TWA) (US)
Aircraft type: Lockheed 049 Constellation (NC-86505)

Operating as Flight 6963 and on a trans-atlantic service from New York City to Paris, France, the four-engine airliner crashed and burned approximately 1 mile

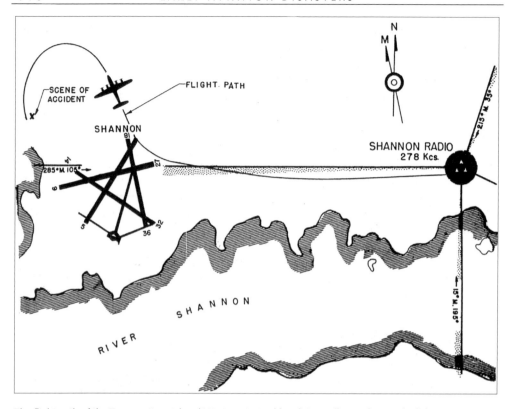

The flight path of the Transcontinental and Western Air Lockheed Constellation that crashed during attempted landing at Shannon Airport. (Civil Aeronautics Board)

(1.5km) west–north–west of Shannon Airport, which was a scheduled en route stop. Including those who succumbed later, thirteen of the twenty-three persons aboard the Constellation lost their lives in the accident, including four members of its crew of nine. The surviving passengers and crew members, the latter of whom included the captain and first officer, suffered various injuries.

Its undercarriage down, NC-86505 had been on its approach to Runway 14 when it initially struck the ground with its port wing tip, then slammed into the muddy terrain on an island in the River Fergus, the impact tearing off its empennage and all four power plants. The crash occurred in early morning darkness and in overcast weather conditions, with a ceiling of 400ft (c.120m) and a visibility of 1 mile (1.5km); the wind was at 5 knots from a direction of 120 degrees.

In its investigative report, the US Civil Aeronautics Board (CAB) attributed the accident to an altimeter error of around 300ft (100m), the primary reason for which was the reversal of the primary and alternate static lines due to the negligence of maintenance personnel. This malfunction caused the pilot to conduct his approach at a dangerously low altitude, with the Constellation losing at least 150ft (50m) in additional height while making a turn on to the proper runway heading. Fogging of the aircraft's windscreen was considered to have been a contributing factor. Although the meteorological conditions had been below the prescribed minima, the pilot apparently thought that the ceiling was higher, along with the aircraft itself, due to the altimeter error. Another factor was the lack of lights on the ground in the area of the crash, which could have provided some reference to the flight crew.

The issue of restriction of visibility due to condensation on the windscreen required corrective action, and later models of the Lockheed 049 would be provided with integral heating elements. And as another enhancement to safety for aircraft landing there, an instrument landing system (ILS) and high-intensity approach and runway lights were subsequently installed at Shannon Airport.

Date: 4 January 1947
Location: Near São Paulo de Olivenca, Amazonas, Brazil
Operator: Panair do Brasil SA (Brazil)
Aircraft type: Sikorsky S-43B (PP-PBN)

The twin-engine flying boat, which had been on a scheduled international service from Iquitos, Peru, to Manaus, Brazil, crashed in the Solimoes River some 600 miles (965km) west-south-west of its destination. All but three of the fourteen persons aboard the aircraft were killed.

Date: 5 January 1947
Location: Near Tsingtao, Shantung, China
Operator: China National Aviation Corporation
Aircraft type: Curtiss-Wright C-46 (XT-T51)

Operating on a scheduled domestic service from Shanghai to Peking (Beijing), the airliner struck a mountain while approaching to land at the airport serving Tsingtao, which was an en route stop. All forty-three persons aboard (thirty-eight passengers and five crew members) were killed in the afternoon accident.

The crash occurred during a low overcast, and the weather conditions were reportedly below the minima prescribed for landing, at least for the standards of the US Navy.

Date: 11 January 1947 (*c.*14:00)
Location: South China Sea
Operator: Far East Air Transport (the Philippines)
Aircraft type: Douglas DC-4 (PI-C-100)

The airliner was ditched in the ocean some 80 miles (130km) north-west of Laoag, on the Philippine island of Luzon. Seven passengers were killed, while the thirty-five survivors, who included the five members of its crew, spent 16 hours on life rafts before being rescued by ship.

Operating on a scheduled international service to Hong Kong from Shanghai, China, PI-C-100 had been diverted by bad weather from its original destination, and was proceeding towards Manila, in the Philippines, when forced down by a fire in its No.2 power plant.

Date: 11 January 1947 (*c.*16:00)
Location: Near Folkestone, Kent, England
Operator: British Overseas Airways Corporation (BOAC)
Aircraft type: Douglas DC-3C (G-AGJX)

The airliner crashed approximately 50 miles (80km) south-east of London, from where it had taken off earlier, and eight of the sixteen persons aboard were killed, including all but one member of its crew of five. All of the survivors, among them the steward, suffered injuries.

Bound for Bordeaux, France, the first segment of a scheduled international service with an ultimate destination of Lagos, Nigeria, G-AGJX had diverted first towards Paris and then proceeded back to England due to bad weather. Low on fuel, it was attempting to reach the Lympne airport when it struck trees while flying in a level attitude, the accident occurring shortly before sunset and in conditions of poor visibility due to fog and rain. There was no fire after impact.

The crash was attributed to improper inflight decision-making on the part of the captain, combined with other operational factors, including the selection of flight crew members who were not familiar with the route.

Date: 12 January 1947 (*c.*01:40)
Location: Near Galax, Virginia, US
Operator: Eastern Air Lines (US)
Aircraft type: Douglas DC-3C (NC-88872)

Designated as Flight 665 and on a US domestic service originating at Detroit, Michigan, with an ultimate destination of Miami, Florida, the transport crashed in the Blue Ridge Mountains some 50 miles (80km) north-west of Winston–Salem, North Carolina, which was a scheduled en route stop, and eighteen persons aboard were killed, including its entire crew of three. One passenger survived but was seriously injured.

During an instrument letdown in preparation for landing at Smith Reynolds Airport, NC-88872 struck the top of a knoll, then slammed into a wooded area, coming to rest at an approximate elevation of 2,500ft (750m). The accident occurred in darkness and adverse weather conditions, which, according to witnesses who were in the vicinity at the time, consisted of intermittent heavy rain and fog obscuring the terrain. The airborne winds in the area reportedly exceeded 50mph (80kmh).

It was concluded by the US Civil Aeronautics Board (CAB) that the pilot must have believed he was south-east of the Winston–Salem radio range station, when in fact the aircraft had been about 50 miles (80km) north-west of the facility, proceeding at an angle of 30 degrees to the left of the proper course and on a bearing of 295 degrees. The DC-3 was thus flying towards the mountainous terrain while descending, its pilot apparently continuing the letdown without positively determining his position.

Contributing to the accident were erroneous navigational procedures, which may have resulted from the fact that the ground speed of the aircraft was slower than the pilot believed, and because the crew had apparently been relying upon their automatic direction finder (ADF), which could have been affected by the atmospheric conditions and thus not been giving them accurate indications. Additionally, two brief power interruptions caused a temporary failure in the radio range and, during this time, the overriding by another station may have resulted in an ADF indication that the DC-3 had flown past the former.

Date: 22 January 1947
Location: Near Puerto Araujo, Santander, Colombia
Operator: Aerovias Nacionales de Colombia SA (AVIANCA)
Aircraft type: Douglas DC-3C (C-108)

All seventeen persons aboard (thirteen passengers and a crew of four) were killed when the airliner, on a scheduled domestic service from Bogotá to Barrancabermeja, crashed in the Andes some 50 miles (80km) south-west of its destination. Its wreckage was found a week later.

Date: 25 January 1947 (*c.*14:00)
Location: Near Liping, Kweichow, China
Operator: China National Aviation Corporation
Aircraft type: Douglas C-47

The airliner was on a scheduled domestic service from Canton to Chungking, Sichuan, when it crashed some 120 miles (190km) south-east of its destination, and all nineteen persons aboard (sixteen passengers and three crew members) were killed. Its wreckage was located nearly two weeks later.

Date: 25 January 1947 (*c.*11:40)
Location: London, England
Operator: Spencer's Airways (Southern Rhodesia)
Aircraft type: Douglas DC-3C (VP-YFE)

The aircraft crashed at Croydon Airport as it was taking off on a non-scheduled international service to Johannesburg, South Africa, via Salisbury, (Southern) Rhodesia. Killed in the accident were twelve persons aboard the DC-3, including the captain, who also owned the airline; the four other crew members and seven passengers survived, most of whom escaped serious injury.

Using Runway 12, VP-YFE reportedly became airborne at 85mph (*c.*135kmh), which was approximately the norm for the type, whereupon its starboard wing dropped. It then rolled to a port wing-down attitude, but as the

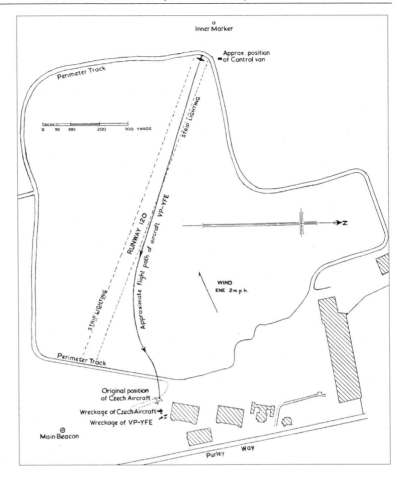

The track of the DC-3 during its attempted take-off from Croydon Airport, ending with its crash into a Czech transport. (Accidents Investigation Branch)

pilot applied and tried to maintain full starboard aileron, the transport veered to the left. As it proceeded at low altitude while continuing to stray to the left of the runway, it banked back to the right, at which time its extended starboard gear may have struck the ground, and the aircraft ultimately slammed into a parked Ceskoslovenske Aerolinie DC-3, the latter of which was knocked backwards nearly 100ft (30m) by the force of the crash. Both aircraft burst into flames and were destroyed. The accident occurred in instrument weather conditions, with the sky obscured and a visibility of around 1,000ft (300m) in light, falling snow. The wind was negligible.

The crash apparently resulted from a loss of control by the captain, who had allowed the heavily-laden aircraft to become airborne in a semi-stalled condition. His actions were attrib-

uted to his flying technique, which was in turn probably related to his lack of experience in the type. It was noted in the UK Ministry of Civil Aviation report on the crash that had the DC-3 lifted off prematurely, it would have had a tendency to 'sink'. If either wing had been allowed to drop while in a semi-stalled condition, the use of a full aileron could have aggravated the situation and caused VP-YFE to swing in the direction of the lower wing. Furthermore, an aircraft would generally bank with much greater ease while in a stall.

One factor that could not be dismissed by the Ministry as contributing to the accident was the presence on the aircraft's lifting surfaces of snow and/or frost, which may have accumulated earlier in the day while the DC-3 was parked outside at the airport, especially considering that it had not been de-iced prior to departure. Another contributing factor could have been the fatigued state of the captain, attributed to a lack of sleep, and which could have affected his judgement.

The investigation found no evidence of prior technical defect or failure in VP-YFE. However, anomalies were identified in the operations of the airline. The owner had neither notified Southern Rhodesian authorities of his intended departure from England, and the aircraft had not been inspected for the purpose of registration and had neither certificates for airworthiness or safety in the country where it was being operated. It had in fact only been officially registered in the US, as NC-32975. It was further noted in the investigative report that the preparation of the flight showed 'a lack of organisation'. And despite the poor visibility, there was evidence that the pilot had taken off using visual flight procedures. One of the recommendations made by the Ministry was that aviation authorities take steps to assure that regulations pertaining to airworthiness issues have been satisfied before an aircraft is allowed to take off.

Date: 26 January 1947 (c.15:30)
Location: Kastrup, Sjælland, Denmark
Operator: Koninklijke Luchtvaart Maatschappij voor Nederland en Kalonien (KLM) (the Netherlands)
Aircraft type: Douglas DC-3C (PH-TCR)

Operating on a scheduled international service to Stockholm, Sweden, the transport crashed and burned shortly after taking off from Kastrup Airport, serving Copenhagen, and all twenty-two persons aboard were killed. The victims included the aircraft's four-member crew; among the passengers were American opera star Grace Moore and Prince Adolf, the son of the crown prince of Sweden.

The DC-3 had stalled and plunged to earth after climbing to an approximate height of 150ft (50m). It was determined that its elevator locking pins had not been removed prior to departure, which would have rendered pitch control ineffective.

Date: 28 January 1947 (c.12:00)
Location: Near Shashih, Hupei, China
Operator: China National Aviation Corporation
Aircraft type: Curtiss-Wright C-46

The airliner crashed and burned about 100 miles (150km) west of Hankou (Wuhan), where it had last stopped during a scheduled domestic flight from Shanghai to Chungking. All but one of the twenty-six persons aboard were killed, including its two-member crew; the surviving passenger, a four-year-old boy, was seriously injured. Reportedly, a fire had erupted in the port power plant of the C-46, ultimately leading to the separation of the corresponding wing.

Date: 1 February 1947 (c.18:45)
Location: Near Lisbon, Portugal
Operator: Air France
Aircraft type: Douglas DC-3C (F-BAXQ)

Operating on a scheduled international service that had originated at Paris and last stopped at Bordeaux, also in France, the airliner crashed and burned in the Cintra Hills some 15 miles (25km) north of the Portuguese capital, where it was to have landed. All but one of the sixteen persons aboard F-BAXQ lost their lives in the accident, including its entire crew of five; the surviving passenger was seriously injured.

The DC-3 had been on its landing approach to the Lisbon airport when it slammed into a mountain, near its peak, the accident occurring shortly before sunset and during a rain.

Date: 6 February 1947 (c.17:00)
Location: Near Pedros Bernados, Extremadura, Spain
Operator: Aerovias Cubanas Internacionales (Cuba)
Aircraft type: Douglas DC-4 (NC-44567)

The airliner crashed and burned about 100 miles (150km) west of Madrid, which was its destination during a scheduled international

A Douglas DC-4, the most widely used four-engine transport during the late 1940s and the type involved in the disaster in Colombia. (Boeing)

service that had originated at Havana, Cuba, and last stopped at Lisbon, Portugal. All eleven persons aboard (four passengers and a crew of seven) were killed.

According to one report, the DC-4 had strayed from the normal course before it struck a peak in the Sierra de Gredos region, the accident occurring in adverse weather conditions, with clouds obscuring the mountains.

Date: 15 February 1947 (*c.*12:15)
Location: Near Subachoque, Cundinamarca, Colombia
Operator: Aerovias Nacionales de Colombia SA (Colombia)
Aircraft type: Douglas DC-4 (C-114)

The first commercial aviation disaster to claim more than fifty lives involving an aircraft on a regular passenger service occurred during a scheduled domestic Colombian flight from Barranquilla to Bogotá. Including an American pilot and three other crew members, all fifty-three persons aboard perished when the DC-4 crashed and burned in the Andes some 30 miles (50km) north-west of its destination.

Cleanly configured, the airliner had been cruising in cloudy weather conditions when it struck El Tablazo, a mountain more than 10,000ft (3,000m) tall. The accident was attributed to the violation by the pilot of the nation's air regulations in conducting the flight below a safe altitude and off the designated airway.

Date: 5 March 1947 (*c.*10:00)
Location: Georgian SSR, USSR
Operator: Aeroflot (USSR)
Aircraft type: Douglas C-47 (SSSR-1952)

The transport crashed in the Caucasus Mountains during a scheduled domestic service from Moscow, RSFSR, to Tbilisi, Georgian SSR, and all twenty-three persons aboard (nineteen passengers and a crew of four) were killed.

Date: 14 March 1947 (*c.*15:00)
Location: Near Château-Bernard, Dauphine, France
Operator: Air France
Aircraft type: Douglas DC-3C (F-BAXO)

The airliner crashed some 15 miles (25km) south-south-west of Grenoble while en route from Nice to Lyon, one segment of a scheduled domestic service with an ultimate destination of Paris. All twenty-three persons aboard (eighteen passengers and five crew members) were killed.

Flying in fog and snow mixed with rain, F-BAXO had slammed into a mountain after an apparent navigational error by the crew. The crash touched off an avalanche, which buried the wreckage and victims' bodies.

Date: 8 April 1947 (*c.*09:30)
Location: Near Caracas, Venezuela
Operator: Línea Aeropostal Venezolana (Venezuela)
Aircraft type: Douglas DC-3C (YV-C-ALO)

Operating on a scheduled domestic service to Caracas from Cumana, Sucre, the airliner crashed and burned in mountainous terrain some 25 miles (40km) east of its destination. All twenty-seven persons aboard (twenty-four passengers and a crew of three) were killed.

Date: 13 April 1947 (*c.*02:40)
Location: Near Dakar, French West Africa (Senegal)
Operator: British South American Airways
Aircraft type: Avro York (G-AHEZ)

Six passengers among the fifteen persons aboard lost their lives when the transport crash-landed at the city's Yoff Airport. Most of the survivors, who included the entire crew of six, suffered injuries in the accident.

Operating on a scheduled international service that had originated at London, with an ultimate destination of Rio de Janeiro, Brazil, G-AHEZ had previously made three unsuccessful attempts to land at Dakar, an en route stop, and at the time of the crash its fuel supply was nearly exhausted, necessitating the forced landing. Its undercarriage down, the York struck a heap of stones, which split open the underside of its fuselage, and one wing then clipped a tree. There was no fire. The crash occurred in early morning darkness and poor meteorological conditions, with heavy fog.

Blamed for the accident was faulty in-flight decision-making on the part of the captain, who should have diverted to another airport after his second landing attempt, when considering his critical fuel situation. Contributing factors included inadequate runway lighting, the absence of landing aids and language difficulties between the crew and control tower personnel. Subsequent to the crash, new information about the airport was published to enhance the awareness of flight crews.

Date: 22 April 1947 (*c.*10:40)
Location: Near Columbus, Georgia, US
First aircraft:
Operator: Delta Air Lines (US)
Type: Douglas DC-3C (NC-49657)
Second aircraft:
Operator: Private
Type: Vultee BT-13 (NC-55312)

Nine persons lost their lives when the transport and the single-engine aeroplane, the latter used as a trainer during the Second World War, collided, and both then crashed and burned at Muscogee County Airport, serving Columbus. The victims included the pilot (and sole occupant) of the BT-13; all of those aboard the DC-3 were company personnel taking a tour of the carrier's route extensions. There were no survivors.

Both aircraft were landing when the collision occurred at a height of only about 10ft (3m) above the ground, with NC-55312 settling atop NC-49657 and lodging in the latter's tail surfaces. After the initial impact, the DC-3 climbed to an approximate height of 150ft (50m) before it plunged to the ground. The local weather at the time was good, with high, thin, scattered clouds and a visibility of nearly 10 miles (15km).

The pilot of the BT-13 had failed to both conform to the standard left-hand pattern during the landing approach, instead making a right turn on to the runway heading, and also failed to keep a diligent lookout for other aircraft.

Date: 28 April 1947 (*c*.23:50)
Location: Near Vancouver, British Columbia, Canada
Operator: Trans-Canada Air Lines
Aircraft type: Lockheed 18 Lodestar (CF-TDF)

Designated as Flight 328 and on a domestic inter-provincial service to Vancouver from Lethbridge, Alberta, the twin-engine aircraft crashed on a wooded slope of Mount Eslay, about 10 miles (15km) north-north-east of its destination. All fifteen persons aboard (twelve passengers and a crew of three) were killed in the accident. The wreckage of the CF-TDF would not be found until September 1994, nearly half a century after its crash.

It was believed that an emergency of an undetermined nature had occurred after the last radio transmission from the Lodestar, with the subsequent accident occurring in darkness and cloudy weather conditions.

Date: 3 May 1947
Location: Near Nicoya, Guanacaste, Costa Rica
Operator: Compañía de Transportes Aéreos Centros-Americanos (TACA de Costa Rica)
Aircraft type: Lockheed 18 Lodestar (TI-84)

All eleven persons aboard (nine passengers and two pilots) lost their lives when the aircraft crashed and burned some 100 miles (150km) west of San José, which presumably was the destination of the scheduled domestic flight that had departed shortly before from the Nicoya airport. The investigation found that, in what may have been an act of sabotage, sand had been poured into one of the Lodestar's two engines.

Date: 16 May 1947
Location: Near Khabarovsk, Russian Soviet Federative Socialist Republic, USSR
Operator: Aeroflot (USSR)
Aircraft type: Douglas C-47 (SSSR-L1048)

The transport crashed during a scheduled Soviet domestic service, killing all twenty-two persons aboard (seventeen passengers and a crew of five).

Date: 29 May 1947 (*c*.12:00)
Location: Northern Iceland
Operator: Flugfélag Islands HF (Iceland Airways Ltd)
Aircraft type: Douglas DC-3C (TS-ISI)

Operating on a scheduled domestic service from Reykjavik to Akureyri, the airliner crashed and burned near its destination, killing all twenty-five persons aboard (twenty-one passengers and a crew of four).

Proceeding in marginal visual meteorological conditions, the pilots had attempted to turn around over Eyjafjordur (fjord) before TS-ISI flew into a cliff on Hedinsfjordur Mountain. Prior to impact, the DC-3 entered an area of instrument meteorological conditions, with fog and rain having significantly reduced the visibility.

Date: 29 May 1947 (*c*.20:05)
Location: New York, New York, US
Operator: United Air Lines (US)
Aircraft type: Douglas DC-4 (NC-30046)

The four-engine transport crashed after an aborted take-off at La Guardia Field, located on the western end of Long Island and serving New York City. All but five of the forty-eight persons aboard the DC-4 lost their lives in the accident, including four members of its crew of five. Four passengers and the pilot, Capt. Benton 'Lucky' Baldwin, survived, with only the latter escaping serious injury.

Designated as Flight 521 and on a US domestic service to Cleveland, Ohio, NC-30046 had accelerated on Runway 18

The wreckage of the United Air Lines Douglas DC-4 that crashed after an aborted take-off at La Guardia Field, serving New York City. (US National Archives)

to more than 90mph (145kmh), but the pilot was unable to actuate its flight controls. The take-off was then abandoned, with brakes being applied approximately 1,000ft (300m) from the end of the runway. Engine power was also cut and a ground-loop attempted, but the aircraft could not be brought to a safe stop while still on the pavement. After smashing through a fence, the DC-4 'half-bounced and half-flew' across Grand Central Parkway, coming to rest some 800ft (250m) beyond the end of the runway, where it almost immediately burst into flames. The accident occurred shortly before sunset and in the 'path' of an approaching thunderstorm; the wind was at the time from a south-westerly direction at around 10mph (15kmh).

The inability of the pilot to manipulate the flight controls probably stemmed from the fact that the aircraft's aileron, elevator and rudder gust locking mechanism was engaged, which would have prevented free movement of the control surfaces. It was concluded by the US Civil Aeronautics Board (CAB) that the mechanism may not have been disengaged by the crew, or may have been re-applied by them after the pre-take-off check due to the gusty winds blowing at the time. The take-off was then hurried by the captain, in an attempt to avoid the rapidly advancing storm, without proper assessment of the position of the gust lock handle. Additionally, the DC-4 was found to have been overloaded by more than 3,000 pounds (1,360kg) according to the correct take-off calculations for this particular runway. However, neither of the latter two factors was considered by the CAB to have been contributory to the accident.

An airworthiness directive issued by the US Civil Aeronautics Administration (CAA) less than three months after the crash of Flight 521 required that the gust lock handle in the type be equipped with a positive latch to hold it in the full 'down' or 'off' position, and in response the manufacturer developed a system to reduce the possibility of inadvertent engagement. Subsequent action by the CAA, CAB and a President's Special Board of Inquiry on Air Safety included requirements that runway gradients be a factor in calculating allowable weight limitations on runways (the slope of the runway was a secondary factor in the United accident); that aircraft weight limitations take into account ambient temperature that could affect take-off loads, with adjustments being made on a scientific basis; and that the CAA in cooperation with the airline industry work out uniform weight limitations for runways used by commercial transports. And pertaining directly to the safety of La Guardia Field, Runway 18 would be closed for use by four-engine aircraft because it was considered too short for a DC-4 operating with a significant gross weight.

Date: 30 May 1947 (c.17:40)
Location: Near Port Deposit, Maryland, US
Operator: Eastern Air Lines (US)
Aircraft type: Douglas DC-4 (NC-88814)

The record death toll in a US commercial aviation disaster, which had been set the previous day in the crash at New York City (see above) was exceeded in this freakish and unexplained accident involving Flight 605, a US domestic service originating at Newark, New Jersey, and bound for Miami, Florida. All fifty-three persons aboard (forty-nine passengers and a crew of four) perished when the four-engine transport went into a sudden descent from its cruising height of 4,000ft (c.1,200m) and plunged into a wooded area some 30 miles (50km) north-east of Baltimore. Although the aircraft disintegrated on impact, and a flash fire did erupt, there was no sustained post-crash blaze. The weather in the area at the time was clear.

As observed by two US Civil Aeronautics Board (CAB) personnel riding in another DC-4, which was carrying them back to Washington after visiting the scene of the United crash, NC-88814 fell nearly vertically and struck the ground in a nearly inverted attitude, as though it had almost completed the first half of an outside loop. During the dive, the aircraft's tail surfaces broke apart, but whether the failure of the empennage and/or its related flight controls was a cause of the descent or the effect of the aerodynamic forces associated with the dive was not known.

A number of theories were considered by the CAB in its investigation of the crash of Flight 605 to explain the sudden loss of control, but no conclusions could be made. One possibility considered by the Board, and which would not only have been consistent with the sequence of events leading to this tragedy but also with a subsequent non-fatal incident involving a DC-4, was the intentional engagement by the pilots of the aircraft's flight control surface gust locking system. Soon after the United accident, it became commonly surmised that the gust locking mechanism had not been released prior to take-off, and this led to the suggestion that the Eastern crew may have tried to experiment with the system on the DC-4 they were flying, especially considering that they had been operating out of Newark, not that far from La Guardia. In view that the captain of NC-88814 had previously worked as a test pilot on large aircraft, such action on his part would have been completely contrary to sound operating procedures during a passenger service, and as a result, the CAB considered this theory 'highly unlikely'. The cause of the uncontrolled descent of Flight 605 therefore remained unknown.

Soon after the Eastern accident, the US Civil Aeronautics Administration (CAA) issued airworthiness directives requiring the inspection in air carrier operations of aircraft rudder and elevator assemblies in order to assure the proper installation and functioning of various components, and that each horizontal stabiliser outer hinge bracket be reworked in the DC-4. This bracket would be replaced in later production aircraft.

Descent below the minimum en route altitude led to the crash of the Pennsylvania Central Airlines Douglas DC-4, in which fifty persons perished. (US National Archives)

Date: 13 June 1947 (*c.*18:15)
Location: Near Charles Town, West Virginia, US
Operator: Pennsylvania Central Airlines (US)
Aircraft type: Douglas DC-4 (NC-88842)

Operating as Flight 410 and on a US domestic service originating at Chicago, Illinois, with an ultimate destination of Pittsburgh, Pennsylvania, the aircraft crashed in the Blue Ridge Mountains some 60 miles (100km) north-west of Washington, DC, which was a scheduled en route stop. All fifty persons aboard (forty-seven passengers and a crew of three) perished.

Already painted in the livery of Capital Airlines, the company's newly adopted name, the cleanly configured DC-4 was in a slight descent when it slammed into a ridge at an approximate elevation of 1,400ft (400m), the late afternoon accident occurring during a low overcast, with the clouds obscuring the terrain, and also in fog and rain. The pilot had descended below the minimum en route altitude under meteorological conditions that prevented adequate visual reference. Contributing to the crash was the faulty clearance to the flight by the Washington air-traffic control centre, which had been 'tacitly' approved by the company dispatcher and accepted by the crew. Specifically, the pilot had not been advised that the clearance was below the minimum height of 3,000ft (*c.*1,000m) provided by the carrier for both contact flight and instrument operations, and also below the minimum altitude prescribed by the airman's guide in instrument conditions. It was further noted in the US Civil Aeronautics Board (CAB) report that the pilot of NC-88842 may have attempted to descend seeking visual contact with the ground while somewhat uncertain of his position.

Changes implemented subsequent to this disaster included the establishment of a 2,000ft (*c.*600m) minimum altitude above terrain in instrument weather and when flying over mountainous regions, and the mandatory installation in passenger-carrying commercial transports that fly at night or in instrument meteorological conditions of terrain-warning indicators, or radio altimeters, effective 15 February 1948. However, reliability issues encountered by operators that had fitted their aircraft with such equipment prompted the CAB to rescind this order the same year it was to have taken effect. Thus, commercial aviation would have to wait nearly three decades for reality of reliable terrain-avoidance technology as a safety feature.

Date: 19 June 1947 (*c.*01:40)
Location: Near Mayadine, Syria
Operator: Pan American World Airways (US)
Aircraft type: Lockheed 049 Constellation (NC-88845)

The airliner crashed some 250 miles (400km) north-east of Damascus during an off-airport forced landing attempt in early morning darkness and with its port wing ablaze. Killed in the accident were fourteen of the thirty-six persons aboard the Constellation, including all but three members of its crew of ten; the survivors suffered various injuries.

Designated as Flight 121, NC-88845 had been en route from Karachi, India (Pakistan), to Istanbul, Turkey, one segment of a service destined for the US, when an exhaust rocker arm in its No.1 power plant broke due to fatigue, and the corresponding propeller was then feathered. Unable to maintain its cruising altitude of 18,500ft (*c.*5,640m) on the three remaining engines, the crew descended to 10,000ft (*c.*3,000m) and continued on towards

Istanbul. Significantly, most of the airfields along the route were closed until dawn.

Nearly three hours after the original malfunction, and possibly due to over-heating, the thrust bearing of the No.2 power plant failed, resulting in the blocking of the passage of oil from the feathering motor to the dome of the corresponding propeller. As a result, a rupture in either the line or a fitting probably sprayed the oil and touched off a fire as the crew tried to feather the propeller. Several minutes later, the No.2 engine dropped from the aircraft, while the fire continued to burn on the port wing. During the attempted wheels-up landing on relatively smooth, hard-packed desert sand, its port wing contacted the ground and was torn off, after which the Constellation swerved violently to the left and skidded backwards to a stop. It was then virtually consumed by the flames.

It was noted in the US Civil Aeronautics Board (CAB) report that the No.2 power plant had showed indications of malfunctioning during the eastbound flight, prompting the change of its spark plugs in its No.18 cylinder at Gander, Newfoundland. However, a special US government technical consultant later stated that the entire engine should have been replaced at that point; he also recommended the overhaul of Constellation engines every 500 hours.

Date: 1 July 1947
Location: Near Eseka, French Cameroons
Operator: Air France
Aircraft type: Amiot AAC.1 Toucan (F-BALF)

All thirteen persons aboard (ten passengers and a crew of three) were killed when the trimotored airliner, on a scheduled domestic service within Camerouns, from Yaounda to Douala, crashed approximately midway between the two cities. Reportedly, the hill that was struck by the Toucan had not been depicted on the navigational chart being used by the flight crew. The morning accident was believed to have occurred in conditions of reduced visibility.

Date: 13 July 1947 (*c*.04:30)
Location: Near Melbourne, Florida, US
Operator: Burke Air Transport (US)
Aircraft type: Douglas DC-3C (NC-79024)

Chartered by a group of expatriated Puerto Ricans with the intention of visiting their native land, the airliner crashed about 50 miles (80km) south-east of Orlando while en route from Newark, New Jersey, to Miami, Florida, the first segment of a service with an ultimate destination of San Juan, Puerto Rico, and fourteen of the thirty-six persons aboard lost their lives, including both of its pilots. Among the survivors, who included the stewardess, all but one passenger suffered serious injuries.

The DC-3 was observed in the pre-dawn darkness at a height of only 300 to 500ft (100–150m) above the ground before it slammed into trees and tree stumps in a nearly level attitude. There was no post-impact fire. It was theorised by the US Civil Aeronautics Board (CAB) that the two pilots of NC-79024, both of whom had flown it from San Juan to Newark and been on duty for nearly 20 hours, had either fallen asleep or were not fully awake and alert as the aircraft cruised while under the control of the autopilot, gradually losing altitude. Awakened by either a malfunction in the left engine, attributed to a defective carburettor, or by the very imminence of the crash itself, they were confronted with an emergency that neither time nor immediate available power permitted them to correct.

It was further determined by the CAB that the DC-3 had been overloaded at the time of take-off, although this would not have been a factor in the accident. The investigation also revealed that maintenance records had not been well kept by the company, and 10 spark plugs from both power plants of NC-79024 were found to be defective. Still another operational violation cited by the CAB was poor record-keeping by the company, with the flight time of pilots only being maintained for pay purposes.

Date: 16 July 1947 (*c*.22:40)
Location: Near Az-Zubayr, Basra, Iraq
Operator: British Overseas Airways Corporation (BOAC)
Aircraft type: Avro York (G-AGNR)

The transport crashed in the desert about 10 miles (15km) south-east of Shaibah, and all six members of its crew were killed. Its twelve passengers survived the accident, while suffering from varying degrees of injury.

Operating on a scheduled international service originating in England, with an ultimate destination of Calcutta, India, G-AGNR had diverted to the airfield at Shaibah due to poor visibility at the city of Basra, which it was originally to have landed, having last stopped at Cairo, Egypt. But while descending in darkness through a low overcast, the York touched the ground, crashing approximately half a mile (0.8km) beyond that point.

The precipitating factor in the accident was deemed to have been the improper decision of the captain in continuing the flight in the unsuitable meteorological conditions, coupled with inadequate cooperation by air-traffic control personnel on the ground. Considered as possible causes of the crash itself were a loss of power due to temporary fuel starvation, which may have been related to the failure of the pilot to utilise his reserve gasoline supply; distraction of the pilot from his instruments during the attempt to make visual contact with the airfield environment, leading to an unintentional descent into the ground; or an uncontrolled impact with the terrain attributed to turbulence.

Date: 2 August 1947 (*c*.14:45)
Location: Near Tupangato, Mendoza, Argentina
Operator: British South American Airways
Aircraft type: Avro Lancastrian 3 (G-AGWH)

The disappearance of the 'Star Dust' would remain as one of the great aviation mysteries for more than half a century, only to be solved when some of its wreckage almost literally came 'out of the earth'.

Operating as Flight 59 and on an international service that had originated at London, and last stopped at Buenos Aires, Argentina, the four-engine airliner crashed while nearing Santiago, Chile, which was its ultimate destination, and all eleven persons aboard (six passengers and a crew of five) were killed. In 1998, a power plant belonging to the Lancastrian was found by a mountain guide at the base of Mount Tupangato, some 50 miles (80km) north-east of the flight's intended destination. Later, more debris and the remains of nine victims were recovered.

Two factors determined to have been significant in the accident sequence were the apparent attempt by the pilot to proceed directly from Mendoza to Santiago, and thus to fly 'diagonally' over the Andes Mountains, and his decision to climb above the overcast. In ascending to a height of 24,000ft (c.7,000m), G-AGWH entered the powerful jet stream, and as a result, its ground speed would have been greatly reduced. When the aircraft began its descent into the clouds covering the mountains, with its undercarriage still retracted, it was not as close to Santiago as the crew believed, resulting in the controlled flight into terrain impact, which would not have been survivable to its occupants.

In the more than fifty years since the accident, the wreckage must have been carried down the slope by the moving ice flow until it came to the surface at the bottom of the glacier.

Date: 23 August 1947 (c.04:00)
Location: Bahrain
Operator: British Overseas Airways Corporation (BOAC)
Aircraft type: Short S.25 Sandringham 5 (G-AHZB)

Ten persons lost their lives when the four-engine flying boat crashed in the Persian Gulf while alighting at the Marine Air Base facility serving Bahrain, which was an en route

stop during a scheduled international service originating at Hong Kong, with an ultimate destination of Poole, England. Those killed included three members of its crew of eight, one of them a cabin attendant; among the sixteen survivors, who were rescued by launches that arrived on the scene, all but four of the passengers were injured.

Its flaps having been fully extended for landing, the aircraft bounced after its initial touchdown, then slammed into the water and was demolished. The accident occurred in pre-dawn darkness, but the local weather at the time was good, with a visibility of around 5 miles (10km) and no clouds. The wind consisted of a slight breeze from a north-westerly direction.

The wreckage of G-AHZB was towed to shallow water and examined a week after the crash. The break-up of the Sandringham was consistent with the aircraft striking the water in a nose-down, right wing-low attitude. No evidence could be found of any pre-impact technical failure or defect in the flying boat, and both its weight and centre-of-gravity were found to have been within the prescribed limits. Nor was the physical condition of the flight crew considered to have been a factor in the accident.

The crash was investigated by the UK Ministry of Civil Aviation, which expressed the opinion that the captain of G-AHZB had misjudged the approach and allowed the aircraft to touch down heavily short of the correct 'flare path', then failed to maintain control during the ensuing bounce.

Date: 28 August 1947 (c.09:00)
Location: Near Lødingen, Troms, Norway
Operator: Det Norske Luftfartselakap A/S (DNL) (Norwegian Air Lines)
Aircraft type: Short S.25 Sandringham 6 (LN-IAV)

Operating on a scheduled domestic service with an ultimate destination of Oslo, the four-engine flying boat crashed and burned about 100 miles (150km) south-west of

The Norwegian Air Lines Short S.25 Sandringham LN-IAV, the same aircraft that crashed in Norway due to an apparent navigational error. (Shorts Aircraft)

Tromsø, from where it had taken off earlier. All thirty-five persons aboard the aircraft (twenty-seven passengers and eight crew members) were killed.

The Sandringham had struck a steep mountain in the Lødingen range in adverse meteorological conditions, with a low overcast and 'patchy' cloud coverage. Prior to the accident, it was observed flying at a low altitude before it started to turn and climb, with the crash occurring shortly after it had disappeared into the clouds.

The accident probably resulted from an error in visual navigation, with a possible factor the confusion by the flight crew of two relatively similar islets, one of which was normally used as a reference for aircraft changing their heading. The other islet in this case led directly to the crash site.

Date: 16 October 1947 (*c.*14:30)
Location: Near Cartagena, Murcia, Spain
Operator: Compagnie Transports Aeriens Intercontinentaux (TAI) (France)
Aircraft type: Bristol 170 Mark I (F-BCJN)

The twin-engine airliner crashed in the Mediterranean Sea off Cape Palos, and forty-

one persons aboard were killed, including three members of its crew of four. One passenger and the flight engineer survived the accident and were rescued by a French naval vessel.

Having last stopped at Marseille, France, F-BCJN had been bound for Oran, Algeria, one segment of a charter service originating at Paris, with an ultimate destination of Casablanca, Morocco, when it transmitted a distress message, reporting a malfunction in its port power plant and that the corresponding propeller had been feathered. It was apparently forced down while attempting to reach the Spanish mainland. Soon afterward, searchers recovered the bodies of sixteen victims from the water, but the main wreckage of the aircraft was not located.

Date: 24 October 1947 (*c.*12:30)
Location: Near Panguitch, Utah, US
Operator: United Air Lines (US)
Aircraft type: Douglas DC-6 (NC-37510)

Only six months after its entry into service, the DC-6 was involved in this catastrophic accident occurring in Bryce Canyon National Park, and which stemmed from a serious design flaw in the four-engine transport.

Flight 608 had been on a US domestic service from Los Angeles, California, to Chicago, Illinois, when a member of its crew radioed that a fire had been detected in the aircraft's baggage compartment and could not be extinguished. It was also reported that the cabin had filled with smoke, and that an emergency landing would be attempted at Bryce Canyon Airport, located just outside the park along its northern boundary; if not there, as stated in a later transmission, the crew would try to land at the 'best place' available. Subsequently, NC-37510 crashed on open terrain approximately 1.5 miles (2.5km) south-east of the airport. All fifty-two persons aboard (forty-six passengers and six crew members) perished. Parts that had fallen off the aircraft were found more than 25 miles (40km) from the main wreckage site.

It was determined by the US Civil Aeronautics Board (CAB) that gasoline had ignited upon entering the cabin heater air intake scoop and after inadvertently overflowing from the No.3 alternate tank vent outlet during the transfer of fuel from the No.4 alternate tank. The underlying factor was the proximity of the vent outlet to the scoop, the latter which had been placed about 10ft (3m) aft and slightly to the left of the former. While operating, the cabin heater could be expected to backfire and thereby propagate flame downstream into the scoop, and fuel would be expected to continue to burn in both it and the duct. Reconstruction of the fuselage of NC-37510 indicated that the in-flight fire took place in an area covering the lower right side of the fuselage beginning at a point in the centre section and extending rearward for more than 20ft (6m) and upward along the right side of the fuselage to the top of the window line, and led to the disintegration of the aircraft's structure in the vicinity of the starboard wing fillet. Control cables passing through the air-conditioning compartment were found to have been partially consumed by flames, and had failed in tension. Contributing to the intensity of the blaze was the ignition of at least one emergency landing flare located at the trailing edge of the starboard wing. The fire was of such intensity as

Shown with one propeller feathered, this Bristol 170 is essentially the same as the aircraft that crashed in the Mediterranean Sea after engine failure. (Philip Jarrett)

The crash of the United Air Lines Douglas DC-6 in Bryce Canyon National Park resulted from an uncontrollable in-flight fire. (US National Archives)

to have overcome and killed most or all of the cabin occupants even before the crash. The presence of down draughts in the area of the accident may have contributed to the descent of the DC-6 into the ground during the in-flight emergency.

Besides the fuel system of the Douglas transport not actually being designed for the transfer of gasoline between tanks, crews flying the type had not been provided with instructions concerning the potential hazards associated with such transfer practices, which were being extensively employed at the time of the disaster. Following a non-fatal accident involving a DC-6 the following month, which helped the CAB better understand the sequence in the United crash, the airline industry voluntarily withdrew the type from service, with the fleet remaining grounded for some four months. Considerable structural modifications were made in the aircraft during this period. These included the relocation of the Nos 2 and 3 alternate fuel tank vent outlets to areas where no hazardous fuel

overflow conditions would exist; guards for all booster pump switches; changes in the electrical system to protect against possible fire hazards emanating from this source; and modifications to serve as a precaution against fuel leakage. And in view of their involvement in this accident, emergency landing flares would be removed from aircraft by their operators.

This would not be the end of trouble experienced by the DC-6 early in its operational history. The mere threat of an in-flight fire would factor in a crash involving the same type (17 June 1948).

Date: 26 October 1947 (*c*. 19:30)
Location: Near Koropi, Attica, Greece
Operator: Aktiebolaget Aerotransport (ABA) (Swedish Air Lines)
Aircraft type: Douglas DC-4 (SE-BBG)

Designated as Flight 1629 and on an international service from Istanbul, Turkey, the transport crashed some 10 miles (15km) south-east of Athens as it was attempting to land at Hassani Airport, serving the Greek capital. All forty-four persons aboard the DC-4 (thirty-six passengers and a crew of eight) perished in the accident, which occurred in darkness and visual meteorological conditions.

Following a premature descent during the landing approach, which was being conducted visually, SE-BBG struck Mount Hymettos and exploded.

Date: 26 October 1947 (*c.*13:45)
Location: Territory of Alaska, US
Operator: Pan American World Airways (US)
Aircraft type: Douglas DC-4 (NC-88920)

All eighteen persons aboard (thirteen passengers and a crew of five) were killed when the transport crashed on Annette Island, in the Alexander Archipelago region. The bodies of the victims were recovered some days later.

Having taken off earlier from Seattle, Washington, as Flight 923, the aircraft was originally scheduled to land on Annette Island, but due to extreme turbulence in the area its crew announced their intentions to continue on to Juneau, its ultimate destination. Shortly afterward, the DC-4 struck Tamgas Mountain at an approximate elevation of 3,400ft (*c.*1,040m), or only about 200ft (60m) from its summit, resulting in a flash fire on impact. The weather in the area around the time of the accident was cloudy, with a ceiling of 1,400ft (*c.*400m) and a visibility of 3 miles (*c.*5km) in light rain. The winds were from the south-east at nearly 30mph (*c.*40kmh), gusting to 40mph (65kmh). Moderate icing and severe turbulence had also been reported by the pilots of another airliner and of a US Army aircraft that had flown through the area.

The US Civil Aeronautics Board (CAB) was unable to determine the cause of the crash or why the flight had not remained on the proper side of the radio range course. However, it was considered possible that the accident resulted from a loss of control due to the aforementioned turbulence or icing conditions.

Date: 18 November 1947 (*c.*15:00)
Location: Near Salerno, Campania, Italy
Operator: AB Trafik-Turist-Transportflyg (T. Flyg) (Sweden)
Aircraft type: Bristol 170 Mark XI (SE-BNG)

Its passengers being pilots, the twin-engine airliner crashed on Monte Carro some 30 miles (50km) south-east of Naples, and twenty-one persons aboard were killed, apparently including its regular crew of four. The four survivors suffered serious injuries.

Having last stopped at Catania, on Sicily, SE-BNG was on a non-scheduled service originating in Ethiopia, with an ultimate destination of Rome. It should have flown directly over the Tyrrhenian Sea, but for some unknown reason, its course was altered to the right after passing the island of Stromboli. Presumably, the pilot thought he had been over the ocean, when in fact the aircraft was actually following the Italian coastline as it proceeded northward.

The Bristol was in the clouds at an altitude of around 3,400ft (1,040m) when it struck the treetops on the mountain. Immediately, the crew initiated a climb, but upon discovering that the aircraft was only some 700ft (200m) from an adjacent peak, he executed a 180-degree turn. Seconds later, SE-BNG struck the mountainside, the impact tearing off its port wing.

Date: 18 November 1947 (*c.*13:00)
Location: Near New Castle, Delaware, US
Operator: Transcontinental and Western Air, Inc. (TWA) (US)
Aircraft type: Lockheed 049 Constellation (NC-86507)

All five occupants lost their lives when the airliner, on a pilot proficiency check flight, crashed about 5 miles (10km) south-west of Wilmington while attempting to land at New Castle Airport. In addition to the four-member flight crew, a US Civil Aeronautics Administration (CAA) inspector was killed in the accident.

Its undercarriage down but flaps still retracted, the Constellation had undershot the runway by approximately 130ft (40m) during its final approach. Initially striking the ground in a nose-high attitude, it became airborne again and then crashed on the runway, and after its starboard wing was torn off it rolled into an inverted position and burst into flames. The main part of the wreckage came to rest some 1,500ft (500m) from the point of initial impact and around 200ft (60m) to the right of the runway. The weather at the time was good, with the sky clear and the wind blowing from the north at 10mph (c.15kmh).

It was ruled by the US Civil Aeronautics Board (CAB) that the judgement error that apparently led to the undershoot may have involved not only inadequate air speed but also the improper use of power and the adoption of an incorrect glide path.

Date: 21 November 1947 (c.18:00)
Location: Near Plouznice, Bohemia, Czechoslovakia
Operator: Transporturile Aérienne Romano-Sovietice (TARS) (Romania)
Aircraft type: Lisunov Li-2P (YR-TAI)

The twin-engine airliner crashed and burned some 30 miles (50km) north-east of Prague, from where it had taken off earlier, on a scheduled international service to Bucharest, Romania. Killed in the accident were thirteen of the twenty-six persons aboard the Li-2, including its entire crew of five, while the survivors suffered various injuries.

Reportedly, the crew had become lost after experiencing radio failure, and during this time YR-TAI descended until it struck trees, the accident occurring in darkness and foggy weather conditions.

Date: 27 November 1947 (c.03:15)
Location: Near Yakutat, Territory of Alaska, US
Operator: Columbia Air Cargo, Inc. (US)
Aircraft type: Douglas DC-3C (NC-95486)

The transport crashed approximately 3 miles (5km) north of Yakutat Airport, where it was to have landed, an en route stop during a non-scheduled service originating at Fairbanks, Alaska, with an ultimate destination of Portland, Oregon. All thirteen persons aboard, including a two-member flight crew, were killed in the accident.

Its undercarriage down, NC-95486 had been conducting a straight-in instrument approach when it struck a tree that rose to 140ft (40m), the impact shearing off its port wing, then plunged into the wooded area and caught fire. The crash occurred in darkness and cloudy weather conditions, with an overcast of 500ft (c.150m) and a visibility of 3 miles (c.5km) in light drizzle.

As straight-in approaches had not been approved for aircraft approaching from the north-west, the pilot had in doing so violated approved procedures, apparently initiating his descent while still over the sea and not allowing for adequate terrain clearance once over land. An altimeter mis-setting may have contributed to the accident.

Date: 27 November 1947
Location: Near Titograd, Montenegro, Yugoslavia
Operator: Jugoslovenska Transportna Aviacija (JAT) (Yugoslavia)
Aircraft type: Douglas DC-3 (YU-BAC)

Operating on a scheduled domestic service, the airliner crashed while attempting to land at the airport serving Titograd, the accident occurring during a 'freak' snowstorm, and all twenty-two persons aboard (nineteen passengers and a crew of three) were killed.

Date: 30 November 1947 (c.14:30)
Location: Near Seattle, Washington, US
Operator: Alaska Airlines (US)
Aircraft type: Douglas DC-4 (NC-91009)

The aircraft crashed while landing at Seattle-Tacoma Airport, striking an automobile before it came to rest. Including its stewardess, eight persons aboard the DC-4 were killed in the accident, as was one occupant of the vehicle. Among the twenty survivors, who included both of its pilots, all but three suffered injuries. There was no fire, but the aircraft was demolished by impact forces.

Having completed a non-scheduled service from Anchorage, US Territory of Alaska, NC-91009 touched down on Runway 20 approximately half a mile (0.8km) beyond its threshold. It then overran the pavement, rolled down an embankment that was some 25ft (7.5m) high, and collided with the vehicle at an intersection. The accident occurred during a low overcast, with the cloud base at 400ft (120m), and a visibility of 1 mile (1.5km) or less in fog and light rain.

The instrument approach that preceded the crash had not been in conformity with the standard procedure, and as a result the aircraft was not properly aligned with the runway. An 'S' turn and a rapid descent were then made to both effect alignment with the runway and to lose excessive altitude. In doing so, the DC-4 landed too far down the runway and at too great a speed for the crew to bring it to a safe stop, especially considering the wet pavement, and despite an attempt to carry out a ground-loop by increasing power to the No.4 engine.

Although the aircraft had been plagued by engine trouble throughout the trip, it was not considered to have been making a precautionary landing when it crashed.

Date: 27 December 1947
Location: Near Karachi, Pakistan
Operator: Air-India
Aircraft type: Douglas DC-3C (VT-AUG)

Operating on a scheduled international service to Bombay, India, the airliner crashed about 10 minutes after taking off from the Karachi airport, killing all twenty-three persons aboard (nineteen passengers and a crew of four).

Prior to its departure, the captain had reported the failure of the aircraft's instrument lighting to a mechanic, who replaced the corresponding fuses, after which the lights operated satisfactorily. Shortly afterward, the pilot reported to the mechanic that only one landing light was functioning, but the former elected to proceed with the flight anyway. Following take-off, VT-AUG was observed to be gradually losing height until it finally struck the ground while in a violent right side slip. It was dark at the time of the accident, and the visibility had been reduced to between half a mile and 1 mile (c.0.8–1.5km) in dust haze, with a gusty westerly wind.

It was believed that the pilot had lost control of the aircraft in the conditions of poor visibility, probably because of inadequate illumination of the flight instruments due to faults in its lighting system. The DC-3 had previously experienced a considerable amount of trouble with its electrical equipment, and the decision by the captain to take off in such conditions with known technical defects was considered to have been a serious error of judgement on his part.

Date: 6 January 1948 (c.19:30)
Location: Gonesse, Ile-de-France, France
Operator: Air France
Aircraft type: Douglas DC-3D (F-BAXC)

The airliner crashed and burned while attempting to land at Le Bourget Airport, serving Paris, killing all sixteen persons aboard (eleven passengers and five crew members). Having nearly completed a scheduled international service from Brussels, Belgium, F-BAXC struck trees in close proximity to the runway during its final approach, the accident occurring in darkness and during a mist and low overcast, meteorological conditions that were in fact worse than had been reported to the pilot. Both the weather and pilot error were considered as causative factors in the crash.

Date: 7 January 1948 (c.07:45)
Location: Near Savannah Beach, Georgia, US
Operator: Coastel Air Lines (US)
Aircraft type: Douglas DC-3C (NC-60331)

The transport crashed approximately 10 miles east-south-east of Savannah, killing eighteen persons aboard, including the captain. Eight passengers and the first officer survived the accident with serious injuries.

Having last stopped at Raleigh, North Carolina, NC-60331 was on a non-scheduled US domestic service originating at Newark, New Jersey, ultimately bound for Miami, Florida, and cruising at 2,000ft (600m) when both engines failed. The pilot then attempted a forced landing in a marsh, but apparently lost control of the aircraft. The DC-3 completed about 1½ left-hand revolutions before it slammed to earth and burst into flames with its undercarriage still retracted. Its port wing was torn off and fuselage broken in two by impact forces, and portions of the fuselage and starboard wing came to rest inverted.

The total power failure had apparently resulted from mismanagement of the aircraft's fuel supply by the crew, and subsequent fuel starvation. Specifically, one main tank was providing gasoline to both power plants until its contents were drained, at which time the pilot must have placed the cross-feed valve in the 'on' position before changing the position of either of the fuel selector valves. (The fuel systems operated independently of each other unless connected by means of the cross-feed valve, which would allow for the transfer of gasoline from engine-to-engine or tank-to-tank.) The subsequent adjustment of the cross-feed and fuel-selector valves made in an attempt to bring in fuel from another tank failed to restart the engines.

But whereas improper fuel management had led to the double engine failure, a lack of crew co-ordination was blamed for the subsequent crash. In this regard, the captain had asked the first officer to go back into the cabin and check to see whether the passengers had been properly secured (there being no cabin attendant on the aircraft), and the latter was then unable to assist in the cockpit during the emergency situation.

Date: 8 January 1948
Location: Near Palestro, Algeria
Operator: Société Algérienne du Transportes Aeriens (SATA) (France)
Aircraft type: SNCAC NC.702 Martinent (F-BDLG)

All nine persons aboard (seven passengers and two crew members) were killed when the twin-engine airliner crashed and burned some 50 miles (80km) south-east of Algiers, from where it had taken off earlier, on a scheduled Algerian internal flight to Baskra. The Martinent had reportedly experienced power plant 'trouble'.

Date: 11 January 1948
Location: Near Yamasa, Dominican Republic
Operator: Compañía Dominicana de Aviación
Aircraft type: Douglas DC-3C (HI-6)

The airliner crashed in mountainous terrain around 15 miles (25km) north-north-west of Ciudad Trujillo (Santo Domingo), and all thirty-two persons aboard were killed, including the three members of its crew; among its passengers was the BBC Santiago baseball team, who had been returning home.

Operating on a scheduled domestic service from Barahona to Santiago, the DC-3 had encountered adverse meteorological conditions and was reportedly unable to land in the darkness at the unlighted airport of its intended destination. It then turned back towards the south in an attempt to reach the capital city. Low on fuel and possibly lost, the aircraft slammed into a hillside, perhaps while attempting a forced landing.

Considered as contributing factors in the accident were the weather and a navigational error by the flight crew while they approached the high terrain.

Date: 13 January 1948 (c.04:35)
Location: Near Oxon Hill, Maryland, US
Operator: Eastern Air Lines (US)
Aircraft type: Douglas DC-3 (NC-28384)

Five persons aboard lost their lives, including both of its pilots, when the aircraft crashed approximately 5 miles (10km) south of Washington National Airport, serving the nation's capital, and where it was to have landed. The cabin attendant and three passengers survived the accident with various injuries.

Operating as Flight 572 and on a US domestic service originating at Houston, Texas, NC-28384 had been conducting an instrument landing system (ILS) approach to Runway 36 when the crash occurred in pre-dawn darkness and adverse weather conditions, with heavy rain and a low overcast, with the cloud base varying from 100–2,000ft (30 –600m). Its undercarriage down, the DC-3 initially clipped a tree with its starboard wing tip, then slammed into a wooded area, the wreckage coming to rest inverted. There was no post-impact fire.

The crew had failed to adhere to the prescribed instrument approach procedure by failing to maintain the minimum altitude of 1,500ft (c.500m) until over the outer marker, which was in the vicinity of where the aircraft crashed.

Date: 20 January 1948
Location: Near Mukden (Shenyang), Liaoning, China
Operator: China National Aviation Corporation
Aircraft type: Curtiss-Wright C-46

The airliner crashed and burned immediately after taking off from the local airport, on a domestic evacuation flight to Peking (Beijing); the accident occurred during a snowstorm. Killed in the crash were eleven of the fifty-four persons aboard the C-46, while approximately thirty of the survivors, who included the three members of its crew, suffered various injuries.

Date: 28 January 1948 (c.10:50)
Location: Near San Ardo, California, US
Operator: Airline Transport Carriers (US)
Aircraft type: Douglas DC-3C (NC-36480)

Operating under contract to the US Immigration and Naturalization Service (INS) and carrying as passengers Mexican deportees, the aircraft crashed some 20 miles (30km) west of Coalinga while on a non-scheduled US domestic intra-state service from Oakland to Imperial County, located in Southern California. All thirty-two persons aboard perished, including the three members of its crew and an INS official.

The DC-3 had been cruising at an approximate height of 5,000ft (1,500m) when smoke and then fire were observed emanating from its left power plant, and seconds later the engine and the port wing separated. It then plummeted into hilly terrain and burst into flames. The weather in the area at the time was clear and not a factor in the accident.

In its investigation of the crash, the US Civil Aeronautics Board (CAB) determined that the in-flight fire had stemmed from a broken gasket in a fuel pump that led to a fuel leak. This in turn may have caused a drop or fluctuation in fuel pressure, prompting the pilot to turn on the booster pumps, an action that would have resulted in gasoline being sprayed in large quantities from the defective pump. Although the source of ignition could not definitely be established, the CAB considered it 'most likely' that the fuel was sprayed through the left side of the engine cowling and ignited by emissions from the exhaust stack. The blaze then progressed through a portion of the power plant nacelle and into the wing panel, its intensity being sufficient to burn through the main wing spar, leading to the structural failure.

The investigation further revealed that NC-36480 had been selected in error by the crew, and at the time of its departure earlier in the day from Burbank, California, it was seven hours past its 100-hour inspection, with there having been no notification of this fact. However, it was noted in the CAB report that the defect in the fuel pump was latent in nature and one that may not have been found in the course of a routine inspection. Additionally, the DC-3 had seats for only

A British South American Airways Avro Tudor IV, one of which vanished over the Atlantic Ocean with thirty-one persons aboard. (BAe Systems)

twenty-six passengers, although the slight overloading of the aircraft was not considered a factor in the accident.

Date: 29 January 1948
Location: North Atlantic Ocean
Operator: British South American Airways
Aircraft type: Avro Tudor IV (G-AHNP)

Having been introduced into regular operation less than three months earlier and possessing less than 600 hours total flying time, the Tudor 'Star Tiger' was a youthful product of the British aviation industry at the time of its departure from Santa Maria, in the Portuguese Azores, bound for Bermuda, one segment of a scheduled international service originating at London, with an ultimate destination of Havana, Cuba. But it would soon become part of history, and the centre of one of the more notable aviation mysteries of the twentieth century.

The four-engine transport, with thirty-one persons aboard (twenty-five passengers and a crew of six), had taken off from Santa Maria Airport early in the afternoon, on the third leg of the trip, which, at approximately 2,250 miles (3,620km) long, was at the time one of the longest non-stop flights in commercial passenger operations.

In the last communication with the flight, transmitted at 22:15 local time, the crew had acknowledged receipt of the bearing information it had requested. The aircraft at that point reported being about 400 miles (650km) from Bermuda, and would have been flying in darkness. After a message sent to G-AHNP a little more than half an hour later elicited no response, an emergency was declared, and soon thereafter a search began, primarily conducted by the US Air Force. The search by aircraft and surface vessels went on for five days, but no trace of the 'Star Tiger' or its occupants was ever found.

A court of inquiry of the UK Ministry of Civil Aviation examined various theories in an attempt to determine the cause of the disappearance. In its investigative report, the court noted that in the complete absence of any reliable evidence, it was unable to do more than suggest possible causes, none of which reached the level 'even of probability.' The report observed that there was 'the incalculable element of the human equation dependent upon imperfectly known factors' as well as a 'mechanical element subject to quite different laws', and that a breakdown could have occurred either separately or working in conjunction. Or there could have been an external cause to 'overwhelm' both.

Among the possibilities not considered likely, due to the availability of back-up systems, were a loss of electrical power and thus of the navigational instruments and total failure of the radio transmitting equipment, the latter of which would have involved the malfunction of both generators and the battery, a remote combination. Also considered unlikely were errors in the altimetry system or multiple engine failure. Causes that could not be eliminated were in-flight fire, despite the fact that such an occurrence should have allowed the crew to send a distress message; a catastrophic mechanical failure, such as the separation of a propeller causing severe structural damage to the aircraft; or a loss of control, possibly related to some technical malfunction, such as failure of the autopilot. The planned cruising altitude of G-AHNP was 2,000ft (c.600m), even though in radio reports it was apparently erroneously given as 20,000ft. Its actual height could not be determined, and the report noted that while flight at a lower altitude would not have been in itself hazardous, it could have reduced the margin of safety in the event of an emergency that affected the aircraft's stability. Fuel exhaustion was another possibility, especially considering that at the time of its final transmission the transport had reached the 'point of no alternate', and, lacking the gasoline to reach another airport, was therefore committed to proceeding on to

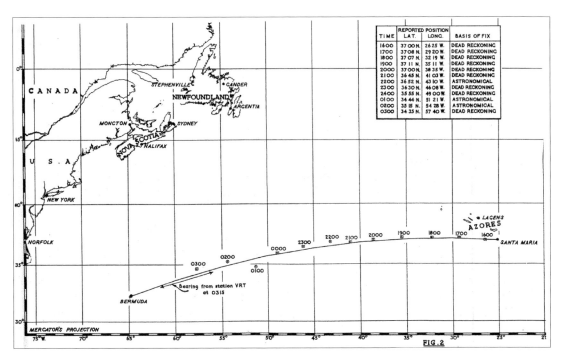

TIME	REPORTED POSITION		BASIS OF FIX
	LAT.	LONG.	
1600	37 00 N.	26 25 W.	DEAD RECKONING
1700	37 08 N.	29 20 W.	DEAD RECKONING
1800	37 07 N.	32 19 W.	DEAD RECKONING
1900	37 11 N.	35 11 W.	DEAD RECKONING
2000	37 00 N.	38 35 W.	DEAD RECKONING
2100	36 45 N.	41 03 W.	DEAD RECKONING
2200	36 52 N.	43 10 W.	ASTRONOMICAL
2300	36 30 N.	46 08 W.	DEAD RECKONING
2400	35 55 N.	49 00 W.	DEAD RECKONING
0100	34 44 N.	51 21 W.	ASTRONOMICAL
0200	35 15 N.	54 28 W.	ASTRONOMICAL
0300	34 35 N.	57 40 W.	DEAD RECKONING

FIG.2

The route of the Tudor 'Star Tiger' that vanished between the Azores and Bermuda, one segment of its transatlantic service, with times given in GMT. (Accidents Investigation Branch)

Bermuda. With regard to this issue, the report noted that the aircraft had taken on a full load of fuel at Santa Maria, so much so that it was determined to have been around 900 pounds (400kg) above its maximum authorised weight at the time of departure. And although this could have been a safety issue during take-off, it would have actually increased the margin of safety during the flight.

There were no known adverse atmospheric conditions, such as thunderstorm activity, severe turbulence or icing, along the route of the Tudor, and the weather was reported by the pilot of a Lancastrian cargo aircraft preceding it as consisting of scattered to broken clouds that became denser closer to Bermuda. The lowest layer of clouds was at 2,000ft (600m). Perhaps significant was the fact that the winds encountered by the Lancastrian were considerably higher than those forecast, and were blowing from a south-westerly direction, rather than from the north, as indicated. Using celestial navigation, its navigator determined that the aircraft had drifted nearly 70 miles (110km) north of the intended track. It was noted in the report that an encounter with head winds that were higher than those forecast was 'fairly common' along the route, particularly during the winter months. On occasion, in fact, a head wind component had prevented a fully fuelled Tudor from reaching its destination.

A review by the court revealed certain irregularities in the operational practices of the airline. Records were found to have been not well kept, and were in many cases incomplete. It was also learned that aircraft had 'not infrequently' taken off on passenger flights with 'not unimportant' defects still to be remedied. Specific to the final flight of G-AHNP, trouble had been reported in one of its compasses during the previous leg of the flight, and had not been rectified before its departure from Santa Maria. The records further suggested that there was a lack of spare parts at stations along the route, and that on some occasions, time had not been allowed for proper servicing and testing them.

An engineer employed by the company at Santa Maria was found to have had an unsatisfactory level of performance in the area of 'care and skill' in the certification of the safety of aircraft when previously employed by British Overseas Airways Corporation (BOAC), even though that company gave him an excellent testimonial for competence when he sought work elsewhere. During the period of employment at British South American Airways, there were complaints regarding his work, which led to the decision to recall him. The notification of this decision was in fact contained in a letter dispatched the previous day, although the 'Star Tiger' had departed on its last flight before the letter arrived. And despite this issue, the investigation found that the maintenance of another Tudor operated by the company, and which was examined by the court, had been carried out carefully.

It was also determined that the airline as a whole did not sufficiently ensure that information about significant changes in the meteorological conditions would be well known by its flight crews. Neither the captain of G-AHNP or the aforementioned Lancastrian had asked at the appropriate time for an amended weather report, with the 'machinery' for such considered by the court as 'not altogether satisfactory'. Flaws were found in the flight plans of both aircraft, and neither captain took written data for wind velocities at different altitudes. Not related to company policy was the fact that the route along which the Tudor was lost lacked the presence of weather-observation ships, as was the case between Europe and North America. Directly related to the practices of the carrier was that information had not been provided to its pilots in certain vital areas, including the procedures pertaining to ditching at sea.

Another possibly significant procedural factor was the length of time between communications with the aircraft, which did not conform to the prescribed guidelines, in which a maximum of 30 minutes would be allowed between contacts with a given flight.

In the case of the 'Star Tiger,' there was no such contact in within that time frame on three occasions, and in one case nearly an hour had elapsed. The third and last communication was only five minutes late, but, upon learning that G-AHNP had not been in direct contact with approach control, the radio operator at Bermuda took no further action. An emergency was therefore not declared for more than an hour and a half after the last contact with the Tudor, and this delayed search operations.

Specific to the aircraft itself, the court found no evidence of design or construction defects in the Tudor. Its certificate of airworthiness did contain the one reservation in that its de-icing equipment had not been tested. This limitation was still in effect when the 'Star Tiger' made its final flight, but for previously mentioned reasons would probably not have been a factor. Among the recommendations made by the court were for improvements in the training of flight crews, greater care in the preparation of flight plans and more strict compliance to schedules in the performance of maintenance.

The mystery surrounding the loss of the 'Star Tiger' would be greatly magnified a year later, when its sister aircraft, the 'Star Ariel' vanished in the North Atlantic under similar circumstances (17 January 1949).

Date: 10 February 1948 (*c.*16:30)
Location: Near Padalarang, Dutch East Indies (Indonesia)
Operator: KLM Interinsulair Bedrijf (Dutch East Indies)
Aircraft type: Douglas DC-3C (PK-REA)

The airliner crashed and burned on the island of Java approximately 10 miles (15km) north-west of Bandung, from where it had taken off earlier, on a scheduled domestic service to Jakarta. All nineteen persons aboard (fifteen passengers and four crew members) were killed.

Date: 12 February 1948 (*c.*13:25)
Location: Near Ulrichstein, Hesse, Germany
Operator: Det Danske Luftfartselskap A/S (DDL) (Danish Air Lines)
Aircraft type: Douglas DC-3C (OY-DCI)

Operating on a scheduled international service from Copenhagen, Denmark, to Zurich, Switzerland, the aircraft crashed and burned in a wooded area some 20 miles (30km) north of Frankfurt, which was an en route stop. Killed in the accident were twelve of the twenty-one persons aboard the DC-3, including its entire crew of four. Nine passengers survived with various injuries.

The crash apparently resulted from an attempt by the pilots to maintain visual flight during the initial phase of a landing approach being conducted under marginal or actual instrument meteorological conditions, with a ceiling of around 2,000ft (600m) and a visibility of 1 to 3 miles (*c.*1.5–5km) in rain, and a 20-knot wind blowing from a south-south-westerly direction.

Date: 21 February 1948 (*c.*14:00)
Location: Near Ste Mère Église, Normandy, France
Operator: Latécoère (France)
Aircraft type: Latécoère 631 (F-BDRD)

All nineteen persons aboard were killed when the six-engine flying boat, which was being test flown by the manufacturer, crashed in the English Channel some 50 miles (80km) west of La Havre, from where it had taken off earlier. The victims included twelve observers in addition to the regular crew. Wreckage and some of the victims' bodies were later recovered.

The aircraft had turned back after encountering adverse weather conditions and was observed flying at a very low altitude in falling snow, which had reduced the visibility to only about 150ft (50m), before it plunged into the water.

A six-engine Latécoère 631 flying boat of the type that crashed in the English Channel during a test flight. (Philip Jarrett)

Date: 23 February 1948
Location: Near Davao, the Philippines
Operator: Commercial Airways (the Philippines)
Aircraft type: Curtiss-Wright C-46 (PI-C-262)

The transport crashed on the island of Mindanao about 5 minutes after its departure from Mati, presumably on a scheduled domestic service. All twelve persons aboard lost their lives in the accident, including its crew of three; most of the passengers were children.

Date: 2 March 1948 (c.21:15)
Location: London, England
Operator: Société Anonyme Belge d'Exploitation de la Navigation Aérienne (SABENA) (Belgium)
Aircraft type: Douglas DC-3C (OO-AWH)

The transport crashed and burned during an attempted landing at London (Heathrow) Airport, at the end of a scheduled international service from Brussels, Belgium. All but two of the twenty-two persons aboard the DC-3 lost their lives in the accident, including

the three members of its crew and one passenger who succumbed to his injuries a few days later. Both survivors were seriously injured.

After completion of a ground-controlled (GCA) approach to Runway 01, the pilot was instructed by the radar controller to 'look ahead and land'. Subsequently, OO-AHW slammed to earth nearly 1 mile (1.5km) beyond the threshold of the runway and some 350ft (105m) to the left, or north of, its extended centreline. Examination of the wreckage indicated that the aircraft had struck the ground in a stalled condition, its undercarriage down and flaps partially extended at the moment of impact. There was no evidence of pre-impact technical failure, altimeter error or in-flight fire. It was dark at the time of the crash, and the weather was overcast, with a ceiling of 8,000ft (c.2,500m) and a visibility of around 600ft (c.180m) in fog. The wind was from the east at 8mph (c.13kmh).

The accident was attributed to misjudgement on the part of the pilot as he tried to land in the conditions of poor visibility. It was believed that after a successful approach, and as the DC-3 neared the last few sodium lights that were present along the first 600ft (c.180m) of the runway, and of which he had been aware, the pilot anticipated making a normal landing, but that just before touchdown his visual contact was impaired by the sudden change in the runway lighting conditions.

Without realising it, he allowed the aircraft to gain height while endeavouring to re-establish visual contact with the ground. At that point, he turned on his landing lights, but the glare would have made his attempt to make visual contact even more difficult. During this time, OO-AWH veered to the left and then stalled at an approximate height of 50ft (15m).

Date: 10 March 1948 (c.23:00)
Location: Chicago, Illinois, US
Operator: Delta Air Lines (US)
Aircraft type: Douglas DC-4 (NC-37478)

Designated as Flight 705 and on a US domestic service to Miami, Florida, the transport crashed on take-off from Chicago Municipal Airport. All but one of the thirteen persons aboard the DC-4 were killed in the accident, including the four members of its crew. The surviving passenger was seriously injured.

After becoming airborne, NC-37478 assumed a near-vertical climbing attitude and ascended to a height of between 300 and 500ft (c.100–150m), then appeared to stall, whereupon its starboard wing dropped. A partial recovery from the stall was made before the aircraft slammed to earth with its undercarriage still extended and burst into flames, coming to rest some 150ft (50m) beyond the north boundary of the airport.

Examination of the wreckage revealed no evidence of prior mechanical or structural failure in the aircraft, and the cause of the longitudinal control loss that led to the crash could not be determined. The accident occurred in darkness and as a light snow was falling, and sub-zero temperatures prevailed at the time, but the atmospheric conditions were not believed to have been factors.

Date: 12 March 1948 (c.21:15)
Location: Territory of Alaska, US
Operator: Northwest Airlines (US)
Aircraft type: Douglas DC-4 (NC-95422)

Chartered to carry the crew of an oil tanker and on a service originating at Shanghai, China, with an ultimate destination of New York City, the transport crashed and burned on Mt Sanford, in the Wrangell range. Including its six crew members, all thirty persons aboard the aircraft were killed.

The accident occurred some 200 miles (320km) north-east of Anchorage, where the DC-4 had last stopped, in darkness and conditions of good visibility, although the peak may have been obscured by a thin layer of clouds or from the effects of the aurora borealis. At the moment of impact, the aircraft was cruising on a north-easterly heading at 11,000ft (c.3,400m), or about 5,000ft (c1,500m) below the level of the peak. Its wreckage then fell into a small glacial cirque, some 2,500ft (750m) below the point of the initial impact, and was not accessible from either the ground or the air.

The US Civil Aeronautics Board (CAB) concluded that the pilot had deliberately tried to fly direct between the Gulkana and Snag radio range stations, and as a result NC-95422 was at the time of the crash 23 miles (37km) south-east of the centreline of the prescribed airway, which had been intentionally deflected to avoid the mountain. It was noted in the CAB report that the captain in command of the DC-4 had made two dozen previous flights along this route, and made numerous other flights along it for the US Army Air Forces during the Second World War.

Date: 15 March 1948
Location: Near Chocontá, Cundinamarca, Colombia
Operator: Agencia Interamericana de Aviación (Colombia)
Aircraft type: Douglas DC-3C (C-1002)

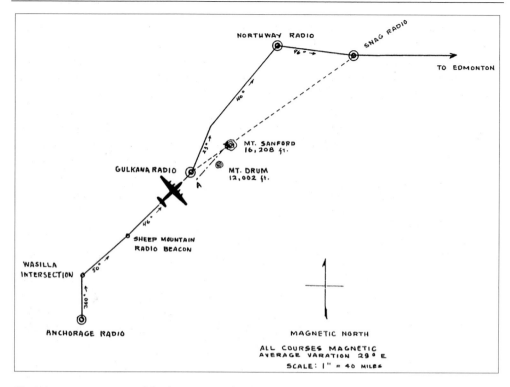

Chart shows correct route and the direct course taken by the Northwest Airlines Douglas DC-4, leading to its crash in Alaska. (Civil Aeronautics Board)

All fourteen persons aboard (ten passengers and four crew members) were killed when the airliner, on a scheduled domestic service to Bogotá from El Secreto, crashed on a hill in the Andes some 50 miles (80km) north-west of its destination.

Date: 27 March 1948 (c.07:30)
Location: French Corsica
Operator: Indian National Airways
Aircraft type: Vickers Viking 1B (VT-CEL)

The twin-engine airliner crashed and burned on Mount Cardo during a scheduled international service that had last stopped at Rome, Italy, having originated at Delhi, India, and with an ultimate destination of London, England. All nineteen persons aboard (fifteen passengers and a crew of four) perished.

Having last stopped at Rome, Italy, the Viking had been cruising at 8,000ft (c.2,500m) when it struck an eastern slope of the moun-

tain, which at the time was obscured by stratocumulus clouds. The weather was clear on the west side.

Date: 5 April 1948 (c.14:30)
Location: Berlin, Germany
First aircraft:
Operator: British European Airways Corporation (BEA)
Type: Vickers Viking 1B (G-AIVP)
Second aircraft:
Operator: Soviet Air Force
Type: Yakovlev Yak-3

This collision occurred in the early days of the Cold War, when the 'Iron Curtain' was a threat, literally and figuratively, to Westerners. Having nearly completed a scheduled international service originating at London, the twin-engine airliner was circling in preparation for landing at RAF Gatow, in (West) Berlin, and the single-engine fighter was in a steep left bank, not in the landing configuration, when they struck head-on. The collision occurred in good weather conditions, with a high ceiling, and at an estimated height of 500 to 1,000ft (*c.*150–300m) above the ground, and after losing its port wing in the impact, G-AIVP plunged to earth and exploded, crashing in the Soviet zone. All fourteen persons aboard the Viking (ten passengers and four crew members) and the pilot of the Yak-3 were killed.

The accident was attributed solely to the Soviet pilot, who had been performing aerobatics for some time beforehand, and whose actions were considered 'in disregard' of the accepted rules of flying as well as procedures of which the USSR had been a participant. Though expressing 'deep regret' over the tragedy, the Soviet government rejected a claim by the UK to compensate for the loss of life and property.

Date: 15 April 1948 (*c.*02:35)
Location: Near Limerick, Ireland
Operator: Pan American World Airways (US)
Aircraft type: Lockheed 049 Constellation (NC-88858)

Designated as Flight 110 and on an around-the-world service originating at and ultimately destined for the US, specifically, San Francisco, California, and New York, New York, the airliner crashed while attempting to land at Shannon Airport, which was a scheduled en route stop. Including all ten members of its crew, thirty persons aboard were killed in the accident; one passenger survived, and in what could also be considered somewhat miraculous, he escaped serious injury.

The crash occurred as NC-88858 was conducting an instrument landing system (ILS) approach to Runway 23 in early morning darkness and during a low overcast, with the cloud coverage 6/10 at 400ft (120m) and 4/10 at 300ft (*c.*100m), and also patchy fog, which had reduced the visibility to 2.5 miles (*c.*4km). Its extended undercarriage had initially struck a stone fence before the Constellation slammed to earth and burst into flames approximately half a mile (0.8km) short of the runway threshold but while directly aligned with its extended centreline. Its speed at impact was estimated to have been around 110mph (175kmh).

A British European Airways Vickers Viking of the type involved in the mid-air collision with a Soviet fighter over Berlin. (British Airways)

A Pan American World Airways Lockheed Constellation, identical to the aircraft that crashed during an attempted landing at Shannon Airport. (Smithsonian Institution)

In its investigative report, the US Civil Aeronautics Board (CAB) attributed the accident to the continuation by the crew of the approach to a height that was below the minimum descent altitude, and which did not provide adequate terrain clearance. The circumstances that led to the premature descent could not be established. There was no evidence of any pre-impact mechanical or structural failure in NC-88858 or a defect in the airport ILS system. And although an altimeter error or a malfunction in some instrument in the aircraft could have been a factor in the crash, the report noted that an ILS approach is not made by reference to any one instrument.

Perhaps significant was the fact that the fluorescent lighting on the pilot's side of the cockpit was known to have previously failed, and that this defect could not be repaired at London, where the flight had last stopped. The report noted that had such a failure taken place again, while at an excessively low altitude and when there would have been either no or only intermittent visual reference, the pilot would have been without an immediate means of orientation at a time when a slight loss of height could prove disastrous. The CAB concluded that this could have been a contributing factor, but not the primary cause of the accident.

Date: 18 April 1948 (*c*.09:20)
Location: Territory of New Guinea
Operator: New Guinea Air Traders (Australia)
Aircraft type: Lockheed Hudson IIIA (VH-ALA)

Leased from a private individual and on an intra-island charter service to Bulolo and Wau, the twin-engine airliner crashed and burned immediately after it had taken off from the airstrip serving Lae, killing all thirty-seven persons aboard (thirty-three passengers and four crew members). This remains even today as the highest death toll in an accident involving an Australian-registered civil aircraft.

The Hudson had climbed to an approximate height of 500ft (150m) when its port power plant failed, whereupon the aircraft plunged into wooded terrain on an island in the Markham River. An investigative panel attributed the engine malfunction to the fatigue failure of the accessory driving gear. However, the resulting crash resulted from error on the part of the pilot, most probably poor technique during the emergency, leading to a loss of control. Considered as a contributing factor was inadequate conversion training of the pilot in Hudson, in that he was not required to demonstrate his ability to fly the aircraft safely with one engine inoperative.

Also considered contributory was improper loading of VH-ALA, which placed its centre of gravity beyond its rearmost limit, thus affecting the aircraft's stability. With regard to this matter, the accident report noted that in operations conducted within New Guinea, it was general practice to carry local inhabitants on a poundage basis, without providing them with seats or seatbelts. However, the panel noted that the disastrous outcome of this particular flight would probably not have been different even had the passengers been seated and restrained unless the occupants been properly distributed in the cabin.

The panel further identified breaches in established regulations by the carrier in not assuring that the passengers were properly secured, and for not having a licensed pilot in the right-hand seat on the flight deck of VH-ALA. It also concluded that the procedures then in effect regarding the dissemination of information and instructions in the loading of aircraft, and the placement of responsibility for such pre-flight planning, were inadequate.

Date: 24 April 1948 (*c*.09:30)
Location: Near Mamakan, Russian Soviet Federative Socialist Republic, USSR
Operator: Aeroflot (USSR)
Aircraft type: Lisunov Li-2 (SSSR-L4460)

The twin-engine airliner, which had been on a scheduled domestic service from Kirensk to Bodaybo, crashed around 20 miles (30km) south-west of its destination. All but one passenger among the twenty-nine persons aboard were killed, including the four members of its crew.

It was reported that the flight crew, who had been drinking the previous night, deviated from the correct route, and had been flying at an altitude only about 300ft (100m) when the Li-2 lost height in a snow shower and plunged into an ice-covered river.

Date: 13 May 1948 (*c.*11:00)
Location: Near Magazini, Belgian Congo
Operator: Société Anonyme Belge d'Exploitation de la Navigation Aérienne (SABENA) (Belgium)
Aircraft type: Douglas DC-4 (OO-CBE)

Operating on a scheduled internal Congolese service to Libenge from Leopoldville (Kinshasa), the transport crashed in the vicinity of its destination, and some 600 miles (950km) north-north-east of the capital city. All but one of the thirty-two persons aboard were killed in the accident, including the entire crew of seven, and the surviving passenger was seriously injured.

The DC-4 had entered an area of clouds and turbulent conditions at an altitude of 700ft (*c.*200m) before it lost height and then slammed into a wooded area. It was believed that OO-CBE had penetrated the active centre of a tornado before being forced to the ground by the severe winds associated with the storm.

Date: 15 May 1948 (*c.*07:20)
Location: Near Vrede, Orange Free State, South Africa
Operator: Mercury Aviation Services Ltd. (South Africa)
Aircraft type: Douglas DC-3C (ZS-BWY)

All thirteen persons aboard (eight passengers and a crew of five) were killed when the air-liner, on a scheduled domestic service from Durban to Johannesburg, crashed and burned approximately 180 miles (290km) south-east of its destination.

Reportedly, ZS-BWY was some 10 miles (15km) off the proper track when it struck a mountain in the Witkoppens range, the accident occurring in adverse weather conditions.

Date: 10 June 1948 (*c.*20:00)
Location: Isle of Man
Operator: Hargreaves Airways Ltd (UK)
Aircraft type: de Havilland 89A Dragon Rapide (G-AIUI)

The twin-engine aeroplane crashed in the vicinity of Port Erin while preparing to land at the Ronaldsway airport, and six persons aboard were killed, including the pilot. Two passengers survived with injuries.

Having nearly completed a charter service from Birmingham, England, G-AIUI was flying in a low overcast when it slammed into a hill and burned. During its approach from the west, the Dragon Rapide had failed to maintain both the proper course to the homing beacon used for landing, deviating to the north of the track, and a sufficient height to clear the terrain. The UK Ministry of Civil Aviation considered it possible that the pilot had been unaware of the fact that the navigational aid was not located at the airport, which could account for these deviations. Also significant was the fact that this had been the pilot's first flight to the Isle of Man.

Date: 17 June 1948 (13:41)
Location: Near Mt Carmel, Pennsylvania, US
Operator: United Air Lines (US)
Aircraft type: Douglas DC-6 (NC-37506)

Its safety already having come into question as a result of a previous fatal crash (24 October 1947), the DC-6 again became the focus of concern in aviation circles as a result of this accident. This time, however, the underlying factor was the aircraft's fire-suppression equipment, rather than an actual fire.

A United Air Lines Douglas DC-6 of the type that crashed after the apparent incapacitation of its flight crew by fire extinguishing agent. (Smithsonian Institution)

Flight 624 had originated in Southern California and last stopped at Chicago, Illinois, during a transcontinental US domestic service with an ultimate destination of New York, New York. Less than five minutes after the crew had acknowledged clearance to descend from its cruising altitude of 17,000ft (*c.*5,200m), another crew heard what they described as 'screaming voices' over their radio, later determined to have emanated from the DC-6. Also heard was the message 'This is an emergency descent!' In a partially intelligible transmission that was recorded from the ground, one or both pilots of Flight 624 reported that the fire extinguisher had been released in the forward cargo compartment.

Witnesses on the ground had observed NC-37506 at a height of 500 to 1,000ft (*c.*150–300m) above the ground, and while at altitude of only about 200ft (60m) it entered a right climbing turn. The aircraft struck a 66,000-volt transformer and severed power lines as it slammed into a hillside some 75 miles (120km) north-west of Philadelphia, disintegrating on impact. All forty-three persons aboard (thirty-nine passengers and four crew members) perished. Its undercarriage was still retracted at the moment of impact, indicating that the transport had descended in that configuration at a speed of approximately 300mph (480kmh), and a flash fire erupted after the crash, scorching and smudging parts of the wreckage throughout the entire area. The weather in the area at the time was good and not a factor in the crash.

The US Civil Aeronautics Board (CAB) determined that the crew had not opened the emergency cabin pressure relief valves after activating the fire-extinguishing system in the forward hold, which went contrary to the approved emergency procedure. Both pilots then must have become incapacitated by a high concentration of carbon dioxide in the cockpit. Depending upon the amount of CO_2, they could have been reduced to a state of 'confused consciousness' or could have rendered completely unconscious. No evidence was found by the CAB of any pre-impact fire in the aircraft, and the only in-flight malfunction was the apparent failure of the fire-detection equipment, which must have resulted in a false warning.

A number of false fire indications had been reported in US air carrier operations employing the DC-6 and other type aircraft even before the United tragedy, prompting tests and research to improve the reliability of smoke detectors. Operators were in fact asked to disconnect detectors that utilised photo-electric cells. After the crash, Douglas developed a modified fire-extinguishing system to permit all necessary steps to be carried out by the activation of a single control, and designed an additional vent to reduce CO_2 build-up in the cockpit in the event of its use. A week after the accident in Pennsylvania the US Civil Aeronautics Administration (CAA) sent out a telegram advising DC-6 flight crews to depressurise the cabin and use emergency oxygen when carbon dioxide was released into any fuselage compartment in the aircraft from any source other than portable fire extinguishers.

Despite the two catastrophic crashes in 1947 and 1948 and the modifications resulting therefrom, the DC-6 would amass an impressive record of safety and reliability and would remain in operation with major scheduled carriers well into the 1960s, and with supplemental and cargo carriers decades after then.

Date: 1 July 1948 (*c.*12:00)
Location: Near Keerbergen, Brabant, Belgium
Operator: Avio Linee Italiane SA (Italy)
Aircraft type: Fiat G.212 (I-ELSA)

The trimotored airliner crashed approximately 10 miles (15km) north-north-east of

Brussels, where it was to have landed. Killed in the accident were eight of the twelve persons aboard the Fiat, including four members of its crew of five; the hostess was among the survivors.

Having nearly completed a scheduled international service from Milan, Italy, I-ELSA reportedly overshot the runway while attempting to land at the Brussels airport, the crash occurring during a heavy rain.

Date: 4 July 1948 (*c.*16:00)
Location: Near Northwood, Middlesex, England
First aircraft:
Operator: Aktiebolaget Aerotransport (ABA) (Swedish Air Lines)
Type: Douglas DC-6 (SE-BDA)
Second aircraft:
Operator: Royal Air Force
Type: Avro York (MW 248)

The airliner and the military transport collided in mid-air approximately 5 miles (10km) north-north-west of Northolt Airport, serving London, where the two had originally planned to land, and both then crashed and burned. All thirty-two persons aboard the DC-6 (twenty-five passengers and seven crew members) and the seven occupants of the York (one a civilian passenger and the rest British service personnel) were killed in the accident.

Operating on a scheduled international service that had originated at Stockholm, Sweden, SE-BDA had about 40 minutes before the collision entered the control zone, and shortly thereafter was transferred to the Northolt control centre. After being cleared down to 2,500ft (*c.*750m), the flight requested permission to proceed to Amsterdam, the Netherlands, apparently due to the poor weather at London. Although it was granted permission to depart from the control zone at the height to which it had been cleared, this message must not have been heard. During this time, MW 248 entered the control zone, and was then authorised for descent down to 3,000ft (*c.*1,000m).

Although the DC-6 had flown in a 'figure-8' circuit during its hold, a south-south-westerly wind of nearly 50mph (80kmh) may have caused it to drift considerably to the north-east of the normal pattern. Additionally, there seemed to be some uncertainty by the captain of the York as to where his aircraft was to circle. But as the two aircraft should have been separated by altitude, neither of these two factors should have been a safety issue. Nevertheless, the two struck at or between the height to which they had been cleared, and in the midst of dense cloud, which was accompanied by rain, having converged at an angle of around 55 degrees. Initial contact appeared to have been between the right outer propeller of the DC-6 and the underside of the York's starboard wing, after which the former's starboard wing slashed into and tore off the latter's aft fuselage section. At the time of the collision, MW 248 had probably been proceeding towards the west, while SE-BDA was flying towards the radio beacon, apparently not having left the holding pattern.

The accident was attributed to 'human fallibility' on the part of both ground and flight personnel. Three errors of duty or erroneous operating practices identified by the investigative court were considered contributing factors. Two of these pertained to the pressure setting given both aircraft by two different facilities that did not correspond to the actual airfield pressure. Additionally, the RAF Area Control Centre at Uxbridge had not broadcast the regional pressure settings at the required times. Due to these failures, the DC-6 could have been some 30ft (10m) above its indicated altitude and the York more than 200ft (60m) below the height indicated by its altimetry system. The minimum height separation for instrument flight rules (IFR) traffic in Great Britain and some other countries had at the time been 500ft (c.150m), but subsequent to this disaster it was increased to 1,000ft (c.300m).

Date: 7 July 1948 (c.09:50)
Location: Near Djirling, French Indochina (Vietnam)
Operator: Air France
Aircraft type: Douglas DC-3C (F-BCYP)

Operating on a scheduled international service from Saigon to Dalat Lien Khang, the airliner crashed on a mountain some 50 miles (80km) south-west of its destination. All twenty-one persons aboard (eighteen passengers and a crew of three) were killed in the accident, which occurred in a monsoon-spawned rainstorm as F-BCYP was reportedly 'near' its planned landing. The crash was attributed to both the adverse meteorological conditions and the absence of adequate ground facilities.

Date: 16 July 1948 (c.18:00)
Location: Near (Portuguese) Macao
Operator: Cathay Pacific Airways (Hong Kong)
Aircraft type: Consolidated Catalina (VR-HDT)

The first airline hijacking ending in disaster occurred during a scheduled service from Macao to Hong Kong. About 10 minutes after take-off, the twin-engine amphibian plunged into the Pearl River estuary, and all but one of the twenty-six persons aboard were killed, including its entire crew of three.

Later, the surviving passenger admitted to being a member of a gang of four robbers who had commandeered the Catalina; he was not prosecuted due to jurisdictional factors and three years after the crime got deported to China. The crash of VR-HDT occurred after its pilot and co-pilot had been shot.

Date: 24 July 1948 (c.17:30)
Location: Near Cap des Rosiers, Quebec, Canada
Operator: Rimouski Airlines (Canada)
Aircraft type: Douglas DC-3C (CF-FKY)

Having been chartered to transport employees of the Consolidated Paper Company to the town of Gaspe from Anticosti Island, also in Quebec, the aircraft crashed on the Gaspe Peninsula, about 10 miles (15km) east of its destination. Including the three members of its crew, all twenty-six persons aboard the DC-3 lost their lives in the accident, the cause of which was probably related to the foggy weather conditions in which it occurred.

Date: 29 July 1948
Location: Near Tsingtao, Shantung, China
Operator: Civil Air Transport (China)
Aircraft type: Curtiss-Wright C-46 (XT-882)

Its passengers comprised of Chinese soldiers, the airliner crashed immediately after taking off an intra-provincial domestic service to Tsinan (Jinan). All nineteen persons aboard the C-46 were killed in the accident, the victims including a crew of three civilians. Reportedly, XT-882 went into a spin after becoming airborne and plummeted to the ground from an approximate height of 300ft (100m).

Date: 29 July 1948 (*c.*09:00)
Location: Near Buenos Aires, Argentina
Operator: Aviación del Litoral Fluvial Argentino (ALFA) (Argentina)
Aircraft type: Short S.25 Sandringham 2 (LV-AAP)

Operating on a scheduled domestic service from Rosario, the four-engine flying boat crashed while alighting on the Plata River, and seventeen persons aboard were killed. Five passengers and two of the aircraft's six crew members survived with various injuries.

After touching down on the water, the Sunderland reportedly struck an obstacle that was not identified, and the aircraft then capsized and sank. Most of the occupants were trapped in the sinking wreckage and probably died of drowning. The accident was attributed to overconfidence by the pilot-in-command and his first officer in attempting

to land atop the water in conditions of fog and poor visibility, which were in fact below the prescribed minima, without flying over beforehand in order to make a visual inspection the landing area.

Date: 1 August 1948 (*c.*00:00)
Location: North Atlantic Ocean
Operator: Air France
Aircraft type: Latécoère 631 (F-BDRC)

The six-engine flying boat was lost with fifty-two persons aboard (forty passengers and a crew of twelve) while on a scheduled international service from Fort-de-France, Martinique, to Port-Etienne, Mauritania. A US Coast Guard vessel later recovered some burnt pieces of debris from the water about halfway between Puerto Rico and Senegal, but no survivors or victims' bodies were found.

Although the cause of the disaster could not be determined, it was concluded that whatever happened to the aircraft must have been 'serious and unexpected'. The crash occurred in darkness, shortly after midnight, but the meteorological conditions in the area were not believed to have been a factor. Following the loss of F-BDRC, Air France discontinued operations with the Latécoère 631.

Date: 29 August 1948 (*c.*17:00)
Location: Near Fountain City, Wisconsin, US
Operator: Northwest Airlines (US)
Aircraft type: Martin 202 (NC-93044)

As was the case with the DC-6, the twin-engine Martin 202 experienced difficulties in its early operational history, and again faulty design was partially to blame. Designated as Flight 421, NC-93044 had been on a US domestic service to Minneapolis, Minnesota, from Chicago, Illinois, when it crashed some 90 miles (145km) south-east of its destination. All thirty-seven persons aboard (thirty-three passengers and a crew of four) perished.

In its last radio transmission, the aircraft was reported to have been descending through

A Northwest Airlines Martin 202, of the type illustrated here, suffered a major accident attributed to faulty design not long after the type entered regular service. (Smithsonian Institution)

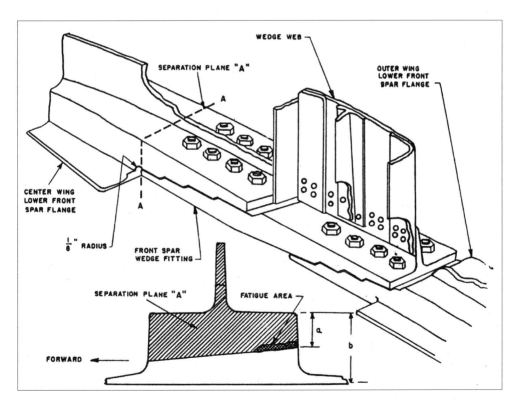

Diagram of the wing fitting indicating the area affected by fatigue, leading to the in-flight break-up of the twin-engine Martin. (Civil Aeronautics Board)

7,000ft (c.2,000m) while on a heading of 335 degrees. After entering a violent thunderstorm it was observed falling to earth in pieces, crashing on a bluff on the east side of the Mississippi River. There was no fire.

It was determined by the US Civil Aeronautics Board (CAB) that the outer panel of the aircraft's port wing had separated in flight. Further examination of the wreckage revealed a fatigue crack approximately 7/8 of an inch (22mm) long and 3/32 of an inch (2mm) deep in the fitting that attached the outer and centre wing front and rear lower spar flanges. The separation of the left front lower spar flange was followed by the failure from tension of the top connections of the outer wing to the centre section. After the wing broke, the Martin rolled to the left, and its fuselage and starboard horizontal stabiliser were struck by debris, whereupon the empennage was severed from the rest of the aircraft. The CAB concluded that the original fatigue crack had been induced by faulty design and been aggravated by the effects of the severe turbulence encountered within the storm.

The investigation of this crash and the discovery of fatigue cracks in other aircraft of the same type showed that the spar flanges, which had been composed of a new aluminium alloy, were inductive to a high concentration of local stress and thus fatigue. As an interim measure, the Martin 202 fleet was given frequent and thorough inspections to check for the development of fatigue cracks, and the front centre section spar flange modified to include five steps, or vertical increases in thickness, until each aircraft could be returned to the manufacturer, where extensive structural changes in the wing could be accomplished. However, it was noted in the CAB report that the gust encountered by NC-93044 may have been of higher velocity than that for which the aircraft had been designed to withstand. The decision to enter or avoid the storm would have been a matter of pilot judgement.

Date: 31 August 1948
Location: Near Elisabethville (Lubumbashi), Belgian Congo
Operator: Société Anonyme Belge d'Exploitation de la Navigation Aérienne (SABENA) (Belgium)
Aircraft type: Douglas DC-3C (OO-CBL)

All thirteen persons aboard (ten passengers and a crew of three) were killed when the transport, on a scheduled internal service with the Belgian Congo to Elisabethville from Manono, crashed on a mountain approximately 30 miles (50km) north-west of its destination. The cause of the accident could not be determined.

Date: 2 September 1948 (c.20:15)
Location: Near Quirindi, New South Wales, Australia
Operator: Australian National Airways
Aircraft type: Douglas DC-3C (VH-ANK)

Designated as Flight 331, the airliner had been on a domestic interstate service from Brisbane, Queensland, to Sydney, New South Wales, when it crashed and burned in the Crawney Pass some 150 miles (250km) north of its destination. Its burned wreckage was found two days later on Square Mountain Peak, with no survivors among the thirteen persons who had been aboard (ten passengers and three crew members).

Apparently due to the failure of its radio range receiver, VH-ANK had deviated by some 135 miles (215km) to the west of its planned course. Unaware of this deviation, the crew had then descended to a height of around 4,600ft (c.1,400m) due to icing, and at the time of impact the DC-3 was proceeding in an easterly direction, in darkness and cloudy weather conditions below the minimum safe altitude for the region. Its heading at the time of the accident indicated that the crew may have realised the original deviation and were attempting to return to the airway.

Date: 2 October 1948 (*c.*10:30)
Location: Near Trondheim, Sør-Trøndelag, Norway
Operator: Det Norske Luftfartselskap A/S (DNL) (Norwegian Air Lines)
Aircraft type: Short S.25 Sandringham 5 (LN-IAW)

The four-engine flying boat crashed in Hommelvika Bay, killing nineteen of the forty-three persons aboard, including three members of its crew of four. Among the surviving passengers was British philosopher Bertrand Russell, then seventy-six years of age, who had been on his way to give a lecture to a student society.

Having nearly completed a scheduled domestic service from Oslo, LN-IAW was initially instructed to land from the north-east, but the crew subsequently received conflicting information concerning the wind conditions. Although the nearby Værnes Airport informed the flight that the wind was blowing from due west at around 20mph (30kmh), a patrol boat operating in the area reported it to the crew as being at least twice that velocity and coming from the south-west, and also noted that the sea had a heavy swell.

The Sandringham alighted towards the south-west and a relatively short distance from the opposite shoreline. Due to the effects of the nearby terrain, the wind would have been blowing from the right side of the aircraft, and its speed could have been more than 45mph (70kmh). To counter this, the captain lowered the starboard wing, but after the corresponding float struck the surface of the bay and was torn off, he initiated an overshoot manoeuvre. However, just after becoming airborne, he realised that he would not be able to clear the terrain and cut the throttles, whereupon the flying boat settled back into the water with such velocity so as to severely damage its front fuselage section. The aircraft then sank. Despite the wind conditions, the visibility was good under the cloud base, with an overcast of 2,700ft (*c.*820m).

Date: 12 October 1948 (*c.*13:00)
Location: Near Yevlakh, Azerbaijan SSR, USSR
Operator: Aeroflot (USSR)
Aircraft type: Ilyushin Il-12 (SSSR-L1450)

Ten persons aboard (four passengers and a crew of six) lost their lives when the twin-engine airliner crashed some 150 miles (250km) west-north-west of Baku, from where it had taken off earlier, on a service to Tbilisi, Georgian SSR. There were no survivors from the accident, which occurred in bad weather.

Prior to the crash, the Il-12 had turned back towards its point of departure after encountering low clouds, rain and icing conditions, as well as navigational difficulties due to poor reception of radio beacons.

Date: 21 October 1948 (*c.*00:35)
Location: Near Prestwick, South Ayrshire, Scotland
Operator: Koninklijke Luchtvaart Maatschappij voor Nederland en Kalonien (KLM) (the Netherlands)
Aircraft type: Lockheed 049 Constellation (PH-TEN)

Operating on a scheduled international service from Amsterdam to New York City, the aircraft crashed in flames some 10 miles (15km) north-east of the city of Ayr, and about 5 miles (10km) east-north-east of Prestwick Airport, which was an en route stop. Including one victim who succumbed to his injuries two days later, all forty persons aboard (thirty passengers and ten crew members) were killed in the accident.

After PH-TEN had performed a ground-controlled (GCA) let-down during the initial approach to Runway 32, a member of the crew announced, 'Overshot. Am going to do a visual circuit for landing on Runway 26.' The Constellation turned left before looping back towards the north-east, but during this manoeuvre, and while proceeding in near-level flight, it struck four cables, three of them

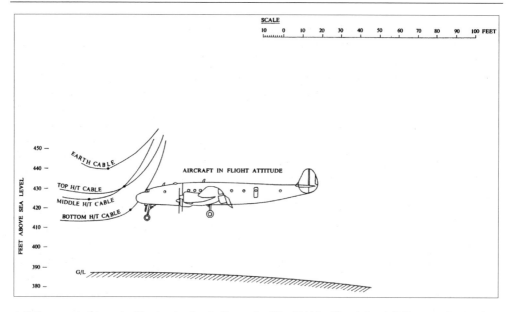

Artist's concept of impact with wires leading to the crash of the KLM Lockheed Constellation near Prestwick, Scotland. (Accidents Investigation Branch)

high-voltage. Severely damaged and set afire by the impact, the transport subsequently slammed to earth at Auchinweet Farm while in a shallow descent and banked to the left, and with its undercarriage down and flaps partially extended. The crash occurred in darkness, with no moon, and cloudy weather conditions, with intermittent drizzle and limited visibility.

An investigative court of the UK Ministry of Civil Aviation attributed the disaster to 'the coincidence of a number of adverse circumstances'. The primary factor was the lack of knowledge on the part of the flight crew of both the prevailing weather and of the terrain along the aircraft's flight path. The court ruled that the non–existence of a uniform system regulating the manner in which meteorological information was to be disseminated had prevented the crew from knowing that the ceiling had lowered since the last weather report they had received. The absence of this information specifically resulted from the failure of the meteorological observer to record it in 'plain' language, rather than code, in either of the reports that he sent to the flying control officer, in the control tower.

As there was no mechanical recording of communications between the control tower and the aircraft, it could not be ascertained exactly what meteorological information had been relayed to the flight. However, there was no evidence that the crew had been informed to the fact that the conditions had deteriorated, with the ceiling down to 300ft (c.100m) and the visibility approximately 1 mile (1.5km). Considering that KLM pilots had been instructed not to use Runway 26 at night if the ceiling was lower than 700ft (200m) and the visibility less than 2 miles (c.3km), the court accepted the fact that the captain of PH-TEN would have abandoned the approach and perhaps diverted to an alternate airport had he been apprised of the situation. Although personnel at the meteorological office were found to have properly assessed the prevailing conditions, inaccuracies were identified in weather logs, such as the ceiling being recorded as 7,000ft rather than 700ft, and there were similar errors in the measurement of visibility. Furthermore, the flying control officer said in subsequent testimony that it was not the normal procedure for the person in his position to relay messages that pertained to a deterioration in the weather, a practice that was 'condemned' by the court. Also faulted was the airline itself, which at the time did not have specific procedures regarding the issuance to its flight crews of updated meteorological information.

The decision of the captain to abandon the landing on Runway 32 was apparently based on the report of a high cross-wind. Though the runway was preferred because of its length, pilots had come to avoid its use if the cross-wind component exceeded 15mph (c.25kmh), although that was the exact velocity as the Constellation made its approach, and this information had been transmitted to the flight by the GCA director. Significantly, no instructions had been provided to KLM Constellation pilots for performing such an overshoot manoeuvre at Prestwick, which would have involved a timing procedure in order to achieve proper alignment with the alternate runway. In any case, it could only be safely executed in conditions in which the pilot could maintain visual reference to the ground. It was possible that the pilot sought to maintain such visual contact by remaining at a low altitude. Had he lost visual contact, it would have been necessary to refer back to his altimeter.

In instructions pertaining to Prestwick Airport appearing in the North Atlantic Route Manual, pilots had been alerted that a circling manoeuvre must be confined to the west side of the airport, since the terrain to the east sloped upward, reaching nearly 400ft (120m) above sea level. The court in fact believed that the height limits for such a procedure did not allow for an adequate margin of safety. Nor was there at the time an official instrument letdown chart available for Prestwick, with the charts being employed by pilots having been derived from US military maps. That such visual aids had been based on information obtained by a foreign agency was deemed 'quite extraordinary' in the court's report. One of the charts found in the wreckage of the Constellation was apparently of this type, and contained incorrect height informa-

tion and no reference to the cables struck by the aircraft; the fact that the chart had been removed from a loose-leaf notebook indicated that it had been used by the crew. Referring to it, the crew would not have been aware of the topography of the terrain over which they were flying after the overshoot. A notice to airmen (NOTAM) had mentioned that obstruction lights on all but one of the surrounding masts were unserviceable and that the radio range facility at the airport was also inoperative, with a non-directional beacon (NDB) available for use in its place. However, the court considered it 'possible' that the beacon may not have been transmitting a continuous signal.

There was no evidence of error in the aircraft's altimeters, nor that an encounter with turbulence could have in any way contributed to the crash. Examination of the wreckage disclosed no indication of a prior technical failure in the Constellation except for the fact that the No.2 propeller was determined to have been rotating slowly at the time of impact with the cables, and that the fire extinguisher cock had been selected to the corresponding power plant. Trouble with the engine could have contributed to the failure of the aircraft to maintain altitude, or at least distracted the crew, during the go-around manoeuvre.

The report also noted that there had been a delay of around 1 hour 40 minutes between the accident and the arrival at the scene of medical aid. One reason for this was uncertainty where, or even whether, the aircraft had crashed. And despite the fact that the airport crash crew had been advised to be ready when they learned of the planned overshoot landing procedure, they did not actually proceed to the scene until about 90 minutes after the accident. This could have been significant when considering that six occupants were actually found alive, even though none ultimately survived. Subsequent to the disaster, new procedures in the area of emergency response were implemented, including the establishment of guidelines in the notification of ambulance and fire services.

Two months after the accident the UK Ministry of Civil Aviation issued official charts for use at Prestwick Airport. Among other recommendations, the court asked for a review of navigational instructions pertaining to airports throughout Great Britain, and suggested that steps be taken to ensure uniformity in the standards by which special weather reports were to be issued.

Date: 23 October 1948 (*c.*14:00)
Location: Near Ohakune, New Zealand
Operator: New Zealand National Airways Corporation
Aircraft type: Lockheed 10A Electra (ZK-AGK)

All thirteen persons aboard (ten passengers and a crew of three) were killed when the twin-engine aircraft, on a scheduled domestic service from Palmerston North to Hamilton, struck Mount Ruapehu, on the country's North Island, at an approximate elevation of 6,000ft (1,800m), or some 700ft (200m) below its summit.

The accident occurred during a low overcast and in intermittent rain, with a visibility of around 2.5 to 5 miles (4–10km), and was attributed to a navigational error by the pilot-in-command, who apparently did not compensate for a wind of nearly 50 knots that was blowing from a north-westerly direction. Another factor was the lack of adequate navigational aids in the area.

Date: 25 October 1948 (*c.*14:00)
Location: Georgian SSR, USSR
Operator: Aeroflot (USSR)
Aircraft type: Lisunov Li-2 (CCCP-4500)

Operating on a scheduled domestic service with a destination of Sukhumi, the airliner crashed in the Caucasus Mountains, and all eighteen persons aboard (fourteen passengers and four crew members) were killed. The accident occurred in adverse weather conditions after the Li-2 had deviated from the prescribed course.

Date: 4 November 1948
Location: North Pacific Ocean
Operator: Alaska Air Express (US)
Aircraft type: Douglas DC-3C (NC-66637)

The airliner vanished with seventeen persons aboard (fifteen passengers and two flight crew members) during a non-scheduled service originating at Anchorage, Territory of Alaska, with an ultimate destination of Seattle, Washington, US.

In its last radio transmission, received at 05:10 local time, NC-66637 was reported cruising at 10,000ft (*c.*3,000m) and at a position approximately 150 miles (250km) south-east of Yakutat, where it had last stopped. Its next en route stop was to have been on Annette Island, also in the Territory of Alaska. Small pieces of material identified as being from a transport-type aircraft, possibly a DC-3, were later found in the water near Chicagof Island, and about 35 miles (55km) south-east of its last reported position.

The disappearance had occurred in pre-dawn darkness, and the weather along the route taken by NC-66637 consisted of scattered clouds at various altitudes, light rain showers, light-to-moderate turbulence and winds ranging from 30 to 45mph (*c.*50–70kmh). It was noted in the investigative report of the US Civil Aeronautics Board (CAB) that these conditions were not believed to have been conducive to either carburettor or airframe icing. However, the CAB was unable to draw any conclusions as to what could have caused the loss of the DC-3.

Date: 11 November 1948 (*c.*18:15)
Location: Near Garston, Lancashire, England
Operator: Mannin Airways (UK)
Aircraft type: de Havilland 89 Dragon Rapide (G-AKOF)

The twin-engine aeroplane was ditched in the Irish Sea near the mouth of the River Mersey, the accident occurring in darkness. Among its eight occupants, who included a two-member crew, only one passenger survived; he was later found on the shore. The others apparently survived the water landing, but none had been wearing life-jackets.

Chartered to fly to the Isle of Man from Dublin, Ireland, G-AKOF had been diverted to Liverpool by adverse weather conditions, with fog and rain, which prevented a successful landing at its intended destination, Ronaldsway Airport. In his last message, the pilot reported that the aeroplane was running out of fuel and that he would attempt to land on a beach.

Although the Dragon Rapide had a sufficient amount of gasoline to reach Liverpool when first advised to divert there, it continued to circle for nearly half an hour in the vicinity of the island before proceeding towards the English mainland. The subsequent exhaustion of fuel apparently resulted from miscalculation by the pilot.

Date: 22 November 1948
Location: Near Ryzhovo, Russian Soviet Federative Socialist Republic, USSR
Operator: Aeroflot (USSR)
Aircraft type: Lisunov Li-2 (SSSR-L4463)

The airliner, which had been on a domestic service from Zyryanka to Srednekymsk, crashed some 70 miles (110km) south-west of its destination. Killed in the accident were twenty-three persons aboard the Li-2, including the five members of its crew; three passengers survived.

After experiencing communications difficulties, SSSR-L4463 attempted to land at a small airfield, at which time it stalled and plummeted into the ice-covered Kolyma River.

Date: 26 November 1948 (*c.*11:00)
Location: Near Vehari, Punjab, Pakistan
Operator: Pakistan Airways
Aircraft type: Douglas DC-3C (AP-ACE)

Operating on a scheduled domestic service from Karachi to Lahore, the transport plunged to earth in flames and exploded in the vicinity of Bahawalpur. All twenty-one persons aboard

(sixteen passengers and five crew members) were killed.

The crash was attributed to the omission of a sealing washer on the carburettor fuel filter in the aircraft's port power plant, which resulted in the leakage of gasoline on to the ignition system and a subsequent fire that ultimately involved the left main fuel tanks. Considered as a contributing factor in the accident was a generally low standard of maintenance by the carrier due to a lack of tools and spares, inadequate lighting, a 'hurried' work environment and inexperience among those in the lower staff grades.

Date: 15 December 1948 (*c.*06:00)
Location: Near Facatativá, Cundinamarca, Colombia
Operator: Limitada Nacional de Servicio Aéreo (LANSA) (Colombia)
Aircraft type: Douglas DC-3C (C-310)

The airliner crashed and burned on a mountain approximately 25 miles (40km) north-west of Bogotá, from where it had taken off shortly before, on a scheduled domestic flight to Barranquilla, Atlantico. All thirty persons aboard (twenty-seven passengers and a crew of three) lost their lives in the disaster.

It was suspected by the carrier that the crash resulted from the apparently accidental detonation of fireworks that were being carried illegally aboard the DC-3, and which reportedly resulted in the in-flight separation of the aircraft's starboard wing.

Date: 21 December 1948 (*c.*14:00)
Location: Hong Kong
Operator: China National Aviation Corporation
Aircraft type: Douglas DC-4 (XT-104)

The transport crashed on Basalt Island some 10 miles (15km) east of Kai Tak Airport, located in the Kowloon section of Hong Kong and where it was to have landed at the end of a scheduled service from Shanghai, China. All thirty-five persons aboard (twenty-eight passengers and a crew of seven) were killed.

Pilot error was blamed for the accident, which occurred as XT-104 was descending through a cloud layer during the visual approach. However, it was also reported that the flight had been given inaccurate meteorological information, and that the pilot had apparently reversed his course and was attempting to climb out of the area when the DC-4 struck the rising terrain and burst into flames.

Date: 21 December 1948 (c.15:00)
Location: Near Kalamata, Peloponnisos, Greece
Operator: Ceskoslovenske Aerolinie (CSA) (Czechoslovakia)
Aircraft type: Douglas DC-3C (OK-WDN)

Designated as Flight 584, the airliner had been on an international service to Athens from Rome, Italy, when it crashed about 100 miles (150km) south-west of its destination. All twenty-four persons aboard (nineteen passengers and five crew members) were killed. It was believed that OK-WDN had been shot down by Greek insurgents, falling into the Tavgetos Mountains after apparently being struck by ground fire.

Date: 23 December 1948 (c.09:30)
Location: Near Gandesa, Catalunya, Spain
Operator: Líneas Aéreas Espanoles SA (Iberia) (Spain)
Aircraft type: Douglas DC-3C (EC-ABK)

Operating on a scheduled domestic service from Madrid to Barcelona, the airliner crashed and burned on a mountain some 100 miles (150km) west-south-west of its destination. All twenty-seven persons aboard (twenty-four passengers and three crew members) perished. The accident occurred during a rain and low overcast, with the weather conditions undoubtedly a primary or contributing factor, although the cause of the crash was not officially reported.

Date: 23 December 1948 (c.15:15)
Location: Near Moscow, USSR
First aircraft:
Operator: Aeroflot (USSR)
Type: Ilyushin Il-12B (SSSR-L1731)
Second aircraft:
Operator: Aeroflot (USSR)
Type: Douglas TS-62 (SSSR-L861)

Twelve persons lost their lives when the two transports, both of which were engaged in ferrying operations, collided in mid-air and crashed in the vicinity of Vnukuvo Airport, from where the TS-62 had just taken off. Those killed included the four crew members of the recently manufactured Il-12; there were no survivors from either aircraft.

The collision occurred in adverse meteorological conditions, with a visibility of around 3.5 miles (6km) in falling snow.

Date: 28 December 1948
Location: Off Florida, US
Operator: Airborne Transport, Inc. (US)
Aircraft type: Douglas DC-3DST (NC-16002)

A disappearance that has widely been linked to the legend of the Bermuda Triangle probably did not even occur in that region, and was most likely related to some technical cause rather than the supernatural.

Leased to the carrier from a private owner, the DC-3 had taken off from San Juan, Puerto Rico, on a non-scheduled service to Miami, Florida, with thirty-two persons aboard (twenty-nine passengers and a crew of three). Prior to departure, the aircraft's batteries were found to be discharged, with their water levels low, and after take-off, the crew had agreed to remain in the vicinity of San Juan until sufficient power was available to transmit on its radio. Around 10 minutes after its departure, an airways communications station would receive a message that the transport had been unable to contact the San Juan airport control tower, but was continuing on to its destination in accordance with its instrument flight rules (IFR) clearance, i.e. at 8,500ft (2,600m). In its last transmission, heard by a New Orleans communications station at 04:13 local time, NC-16002 was reported at a position of around 50 miles (80km) south of its destination. An extensive search of the sea and adjacent land areas went on for six days, but no trace of the DC-3 or its occupants was ever found.

Despite there being insufficient evidence to determine the reason for the loss of the aircraft, the US Civil Aeronautics Board (CAB) considered it possible that an electrical system failure had rendered its radio and automatic compass inoperative. The meteorological conditions in the area at the time were good, with scattered clouds at 2,500ft (c.750m), a visibility of 12 miles (c.20km) and light, variable winds. However, the CAB observed that there had been a change in wind direction from the north-west to the north-east, with no change in velocity, which could have caused a drift to the left of course by approximately 40 to 50 miles (65–80km), without the knowledge of the crew. (It could not be determined whether a message reporting this change had been received by the pilots.)

It was further noted in the CAB report that at the time of the last transmission, NC-16002 had less than 90 minutes of fuel remaining, and that the pilot may have been in error as to his reported position, possibly mistaking the lights of the Florida Keys for Miami. Had it missed the southern tip of the state, it could have continued out over the Gulf of Mexico until fuel exhaustion, resulting in an unsuccessful ditching in the pre-dawn darkness.

The Board noted that the company's maintenance records were incomplete, and due to the aforementioned technical anomaly, the aircraft did not at the time of departure meet the requirements of its operating certificate. It may also have been approximately 120 pounds (55kg) overweight, and although this should not have been a factor in the disappearance, it was a reflection of the carrier's faulty operating practices.

Date: 31 December 1948 (c.17:50)
Location: Near Orbetello, Tuscany, Italy
Operator: Pan African Air Charter Ltd (South Africa)
Aircraft type: Douglas DC-3C (ZS-BYX)

All thirteen persons aboard (eight passengers and a crew of five) were killed when the airliner crashed and burned on Mount Arbetello, some 75 miles (120km) north-west of Rome, during a non-scheduled service from Athens, Greece, to Nice, France.

The accident occurred in darkness and conditions of poor visibility, the latter of which was considered a contributing factor, as were certain geographical features that could have misled the pilot as to his position. With regard to the latter issue, Orbetello Lagoon, over which ZS-BYX had flown, could have given someone unfamiliar with the area the impression of being the open sea, thus making the pilot believe it was safe to descend to a lower altitude.

Date: 2 January 1949 (c.22:00)
Location: Seattle, Washington, US
Operator: Seattle Air Charter (US)
Aircraft type: Douglas DC-3C (NC-79025)

Its passengers comprised of a group of students returning to school at Yale University, in Connecticut, US, after their Christmas vacation, the aircraft crashed at Boeing Field, at the beginning of the non-scheduled US domestic service. Including all three members of its crew, fourteen of the thirty persons aboard the DC-3 lost their lives in the accident; the survivors suffered various injuries.

Taking off from Runway 13, NC-79025 began to swerve to the left following a ground run of approximately 1,000ft (300m), and after becoming airborne, its port wing dropped, with the tip dragging along the ground for more than 100ft (30m). Power was then retarded, and the aircraft rolled or skidded on its extended undercarriage for some 700ft (200m) before it slammed into a revetment hangar, the impact touching off a fire that ultimately consumed most of its fuselage. It was dark at the time of the crash, and visibility had been reduced to less than 1,500ft (500m) by fog. However, the ceiling was reported as unlimited.

It was determined that the crew had proceeded with the flight despite a layer of clear ice covering the underside of both of the aircraft's wings, and patches of heavy frost on the top surface of the port wing. This coupled with the fact that the DC-3 had been overloaded by about 1,500 pounds (680kg) had reduced the margin of safety and prevented a successful take-off. In its report on the accident, the US Civil Aeronautics Board (CAB) noted that NC-79025 had been parked at the airport without wing covers, and that snow had fallen on it, leaving a film of water that later froze. Attempts to remove the ice, which included the use of an alcohol solution, had been made prior to departure, but were not made on that which had built up on the underside of the wings.

The weather was probably not a significant factor in the crash, as the pilot had reported to the control tower that he could see the green range lights at the opposite end of the runway before being cleared for take-off. Among those killed in the accident was the owner of the airline, whose company's practices did significantly factor in the tragedy.

Date: 16 January 1949
Location: Near Srinagar, Jammu and Kashmir, India
Operator: Dalmia Jain Airways (India)
Aircraft type: Douglas DC-3C (VT-CDZ)

The airliner crashed in the Banihal Pass region of the Himalayas during a scheduled domestic service to Srinagar, and all thirteen persons aboard (nine passengers and a crew of four) were killed.

Date: 17 January 1949
Location: North Atlantic Ocean
Operator: British South American Airways
Aircraft type: Avro Tudor IVB (G-AGRE)

An aviation mystery that began with the loss of the 'Star Tiger' (29 January 1948) would develop into one of the great aviation ironies a little less than a year later when its sister aircraft, the 'Star Ariel', vanished in the same general region and under similar circumstances. The two tragedies would, decades later, help formulate the legend of the Bermuda Triangle. Mystery, it seems, is cheap fodder for those hungering for the supernatural.

Designated as Flight 401 and carrying twenty persons (thirteen passengers and a crew of seven), G-AGRE departed from Bermuda, bound for Kingston, Jamaica; one segment of a service with an ultimate destination of Santiago, Chile. The flight plan stipulated a cruising altitude of 18,000ft (c.5,500m). In the last message from the flight, sent at 08:42 local time, the aircraft was reported passing through the 30-degree parallel, which would have placed it approximately 200 miles (320km) south-west of Bermuda. The first hint of something amiss came more than four hours later, when the carrier's office at Kingston requested information about the Tudor from the Bermuda air-traffic control centre. Finally, more than six hours after the last message from G-AGRE, air/sea rescue services at Bermuda were notified, although before then another company aircraft had been dispatched from Nassau with the intention of searching for the 'Star Ariel'. The search operation, conducted largely by the US Navy and involving seventy to eighty aircraft every day, ended, unsuccessfully, on 23 January.

With the absence of wreckage and an otherwise thorough lack of evidence, the cause of the disappearance G-AGRE would remain unknown. There were no known meteorological complications along the route of the flight, with the weather consisting of clouds below 10,000ft (c.3,000m) and unlimited visibility above them. Nor was there evidence of any technical anomalies in the aircraft at the time of its departure from Bermuda. And although a UK Ministry of Civil Aviation court of inquiry ruled that sabotage could not be entirely eliminated as a cause, there was no indication of such a criminal act.

Similarly with the case of the 'Star Tiger' a year earlier, air/ground radio communications were not being conducted in accordance with company procedures pertaining to transoceanic operations. The requirement in place at the time was that contact would have to be made with a flight every 15 minutes, and that rescue services were to be notified if there had been no contact with an aircraft for more than half an hour. The company operations officer at Kingston believed that G-AGRE had still been under the control of Bermuda, despite the fact that in its last message the flight reported changing to the Kingston frequency.

Subsequent to the disappearance of the 'Star Ariel', an independent committee was established to carefully examine the airworthiness of the Avro Tudor. However, its findings did nothing to help explain the loss of the aircraft. The type was withdrawn from use by British South American Airways after the loss of the second aircraft, and later that same year, the airline itself disappeared, being merged into British Overseas Airways Corporation (BOAC).

Date: 20 January 1949 (*c.*20:00)
Location: Territory of Alaska, US
Operator: Alaska Airlines (US)
Aircraft type: Douglas DC-3C (NC-91006)

Five persons aboard (three passengers and two crew members) were killed when the transport, operating as Flight 8, crashed on the Kenai Peninsula about 25 miles (40km) northeast of Homer, from where it had taken off some 15 minutes earlier, on an internal service to Anchorage. Only the captain, who was seriously injured, survived the accident.

The DC-3 had struck Ptarmigan Head at an approximate elevation of 2,800ft (850m), or some 300ft (100m) below the summit of the mountain, while proceeding under visual flight rules (VFR) procedures off the designated airway and at an insufficient altitude.

It was dark at the time of the accident, and although reported as unlimited, the visibility at the top of the mountain at the time may have been reduced by blowing snow.

Date: 2 February 1949 (*c.*16:00)
Location: Near Trinity, Newfoundland
Operator: Saint Lawrence Airways (Canada)
Aircraft type: Avro Anson V (CF-FEO)

The twin-engine aeroplane crashed some 60 miles (100km) north-north-west of St John's, and shortly after it had taken off from the airport serving Trinity, bound for Rimouski, in New Brunswick, Canada. Six persons lost their lives in the accident, and four others aboard survived.

Date: 8 February 1949 (*c.*20:00)
Location: Near Kastrup, Sjælland, Denmark
Operator: Det Danske Luftfartselskap A/S (DDL) (Danish Air Lines)
Aircraft type: Vickers Viking 1B (OY-DLU)

The twin-engine aircraft crashed in the Oresund sound while attempting to land at Kastrup Airport, serving Copenhagen. All twenty-seven persons aboard (twenty-three passengers and a crew of four) were killed.

Having nearly completed a non-scheduled international service that had originated at Madrid, Spain, OY-DLU was originally instructed to hold for landing due to the adverse meteorological conditions in the area. Subsequently, it was cleared to the south-western leg of the radio range course preparatory to landing on Runway 22. There were indications that the Viking had been flying slightly obliquely to the final approach course before it slammed into the water. Its sunken wreckage was found a month later at an approximate depth of 80ft (25m). The accident occurred in darkness and during a heavy fog.

Examination of the recovered debris and other information obtained during the investigation revealed nothing that could explain the crash.

Date: 10 February 1949 (c.11:00)
Location: Near Huanuco, Peru
Operator: Compañía de Aviación Faucett SA (Peru)
Aircraft type: Douglas DC-3C (OB-PAV-223)

Operating on a scheduled domestic service from Tingo Maria, also in the department of Huanuco, the airliner crashed on a mountain, which was probably obscured by dense fog, while approaching to land at the airport serving the town of Huanuco. All sixteen persons aboard (thirteen passengers and a crew of three) were killed.

Date: 19 February 1949 (c.09:45)
Location: Near Exhall, Warwickshire, England
First aircraft:
Operator: British European Airways Corporation (BEA)
Type: Douglas Dakota C.3 (G-AHCW)
Second aircraft:
Operator: Royal Air Force
Type: Avro Anson (VV 243)

The airliner and the twin-engine military aircraft collided in mid-air about 3.5 miles (5.5km) north of Coventry, and both then crashed. Killed in the accident were all ten persons aboard the C.3 (six passengers and four crew members) and the four occupants of the Anson (all of them British service personnel).

Having taken off earlier from Northolt Airport, serving London, G-AHCW was on a scheduled domestic service to Glasgow, Scotland, while VV 243 was on a navigation training exercise. The collision occurred in good weather conditions at a height of 4,500ft (c.1,400m), and while both aircraft were operating under visual flight rules (VFR) procedures, with the Anson flying in a straight-and-level attitude towards the sun. Impact was 25 to 30 degrees from the head-on position, and slightly to the left side of the Dakota.

There was no evidence of evasive action by either aircraft prior to impact, and the accident apparently resulted from the failure of both crews to maintain an adequate lookout for conflicting air traffic.

Date: 24 February 1949 (c.11:00)
Location: Hong Kong
Operator: Cathay Pacific Airways (Hong Kong)
Aircraft type: Douglas DC-3C (VR-HDG)

All twenty-three persons aboard (nineteen passengers and a crew of four) were killed when the aircraft crashed and burst into flames near the Braemar Reservoir. Having nearly completed a scheduled international service from Manila, the Philippines, VR-HDG had initiated an overshoot manoeuvre after abandoning a landing approach to Kai Tak Airport before it slammed into a hill, the accident occurring in conditions of poor visibility due to fog. The crash was attributed to pilot error.

Date: 10 March 1949 (c.11:15)
Location: Near Coolangatta, Queensland, Australia
Operator: Queensland Airlines (Australia)
Aircraft type: Lockheed 18 Lodestar (VH-BAG)

The twin-engine transport crashed and burned immediately after its departure from the Coolangatta airport, on a scheduled domestic intra-provincial service to Brisbane, located some 40 miles (65km) to the north-west. Including its crew of three, all twenty-one persons aboard the Lodestar lost their lives in the accident; among the passengers were two children riding on their parents' laps.

Taking off towards the east, VH-BAG climbed to a height of between 150 and 300ft (50–100m), whereupon it appeared to stall, then rolled to the left. It had levelled out laterally before it slammed into a swamp almost vertically and in a flat attitude, its undercarriage retracted at the moment of impact.

It was determined that at the time of departure, the Lodestar had been approximately 90 pounds (40 kg) heavier than its calculated weight. More significantly, the aircraft had been loaded so that its centre-of-gravity was considerably beyond the aft limit specified in the certificate of airworthiness. This condition must have resulted in longitudinal instability, which caused a loss of pitch control. Although the elevator trim control mechanism in the cockpit was destroyed in the crash, and no determination could be made as to its setting, the use of insufficient 'nose-down' elevator trim by the crew during the take-off could have contributed to the accident.

One of the recommendations made in the investigative report was for the responsibilities of the safe loading of aircraft be defined in the Air Navigation Orders and disseminated immediately.

Date: 18 March 1949 (*c.*10:00)
Location: Near Paraparaumu, New Zealand
Operator: New Zealand National Airways Corporation
Aircraft type: Lockheed C-60A Lodestar (ZK-AKX)

Operating on a scheduled domestic service from Auckland, the twin-engine transport crashed and burned on the country's North Island some 7.5 miles (12km) east of Paraparaumu Aerodrome, serving Wellington, where it was to have landed. All fifteen persons aboard (thirteen passengers and two pilots) were killed in the accident.

The weather in the vicinity at the time consisted of a low overcast, with 6/8 to 8/8 cloud coverage at around 1,000ft (300m), and winds out of the west at approximately 30 knots. A navigational error by the pilot-in-command was blamed for accident, which occurred as the Lodestar was descending from its cruising altitude in preparation for landing.

Date: 29 April 1949 (*c.*12:20)
Location: Near Mironovo, Russian Soviet Federative Socialist Republic, USSR
Operator: Aeroflot (USSR)
Aircraft type: Lisunov Li-2 (SSSR-L4464)

The twin-engine airliner, on a scheduled domestic service from Yakutsk to Kirensk, crashed approximately 75 miles (120km) east of its destination, and fourteen of the twenty-four persons aboard were killed, including three members of its crew of six.

After SSSR-L4464 had reportedly deviated by some 60 miles (100km) off the proper course, the crew had apparently initiated a descent without either establishing their position or making visual contact with the ground. The Li-2 subsequently slammed into a mountain at an elevation of around 4,300ft (1,300m), the accident presumably occurring in instrument or at least marginal weather conditions.

Date: 4 May 1949 (*c.*17:00)
Location: Near Turin, Piedmont, Italy
Operator: Avio Linee Italiane SA (Italy)
Aircraft type: Fiat G.212 (I-ELCE)

The trimotored airliner crashed while attempting to land at Aeritalia Airport, serving Turin. All thirty-one persons aboard lost their lives in the accident, including a crew of four; among the passengers were eighteen members of the Turin Calcio football (soccer) team.

Having nearly completed a non-scheduled international service that had originated at Lisbon, Portugal, I-ELCE was on its descent when it struck the back wall of a basilica located atop Superga Hill. The accident occurred in poor meteorological conditions, with a ceiling of around 1,300ft (400m) and a visibility in the immediate area of only about 120ft (40m). The weather was considered to have been a contributing factor in the crash, as were inadequate radio-navigational aids on the ground, with the primary cause an error in judgement on the part of the pilot.

Date: 6 May 1949 (*c.*12:10)
Location: Near Portland, Dorset, England
Operator: Bristol Aeroplane Company (UK)
Aircraft type: Bristol 170 Freighter 31 Mark II (G-AIFF)

The twin-engine transport crashed in the English Channel approximately 15 miles (25km) from Portland Bill Lighthouse, on the Portland Bill promontory. All seven of the aircraft's crewmen, who were its only occupants, lost their lives in the accident.

Having taken off about an hour earlier on a test flight, G-AIFF was observed to plunge into the sea, while at the same time several smaller objects were seen fluttering down separately. Along with the bodies of two victims, a small amount of debris was recovered from the water. However, the main wreckage of the aircraft was never found, and the cause of the apparent in-flight structural failure remained unknown.

Date: 7 May 1949
Location: The Philippines
Operator: Philippine Air Lines
Aircraft type: Douglas DC-3C (PI-C-98)

The transport crashed in Lamon Bay off Alabat Island while en route to Manila from Daet, Camarines, one segment of a scheduled domestic service originating at Tacloban, on Leyte. All thirteen persons aboard (ten passengers and three crew members) were killed.

Radio communications with the flight had ended shortly after 16:00 local time. The following week, some wreckage and the body of the pilot were recovered, and examination of the former indicated a sudden explosion in the aircraft's tail assembly. Two ex-convicts later confessed to planting a time bomb aboard the DC-3 in order to kill the husband of a woman who was involved with another man. Their payment for the mass murder was 185 pesos, or less than $100 US. But their payment for the crime was much greater: both would later be sentenced to death.

Date: 6 June 1949 (*c.*19:00)
Location: Near Dhekelia, Attica, Greece
Operator: Technical and Aeronautical Exploitations Company (TAE) (Greece)
Aircraft type: Douglas DC-3C (SX-BAI)

Operating on a scheduled domestic service to Athens from Kavalla, Macedonia, the airliner crashed some 15 miles (25km) north of its destination. All twenty-two persons aboard (eighteen passengers and a crew of four) were killed. The DC-3 reportedly suffered structural failure while flying through an area of thunderstorm activity, then plummeted to earth in flames.

Date: 7 June 1949 (*c.*00:30)
Location: Near San Juan, Puerto Rico
Operator: Strato-Freight, Inc. (US)
Aircraft type: Curtiss-Wright C-46A (NC-92857)

The twin-engine airliner was ditched in the Atlantic Ocean some 600ft (180m) off shore from Punta Salinas and approximately 5 miles (10km) west of Isla Grande Airport, serving San Juan, from where it had taken off shortly before, on a non-scheduled service to Newark, New Jersey, US. Among the eighty-one persons aboard the C-46, who included nineteen infants and children, fifty-three lost their lives in the accident, which occurred in darkness and overcast weather conditions, with a ceiling at San Juan of 2,500ft (*c.*750m), a visibility of more than 10 miles (15km) and no wind reported. The survivors included all but one of its six crew members; most of the victims' bodies were subsequently recovered.

Only a minute after its departure, the aircraft's starboard engine began to backfire and lose power, and the crew then declared an emergency and was given immediate clearance to return to the airport. However, NC-92857 had at that point yet to attain the optimum single-engine climbing speed, and this coupled with the fact that the transport was about 3,700 pounds (1,800kg) overweight, led to the loss of height and the necessity of the crew to carry out the forced water landing. Following the ditching, the C-46 remained afloat for only about six minutes. Before it sank, the crew had deployed two life rafts and distributed several lifejackets, but none of the passengers had received instructions in their use, resulting in considerable confusion and panic.

Recovery of the wreckage revealed that the failed power plant had been in poor condition, with heavy carbon deposits in the carburettor. Moreover, all but six of the thirty-six spark plugs used in the engine were of the type that had not been approved by the manufacturer. Additionally, some of the plugs were chipped or cracked, or showed excessive heat damage. Possibly contributing to the latter condition was the fact that the crew had kept the magneto switch in the 'left' position, which meant that the engine had only been operating on the rear set of plugs.

With regard to the specific errors of the crew that led to the crash, the US Civil Aeronautics Board (CAB) noted that although the aircraft's undercarriage and flaps had been properly retracted, no attempt had been made to feather the starboard propeller, and its cowl flaps were left fully open and its landing lights remained extended. The combined effects of these failures would have increased drag and reduced air speed, thus contributing to the inability of the pilots to maintain altitude.

In view of this accident and previous violations, the carrier's operating certificate was revoked in November 1949, and the following year, the pilot certificate of the designated captain of NC-92857 at the time of the crash was suspended for six months. It was noted in the CAB report that he had been riding in the cabin and did not enter the cockpit until the engine started backfiring.

Date: 23 June 1949 (c.10:55)
Location: Near Bari, Apulia, Italy
Operator: Koninklijke Luchtvaart Maatschappij voor Nederland en Kalonien (KLM) (the Netherlands)
Aircraft type: Lockheed 749 Constellation (PH-TER)

The transport crashed in the harbour area while en route to Rome from Athens, Greece, one segment of a scheduled international service originating at Jakarta, Dutch East Indies

(Indonesia), with an ultimate destination of Amsterdam, the Netherlands. All thirty-three persons aboard (twenty-three passengers and ten crew members) perished.

Following an in-flight break-up, the Constellation fell in flames from an approximate height of 15,000ft (5,000m) and into water that was around 100ft (30m) deep less than 1 mile (1.5km) off shore. The remains of about half of the victims were recovered the same day, but little wreckage was found.

Although the cause could not be determined with certainty, one possibility was that the disaster resulted from the malfunctioning of the aircraft's autopilot, which led to uncontrolled flight deviations and, in turn, structural failure of the tail planes. The type autopilot then in use was subsequently removed from KLM aircraft for modification. Also, the airline advised its pilots to keep their seatbelts fastened when flying on autopilot in the event of a sudden disconnection or malfunction.

Date: 2 July 1949 (c.02:15)
Location: Near Perth, Western Australia
Operator: MacRobertson Miller Aviation Co. Ltd (Australia)
Aircraft type: Douglas DC-3C (VH-MME)

Designated as Flight 772 and on a domestic service to Darwin, Northern Territory, the airliner crashed about a minute after its departure from Guildford Aerodrome, serving Perth, killing all eighteen persons aboard (fourteen passengers and a crew of four).

Following lift-off from Runway 01, VH-MME climbed to a height of between 500 and 600ft (c.150–180m), then suddenly nosed down, and after its port wing had dropped it plunged to earth and burst into flames with its undercarriage and flaps in the retracted position. Occurring in darkness and as a light rain was falling, the accident had apparently resulted from a stall, leading to a loss of control. A tail-heavy condition at the time of take-off, attributed to improper loading of the DC-3, and which resulted in its centre of gravity being beyond the permissible limit, was a possible factor in both causing the stall and preventing the pilots from regaining control.

Though none proved to be conclusive, among the theories considered possible as the initial precipitating factor in the stall were defective flight instruments, improper use of the autopilot, a malfunction in the aircraft's elevator system or a control lock being left on an aileron or elevator. Among the theories discarded were engine failure, a design or structural defect or interference with the flight crew.

The investigation revealed deficiencies in the abilities of the captain in command of the fatal flight, including his incorrect use of the artificial horizon, and in the carrier's record-keeping in the areas of loading and servicing its aircraft. A careful review of the qualifications of a pilot being considered for command status was one of the recommendations made in the accident report.

Date: 12 July 1949 (c.09:20)
Location: Near Bombay, India
Operator: Koninklijke Luchtvaart
Maatschappij voor Nederland en Kalonien
(KLM) (the Netherlands)
Aircraft type: Lockheed 749 Constellation
(PH-TDF)

The aircraft struck a hill and burst into flames approximately 3.5 miles (5.5km) north-north-east of Santa Cruz Airport, serving Bombay, where it was to have landed. All forty-five persons aboard (thirty-four passengers and eleven crew members) were killed.

Having last stopped at Delhi, India, during a non-scheduled service originating at Jakarta, Dutch East Indies (Indonesia), with an ultimate destination of Amsterdam, the Netherlands, PH-TDF arrived in the area about half-an-hour before the accident. The pilot must have elected to hold at 3,000ft (c.1,000m) until the weather improved; however, he did not notify air-traffic control (ATC) authorities of his intentions, which was considered to have been an error of judgement on his part.

After receiving authorisation by the control tower for descent down to 500ft (c.150m), the crew reported making visual contact with the ground, and were then cleared to land on Runway 05, according to the written ATC log. The Constellation then flew over the airport on an easterly heading at an estimated height of 300ft (100m). Shortly thereafter, while proceeding in a north-north-easterly direction, it began a left turn in order to land from the opposite direction, i.e. on Runway 23. Its undercarriage down and flaps partially extended, the aircraft was in a slight climb when it crashed at an elevation of around 600ft (180m), or some 75ft (20m) below the crest. At the time, the hill was shrouded by rain and low clouds. The wind at the airport was blowing from a south-westerly direction at 15 knots.

Blamed for the accident were two other significant errors of judgement on the part of the pilot-in-command, first, his attempt to land at an airport with which he was not acquainted, in meteorological conditions that were below the prescribed minima, and his subsequent action in flying at too low an altitude over the hazardous terrain. Despite inconsistencies pertaining to their exact location, the hills east of the airport had been depicted on the approach chart in possession of the pilot, which should have provided him with a clear warning. Additionally, he had received a briefing regarding the terrain around Bombay and also had access to a photograph of the area posted in the ATC station prior to his departure from Delhi. It was therefore considered unlikely that he had not been aware of the hazard. And although the conditions at Bombay were worse than indicated in the forecast provided him during his last stop, the latest weather information had been given the pilot by approach control upon the arrival of the aircraft over Bombay.

Since Santa Cruz Airport was not normally served by KLM, the airline had no specific minima for operations there. Under the circumstances, a pilot would customarily adopt the minima of other operators that frequently served the airport, which in this case would have been British Overseas Airways Corporation (BOAC) or the US carrier Transcontinental and Western Air (TWA), whose standards were more rigid than the national flag airline, Air-India. The minima at the time was, however, below those of any of these three operators.

The Indian investigative board noted that, when considering their lack of experience at Santa Cruz, the crew should have been provided by ATC personnel with more than the usual assistance. Their failure to advise the pilot to delay the landing or abandon it altogether and divert to another airport was in fact considered by the board as a contributing factor in the accident, as was the designation of a runway to be used for landing that necessitated flying over the obstacles. When PH-TDF did not land, the crew was apparently instructed to ascend to 800ft (*c.*250m), and the board considered the decision by the pilot not to initiate an immediate climb as an additional error in judgement. However, the instructions were tardy and could have been misleading to the pilot, since 800ft would not have been a normal circuit altitude. Furthermore, that height would have provided very little terrain clearance, and the instructions may have led the pilot to believe he should not climb any higher due to the possible presence of another aircraft.

It was noted in the accident report that during the low pass, the pilot should have had a sufficient opportunity to assess the local weather; however, he could not at that time have been able to see the hills to the east because of the poor visibility conditions. As a result of this disaster, obstruction lights were later installed atop the hills surrounding the airport, whose presence alone may have prevented the tragedy.

Date: 12 July 1949 (*c.*07:45)
Location: Near Chatsworth, California, US
Operator: Standard Airlines (US)
Aircraft type: Curtiss-Wright C-46E (N-79978)

The transport had been on a non-scheduled US domestic transcontinental service originating at New York, New York, with an ultimate destination of Long Beach, California, when it crashed and burned in the Santa Susana Mountains some 12 miles (20km) north-west of Lockheed Air Terminal, in Burbank, where it was to have landed. Killed in the accident were thirty-six persons aboard the C-46, including both of its pilots and one cabin attendant; two other stewardesses and ten passengers survived with various injuries.

Cleared for a straight-in instrument approach to Runway 07, the crew of N-79978 was last reported 'approaching Burbank range'. Subsequently, and with its undercarriage extended, the aircraft brushed the sloping terrain while on a magnetic heading of around 240 degrees and then slammed into a mountain at an approximate elevation of 2,000ft (600m), or some 400ft (120m) below its summit. The accident occurred in cloudy weather conditions, with a measured ceiling of 800ft (250m) and a visibility of 2 miles (3km) at the airport.

It was determined by the US Civil Aeronautics Board (CAB) that the C-46 had descended by about 1,000ft (300m) below the prescribed minimum altitude during the procedural turn portion of the approach. The site of the impact was in fact almost exactly on the outbound leg of the manoeuvre from the Chatsworth fan marker, and the direction of the flight almost exactly as that prescribed for that leg of the procedure. There was speculation that the pilot may have believed that the low layer of stratus clouds he descended into would rapidly dissipate. Or he may have descended into a clear area within the clouds and was then unable to maintain visual reference, reverting back to instrument flight at too low an altitude to prevent the crash. Another possibility was that crew fatigue had led to the deviation from the correct letdown procedure. In its report, the CAB noted that the accident may have resulted from a combination of factors. However, a fight between two passengers that had been reported by the crew less than an hour earlier was not believed to have been a factor in the crash.

The carrier suspended operations less than a month after the accident, but this action was related to an ongoing conflict with the CAB because it had conducted scheduled flights, in violation of the Civil Aeronautics Act, rather than to safety matters.

Date: 19 July 1949 (*c.*22:00)
Location: Seattle, Washington, US
Operator: Air Transport Associates, Inc. (US)
Aircraft type: Curtiss-Wright C-46F (N-5075N)

The airliner crashed in a residential area immediately after its departure from Boeing Field. Five persons on the ground and two passengers among the thirty-two occupants of the C-46 lost their lives in the accident; among the survivors, who included the four members of its crew, twenty-one suffered injuries, as did four fire fighters.

During its take-off from Runway 31, on a non-scheduled US domestic service to Chicago, Illinois, one of the aircraft's power plants was heard to sputter and backfire, and an unusual amount of torching or exhaust flame was observed coming from both engines. The transport became airborne after a ground run of around 3,500ft (1,050m), but as the port engine did not seem to be developing full power, the captain retarded the throttles, and the aircraft settled back on to the pavement. Seeing in the darkness the green threshold lights ahead, the pilot at that point did not believe he had sufficient runway remaining to come to a safe stop, and so he increased power, whereupon N-5075N became airborne again, at a velocity of 105mph (*c.*170kmh). Its undercarriage was then retracted, and the C-46 passed over the north end of the runway at an above-ground altitude of approximately 50ft (*c.*15m), which was not of sufficient height to clear the obstacles in its path. The aircraft initially

struck poles and high-tension power lines before it slammed into a single-storey dwelling less than 1 mile (1.5km) from the end of the runway and caught fire.

Examination of the wreckage revealed numerous defects in the port power plant, including a substantial 'crater and cone' condition in the contact points of both magnetos, excessive end movement in one of the rocker arm bearings, and a wet or oily condition in the combustion chambers, diffuser section and intake pipes. Though not as pronounced, a similar condition was also found in the starboard power plant. Of greater significance was the finding that N-5075N had been using in both its engines 91 octane gasoline, instead of the standard 100 octane. The US Civil Aeronautics Board (CAB) concluded that although the aforementioned technical anomalies could have contributed to the power loss, the use of a lower octane fuel probably caused the malfunctioning of the engine. Further to this issue, its use would have necessitated the operation of the engines in excess of their approved operating limitations.

Regardless of the technical factors, the CAB determined that the primary cause of the crash was the indecision on the part of the captain with regard to continuing or discontinuing the flight. His initial error was not in abandoning the take-off at the first indication of a power plant malfunction. The CAB report noted that the decision to abandon it consumed considerable runway that could have been used in accelerating to a higher speed, which may have made possible a successful climb-out from the airport. On the other hand, had the pilot not attempted to take-off after reversing his decision, there would have been ample runway remaining on which to stop safely. His indecision stemmed from his lack of knowledge of the minimum air speed required for a safe single engine take-off. The local weather at the time was good, with a high overcast, a visibility of nearly 10 miles (15km) and only a slight breeze from the north-east, and did not factor in the accident.

Date: 30 July 1949 (*c.*11:30)
Location: Near Chesterfield, New Jersey, US
First aircraft:
Operator: Eastern Air Lines (US)
Type: Douglas DC-3 (NC-19963)
Second aircraft:
Operator: US Navy
Type: Grumman F-6F-5 Hellcat (72887)

The commercial transport and the single-engine fighter collided in mid-air some 10 miles (15km) south-east of Trenton, and both then crashed. Among the sixteen persons killed in the accident was the pilot (and sole occupant) of the F-6F, who was thrown out of his aircraft in the collision; there were no survivors among the occupants of the DC-3 (twelve passengers and a crew of three).

Designated as Flight 557, NC-19963 had at the time of the accident been en route from New York, New York, to Wilmington, Delaware, one segment of a US domestic service originating at Boston, Massachusetts, with an ultimate destination of Memphis, Tennessee, while 72887 was on a pilot proficiency flight, bound for the naval air station at Quonset Point, Rhode Island. Occurring at an approximate altitude of 2,000ft (600m) and in good weather conditions, with a visibility of 10 miles (*c.*15km) and scattered clouds at 12,000ft (*c.*3,700m), the collision sheared off the fighter's port wing and the outer portion of the airliner's port wing. Both aircraft then fell uncontrollably, and although DC-3 burned after its impact with the ground, the F-6F did not. The two aircraft had been at the time operating under visual flight rules (VFR), with the transport proceeding along a prescribed airway in a south-westerly direction.

Based on witness accounts, 72887 had buzzed a light aeroplane before pulling up and striking nearly head-on NC-19963. In its report, the US Civil Aeronautics Board (CAB) attributed the accident to what it described as the 'reckless' conduct of the fighter pilot in performing aerobatic manoeuvres in a civil airway. Subsequently, a programme was launched by US military forces and civilian agencies, including the US Civil Aeronautics Administration (CAA), with the intention of apprehending violators of Civil Air Regulations pertaining to 'buzzing' or other types of reckless flying.

Date: 6 August 1949
Location: Near Pelileo, Tungurahua, Ecuador
Operator: Anglo Saxon Petroleum (Shell Oil)
Aircraft type: Bristol 170 Freighter Mark 21 (HC-SBU)

The Ecuadorean-registered twin-engine aircraft, which was on a non-scheduled domestic earthquake relief flight from Mers Nueva to Ambato, crashed in the Andes about 10 miles (15km) south-east of its destination. All thirty-four persons aboard (thirty-one passengers and a crew of three) were killed in the morning accident.

Date: 13 August 1949 (*c.*13:30)
Location: Near Bogotá, Colombia
Operator: Empresa Sociedad Aeronautica (SAETA) (Colombia)
Aircraft type: Douglas DC-3C (HK-1200)

All thirty-two persons aboard (twenty-nine passengers and a crew of three) were killed when the airliner crashed and burned shortly after taking off from the capital city, on a scheduled domestic service to Ibague, Tolima.

The poor meteorological conditions and rugged terrain in which the accident occurred, with the mountain peaks nearly always obscured by clouds, were believed to have been primary or contributing factors.

Date: 15 August 1949 (*c.*03:40)
Location: North Atlantic Ocean
Operator: Transocean Air Lines (US)
Aircraft type: Douglas DC-4 (N-79998)

The transport was ditched approximately 7 miles (11km) north-west of Lurga Point, Ireland, and south-west of Galway Bay. Among the fifty-eight persons aboard the DC-4, who included nine crew members, seven passengers and the radio operator lost their lives, their deaths attributed to exposure or drowning.

Having taken off the previous day from Rome, Italy, on a non-scheduled international service, N-79998 was to have landed at Shannon Airport, in Ireland. However, and unbeknown to the crew, it flew past Shannon and continued out over the ocean. After obtaining a celestial fix, they finally determined their position as 175 miles (280km) north-west of their intended destination, and turned back on to a heading of 130 degrees. But at that point, the DC-4 had an insufficient amount of gasoline to reach land, and after experiencing fuel exhaustion, it was landed at sea in the early morning darkness, remaining afloat for about 15 minutes before it sank. The survivors were rescued from life rafts by a British trawler after daybreak.

Since flight documents, logs, charts and instruments were lost with the aircraft, available navigational data were incomplete, and the investigation had to depend entirely upon recorded radio transmissions, weather reports and the testimony of the crew. It was concluded by the US Civil Aeronautics Board (CAB) that N-79998 had progressed much faster over the route than had been either computed or realised by any of the flight crew members. Only one of the radio position reports seemed to be consistent with the known facts. The transport was apparently flown to the west of both its intended course and the navigator's planned route.

In its report, the CAB attributed the accident to 'inadequate flight planning and haphazard performance of flight duties' on the part of the crew. Specific to these failings, the Board found that the hourly positions of the aircraft were not determined accurately, radio facilities had not been used to their best advantage and celestial navigation had not been adequately employed. The latter failure was in spite of the fact that darkness had set in during the trip, and considering the good meteorological conditions along the route, with only scattered cumulus clouds, the stars would

have been visible for navigational purposes. Additionally, the wind and weather reports being used by the crew were not applicable to the route actually taken, and no attempt was made to secure the correct information. There must also have been the misidentification of landmarks, including the coast of southern Ireland for Land's End, in England. It was noted in the report that as fuel was consumed, the weight of the aircraft would have been reduced, resulting in an increase in air speed unless power adjustments were made.

During the planning stage of the flight, members of the flight crew did not confer with one another, and they had no agreement with nor accurate knowledge of the route, fuel requirements or the duration of the flight. The primary factor was determined by the CAB to have been the failure of the captain to exercise proper supervision over his crew. This failure had occurred before the flight, with the pilot apparently not examining any of the flight documents prepared by the other crewmen, and while en route.

Date: 19 August 1949 (c.13:00)
Location: Near Stockport, Cheshire, England
Operator: British European Airways Corporation (BEA)
Aircraft type: Douglas DC-3C (G-AHCY)

Operating on a scheduled domestic service from Belfast, Northern Ireland, the airliner crashed about 15 miles (25km) north-east of Ringway Airport, serving Manchester, and where it was to have landed. Including the three members of its crew, twenty-four of the thirty-two persons aboard the DC-3 were killed, while the surviving passengers suffered various injuries.

The accident occurred during a standard beam approach (SBA) procedure, which used a radio transmitter located in close proximity to the airport and two marker beacons to determine the position and proper alignment of the aircraft. Only minutes earlier, and responding to the concern of a pilot who had landed about half an hour before the crash, the

Designed in the 1930s, the Douglas DC-3 would remain in service well after the Second World War with major airlines, including BEA, which lost one in an accident in August 1949. (British Airways)

air-traffic control centre had transmitted to G-AHCY the message, 'Beam reported fading at Stockport, please check.' The final transmission from the flight was acknowledgement of the message, and ended with it reporting, 'Procedure turn'.

At around this time, the DC-3 was observed flying in an approximately south-westerly direction with its undercarriage extended, and soon thereafter it struck Wimberry Moss Hill (Kinders Intake) at an elevation of around 1,400ft (430m). There was no fire after impact. The airport weather shortly beforehand consisted of a low overcast, with 8/8 coverage at 1,200ft (c.350m) and clouds obscuring the top of the hill.

A UK Ministry of Civil Aviation court found no evidence that G-AHCY had been in anything but an airworthy condition at the time of its departure from Belfast, and the one altimeter that was recovered from the wreckage showed no indication of a prior defect or failure. However, a defect in one of the aircraft's SBA receivers, which could have affected the reception of signals, could not be completely discounted.

Although it was unable to determine with certainty the underlying reason for the accident, the court identified as the primary contributing factor the failure of the captain to follow the prescribed SBA procedure, as he had done, according to pilots who had flown with him, in his previous landings at Ringway Airport, which numbered nearly ninety. The normal procedure involved flying to the point where the back beam signal was being received, then proceeding directly over the transmitter and through its 'cone of silence', after which the aircraft would execute a procedural turn back towards the airport while commencing the final letdown.

In the case of G-AHCY, its track had been displaced farther to the east than was normal as it approached the airport from the north-west. The next event in the sequence leading up to the crash was that the aircraft had not turned right on to a heading of 125 degrees, despite the entry in its log stating that it had. This placed the DC-3 considerably to the north-east of the transmitter. Another factor was overconfidence on the part of the pilot with regard to his navigation, which must

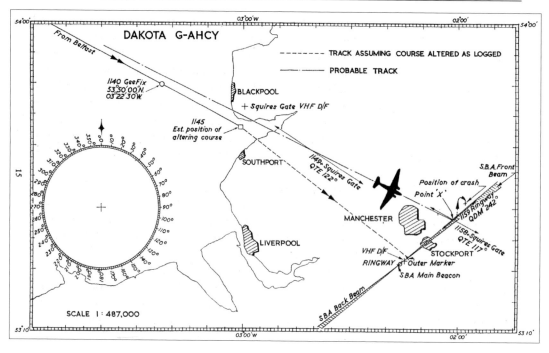

Chart indicates correct course and displaced flight path of G-AHCY, leading to its crash near Manchester's Ringway Airport. (Accidents Investigation Branch)

have led him to assume when he initiated the procedural turn that he was nearer to the airport than was actually the case. Unaware of his position, he then proceeded to descend below a safe altitude. Despite the report from the other pilot, no evidence of a fading signal emanating from the SBA facility was found.

Among the recommendations made in the court's report on the accident was for the introduction of a standard procedure at the airport in which the position of an aircraft must be determined through the use of a reliable ground navigational aid. The radio beacon installed at Ringway had not been brought into service at the time of the crash, but would be soon afterward, increasing the margin of safety at the airport.

Date: 27 August 1949 (*c.*08:00)
Location: Near Leopoldville, Belgian Congo
Operator: Société Anonyme Belge d'Exploitation de la Navigation Aérienne (SABENA) (Belgium)
Aircraft type: Douglas DC-3C (OO-CBK)

Five persons lost their lives when the transport crashed immediately after its departure from N'Dolo Airport, serving the capital city, on a scheduled internal Congolese flight to Elisabethville (Lubumbashi). Those killed included the aircraft's crew of three; all but two of its seventeen passengers survived without serious injury.

The DC-3 had failed to achieve the desired climb rate after becoming airborne, and plummeted to the ground during a low-altitude turn. It was believed that the accident resulted from a loss of power due to both water in its fuel supply and abnormal lead deposits on its spark plugs.

Date: 9 September 1949 (*c.*10:45)
Location: Near St Joachim, Quebec, Canada
Operator: Quebec Airways (Canada)
Aircraft type: Douglas DC-3C (CF-CUA)

Operated by a subsidiary of Canadian Pacific Air Lines and on a scheduled domestic service originating at Montreal, with an ultimate destination of Comeau Bay, the aircraft crashed some 40 miles (65km) north-east of Quebec City, which was an en route stop and from where it had taken off about 20 minutes earlier. All twenty-three persons aboard (nineteen passengers and a crew of four) were killed.

The DC-3 had been observed over the St Lawrence River when an explosion occurred in its front fuselage area. It then turned to the right and started to descend, and subsequently slammed into a hill on the northern side of the river. There was no fire.

Investigation revealed that CF-CUA had been sabotaged in an elaborate scheme carried out by three conspirators. The detonation of the explosive device in the forward baggage compartment must have either killed or incapacitated both pilots, leading to the uncontrolled descent. The mastermind of the plot was Joseph Albert Guay, a jeweller, whose

wife had been a passenger on the flight and who had been insured for C$10,000, with her husband named as beneficiary. A woman, with whom he had been romantically linked, Marguerite Pitre, had apparently placed the bomb aboard the aircraft, and her brother, Genereux Ruest, was also implicated in the crime. Canadian law was harsh at the time, and the trio would hang for the mass murder.

Date: 26 September 1949 (*c*.13:30)
Location: Near Amecameca, Mexico
Operator: Compañía Mexicana de Aviación SA
Aircraft type: Douglas DC-3C (XA-DUH)

The airliner crashed and burned on Popocatepetl Volcano, approximately 50 miles (80km) south-east of Mexico City, which was its destination during a scheduled domestic service that had originated at Tapachula,

The wreckage of the Quebec Airways DC-3 after a crash that was attributed to an act of sabotage. (Canadian National Archives)

Chiapas. All twenty-five persons aboard (twenty-two passengers and a crew of three) were killed.

At the time of the accident, the pilot was apparently proceeding visually through an area of instrument meteorological conditions, consisting of a low overcast. Subsequently, the Mexican government ordered the airline to alter this particular route in order to assure a greater margin of safety.

Date: 28 October 1949 (c.01:50)
Location: Portuguese Azores Islands
Operator: Air France
Aircraft type: Lockheed 749 Constellation (F-BAZN)

Designated as Flight 009 and on a transatlantic service from Paris to New York City, the airliner crashed and burned on São Miguel Island as it was preparing to land at the airport on the nearby island of Santa Maria, which was a scheduled en route stop. All forty-eight persons aboard (thirty-seven passengers and eleven crew members) were killed.

More than an hour before the accident, the crew reported their position as 150 nautical miles (c.275km) from Santa Maria, and shortly afterwards gave its estimated time of arrival (ETA) as 01:45 local time. Subsequently, it transmitted a revised ETA of 10 minutes later than its first estimate, and reported being at 5,000ft (c.1,500m). The flight was then authorised for descent down to 3,000ft (c.1,000m). Only about a minute before the crash, the crew announced that it was proceeding under visual flight rules (VFR) at the altitude to which it had been cleared and that the airport was in sight, and also requested and acknowledged landing instructions. There were no further communications with the Constellation, which had struck Redondo Mountain at around its last reported height, and while flying in a south-south-westerly direction. The accident occurred in darkness but generally good meteorological conditions, with broken clouds and unlimited horizontal visibility.

Due to the lack of data, the investigative commission had difficulty in reconstructing the position of the aircraft during the final moments of the flight. It also had trouble in securing useful information from local witnesses, and its task was rendered more difficult by the inaccessibility of the crash site and the considerable movement and pilfering of the wreckage that had occurred before its members arrived on the scene. However, the commission was able to conclude that the disaster apparently resulted from the following causative factors: 1) Failure of the crew to utilise either one of the two prescribed approach procedures in use at Santa Maria, which led to a descent and subsequent flight below the proper altitude of 5,000ft (c.1,500m) over São Miguel; 2) An erroneous position indication about 15 minutes prior to impact, wherein the crew reported being abeam of the radio beacon designated BB7, even though the accident occurred before F-BAZN had even reached that location; 3) Faulty navigation, so that the crew mistook São Miguel for Santa Maria Island; and 4) The failure of the pilots to identify the airport while flying in VFR conditions, their final message coming before the Constellation crashed while still some 55 miles (90km) away.

Among the recommendations made by the commission were that astronomical navigation be given preference over radio procedures; that night flying should not be attempted under VFR, even in good weather, because of the difficulty in accurately judging distances in darkness; and that the term 'VFR' be deleted from regular terminology at night within respective control areas.

Date: 1 November 1949 (c.11:45)
Location: Near Alexandria, Virginia, US
First aircraft:
Operator: Eastern Air Lines (US)
Type: Douglas DC-4 (N-88727)
Second aircraft:
Operator: Universal Air Marine and Supply Company (US)
Type: Lockheed P-38 Lightning (NX-26927)

The aft portion of the Eastern Air Lines Douglas DC-4 rests on the west bank of the Potomac River after the disaster that claimed the lives of fifty-five persons. (US National Archives)

Despite continued improvement in safety in the years after the Second World War, particularly for scheduled airlines, the US aviation industry was jolted by this collision near the nation's capital, which resulted in the highest death toll in a commercial aviation disaster occurring during a regular passenger service prior to 1950.

Having been purchased by the private firm for subsequent transferral to the Bolivian government, the twin-engine fighter had just taken off from Washington National Airport, located just across the Potomac River from the District of Columbia, on an acceptance flight in preparation for delivery to its new owner. The P-38 was being flown by a Bolivian Air Force officer, Capt. Erick Rios Bridoux. Moments into the flight, he reported power plant trouble and requested permission to land. During this time, the transport had begun its approach to land at the airport at the end of a US domestic service to Washington from Boston, Massachusetts, as Flight 537.

The two aircraft collided approximately half a mile (0.8km) south of the airport, at an altitude of around 300ft (100m), with the fighter striking the top of the airliner and its port propeller slashing into the latter's fuselage, which broke near the trailing edge of the wing. The forward portion of the DC-4 fell into the Potomac with the P-38, in water some 30ft (10m) deep, and the former's aft portion came to rest on the west bank of the river. All fifty-five persons aboard the transport were killed, including its four crew members, while Captain Bridoux survived but was seriously injured. Most of the wreckage was subsequently recovered, as were the bodies of the victims. The local weather at the time was good, with the cloud base above 6,000ft (1,800m) and a visibility of 15 miles (c.25km).

The US Civil Aeronautics Board (CAB) attributed the accident primarily to the actions of the fighter pilot, who had executed the long, straight-in final approach without

Emergency personnel search through the wreckage of the Eastern Air Lines DC-4 involved in the collision near Washington with a P-38 fighter. (US National Archives)

obtaining proper clearance and without exercising necessary vigilance. In its investigative report, the CAB noted that he could have manoeuvred his aircraft in such a manner so to assure that his flight path had been clear of traffic. Although Captain Bridoux later claimed that he had been cleared for an immediate landing, tower controllers recalled only clearing him to enter the traffic pattern, saying that he was second behind the airliner. Failing to acknowledge or to comply with a request to make a 360-degree turn, NX-26927 was then ordered to turn left, again to no avail. During this time, its flaps and undercarriage were extended, and the aircraft descended rapidly while proceeding towards the airport from the south. Meanwhile the DC-4, its gear also extended for landing, had just rolled out of a left turn and on to the final approach course to Runway 03 when instructed to turn left in order to clear the path for the fighter that was overtaking it

from behind. The crew responded immediately by increasing power, levelling off and starting to turn, but the action failed to prevent the collision seconds later.

Additionally, the Board imputed what it described as 'poor judgement' on the part of control tower personnel for their failure to give the airline crew a more timely warning of the potential conflict with the fighter. But when considering the time available, and especially the 'unpredictable' actions of the fighter pilot, it was admitted by the CAB that different or additional actions by tower personnel may not have averted the collision.

The US pilot licence of Captain Bridoux was subsequently revoked. It was also noted in the CAB report that ownership of the P-38 was in 'legal' dispute, with complete records not available for review, and it in fact had no authorisation from the US Civil Aeronautics Administration (CAA) to make the flight that ended in an accident.

Date: 20 November 1949 (*c.*17:00)
Location: Near Oslo, Norway
Operator: Aero Holland
Aircraft type: Douglas DC-3C (PH-TFA)

Its passengers comprising mostly Jewish refugee children, the airliner crashed and burned some 20 miles (30km) from Fornebu Airport, serving Oslo, where it was to have landed. All but one of the thirty-five persons aboard the DC-3 lost their lives in the accident, including the four members of its crew; the twelve-year-old boy who survived escaped serious injury.

Having nearly completed a non-scheduled service from Brussels, Belgium, PH-TFA slammed into a hill during its approach, the crash occurring in darkness and during a rain and a low overcast, with the clouds completely obscuring the higher terrain. The accident was believed to have resulted from the attempt by the pilot to continue into the instrument meteorological conditions under visual flight rules (VFR) procedures.

Date: 26 November 1949 (*c.*12:00)
Location: Near Bucaramanga, Santander, Colombia
Operator: Limitada Nacional de Servicio Aéreo (LANSA) (Colombia)
Aircraft type: Douglas DC-3C (HK-305)

All twelve persons aboard (nine passengers and a crew of three) were killed when the airliner, on a scheduled domestic service to Cucuta, in Norte de Santander, struck a mountain shortly after its departure from the Bucaramanga airport.

Date: 27 November 1949 (*c.*16:00)
Location: Near Dong Khe, Indochina (Vietnam)
Operator: Société Aigle Azur (France)
Aircraft type: Douglas DC-3C (F-OABJ)

The transport crashed some 50 miles (80km) north-east of Hanoi during a non-scheduled supply-dropping operation, killing all ten persons aboard. According to one report, the DC-3 had been shot down.

Date: 29 November 1949 (*c.*05:50)
Location: Dallas, Texas, US
Operator: American Airlines (US)
Aircraft type: Douglas DC-6 (N-90728)

Designated as Flight 157 and on an international service from New York City to Mexico City, the four-engine transport crashed and burned at Love Field, the Dallas municipal airport and the second of two scheduled en route stops. Among the twenty-eight persons killed in the accident were both of the aircraft's cabin attendants; its three flight crewmen and fifteen passengers survived with various injuries.

During the second leg of the trip, having last stopped at Washington, DC, and as N-90728 was in the vicinity of Nashville, Tennessee, its No.1 power plant started backfiring and had to be shut down. The flight continued on to Dallas otherwise normally, but the earlier loss of the engine would become a critical factor in the attempted landing at Dallas.

Following a turn to begin its final approach to Runway 36, an 'S' turn was made to correct its misalignment with the proper heading, during which the aircraft 'skidded' to the left, and this in turn caused it to settle rapidly with an abrupt drop in its air speed. It was then that the relatively small amount of gasoline in the No.4 tank moved centrifugally to the right, leading to the starvation of the right outboard power plant.

Immediately thereafter, and when power to engines 2, 3 and 4 was increased, the latter surged, resulting in an asymmetrical power condition. This in turn caused the transport to yaw to the left and its port wing to drop, and the condition would have been aggravated by the imbalance in the fuel supply, attributed to the fact that considerably more gasoline remained in the No.1 tank.

Retracting the aircraft's undercarriage, the crew was still unable to maintain control, and considering its low altitude, nose-high attitude and with its flaps remaining in the fully extended position, neither a safe landing nor a missed approach procedure were possible. A stall developed just before the DC-6 struck the top of a hangar and then slammed to earth, the second impact breaking off its entire cockpit section. The accident occurred in pre-dawn darkness, but the weather conditions were good, with an unlimited ceiling and a visibility of 15 miles (c.25km).

The underlying cause of the crash was determined to have been the faulty three-engine approach procedure employed by the crew. This error involved the failure of the pilots to assure that the aircraft was in close alignment with the runway well before beginning the final approach, which would have made unnecessary the aforementioned 'S' manoeuvre. Another significant factor was mismanagement of the fuel supply by the crew after the No.1 engine had been shut down. Specifically, their failure to transfer fuel from the No.1 tank resulted in there being approximately 1,400 pounds (640kg) of additional weight on the aircraft's left side, which could have contributed to the final loss of control. Not considered to have been a factor in the accident was the feathering of the No.4 propeller, only seconds before impact, by first officer, who believed that the engine had failed.

Date: 29 November 1949 (c.16:45)
Location: Near Saint Just-Chaleyssin, Lyonnais, France
Operator: Air France
Aircraft type: Douglas DC-4 (F-BELO)

Five persons aboard lost their lives when the airliner crashed and burned about 10 miles (15km) south-south-east of Lyon-Bron Airport, serving Lyon, where it was to have landed during a scheduled international service from Paris to Tunisia. Among the thirty-three survivors, who included two of its five crew members, all but three escaped serious injury.

The accident occurred shortly before sunset and in foggy weather conditions after the pilot had apparently misjudged his height during the final approach.

Date: 1 December 1949 (c.19:00)
Location: Near Rebeirão Claro, Paraná, Brazil
Operator: REAL Transportes Aéreos (Brazil)
Aircraft type: Douglas DC-3C (PP-YPM)

Operating on a scheduled domestic service to Jacarézinho, the aircraft crashed in mountainous terrain approximately 15 miles (25km) east of its destination, and all but two of the twenty-two persons aboard were killed, including the entire crew of four. Both surviving passengers, a woman and her month-old child, suffered serious injuries.

The accident occurred during a rainstorm and was believed to have resulted from crew error, specifically, imprudence and a lack of discipline, combined with the erroneous decision by the carrier's chief of operations for allowing the flight to continue in the adverse weather conditions.

Date: 7 December 1949 (c.17:15)
Location: Near Vallejo, California, US
Operator: California Arrow Airlines (US)
Aircraft type: Douglas DC-3C (NC-60256)

All nine persons aboard (six passengers and a crew of three) were killed when the aircraft crashed and burned some 15 miles (25km) north-north-east of Oakland, from where it had taken off about 20 minutes earlier, on a scheduled US domestic intra-state service to Sacramento.

As part of its instrument flight rules (IFR) clearance, NC-60256 was to have proceeded towards its destination at 4,000ft (c.1,200m). The DC-3 was approximately 3,000ft (1,000m) lower than the specified height when it slammed into a hill 200ft (c.60m) below its crest, while on a near-northerly heading. At the moment of impact, the cleanly configured transport was in a steep climbing attitude, and its engines were developing considerable power, indicators that a last-second evasive manoeuvre had been initiated by the pilot. The accident occurred in twilight and overcast weather conditions, with clouds at lower altitudes obscuring the tops of the hills in the area, presumably including the one struck by the DC-3. No icing and only light turbulence had been reported by other aircraft in the area.

In its investigative report, the US Civil Aeronautics Board (CAB) found no evidence of prior mechanical or structural failure in NC-60256, concluding that the pilot must have intentionally attempted to fly by visual reference to the ground at an altitude much lower than his clearance had authorised.

Date: 9 December 1949
Location: Near Lanzhou, Gansu, China
Operator: Civil Air Transport (China)
Aircraft type: Curtiss-Wright C-46D (XT-820)

The twin-engine airliner crashed while on an apparently non-scheduled service, possibly to Hong Kong, and all thirty-eight persons aboard were killed.

Date: 10 December 1949
Location: Near Haikou, Hainan, China
Operator: Civil Air Transport (China)
Aircraft type: Curtiss-Wright C-46D (XT-814)

The airliner crashed on Hainan Island during an evacuation flight to Haikou from Chengtu, on the Chinese mainland. Killed in the accident were at least seventeen of the forty persons aboard the C-46.

Date: 12 December 1949 (c.22:00)
Location: Near Jungshahi, Sindh, Pakistan
Operator: Pak Air Services (Pakistan)
Aircraft type: Douglas DC-3C (AP-ADI)

Operating on a scheduled domestic service from Lahore to Karachi, the aircraft crashed about 40 miles (65km) north-east of its intended destination. All twenty-six persons aboard (twenty-two passengers and a crew of four) were killed.

Proceeding in darkness under visual flight rules (VFR), the DC-3 had struck a hill at an approximate elevation of 1,300ft (400m) shortly after the pilot reported being at a distance of 30 miles (50km) from the Karachi airport and at a height of 2,500ft (c.750m). However, it was apparent that due to a navigational error on his part, AP-ADI had not been as close to the airport as he believed; additionally, it was below his last reported altitude.

The operations of Pak Air were suspended by the government of Pakistan in the wake of this accident.

Date: 12 December 1949 (20:41)
Location: Near Alexandria, Virginia, US
Operator: Capital Airlines (US)
Aircraft type: Douglas DC-3 (NC-25691)

Designated as Flight 500 and on a US domestic service that had originated at Memphis, Tennessee, and last stopped at Norfolk, Virginia, the transport crashed in the vicinity of Washington National Airport, where it was scheduled to land. Six persons aboard the DC-3 were killed in the accident, including both of its pilots; the cabin attendant and sixteen passengers survived with various injuries.

After it had circled for about an hour, when there was an improvement in the weather, the aircraft received authorisation for descent to 1,500ft (c.500m), and subsequently, clearance for landing on Runway 36. During the instrument landing system (ILS) approach, NC-25691 was observed on radar to drift sharply to the right, then turn to the left and disappear from the scope. Its undercarriage down and flaps fully extended, the aircraft had slammed into the Potomac River around 2,000ft (600m) south-east of the runway threshold, crashing in a steep nose-down, left-turning attitude and coming to rest in water that was about 5ft (1.5m) deep. It was dark at the time, and the local weather consisted of a low overcast, with a ceiling of 400ft (c.120m) and a visibility of slightly less than 1 mile (1.5km) in rain and fog. The wind was blowing from a south-south-westerly direction at approximately 10mph (15kmh).

The condition of the wreckage and testimony of survivors indicated that NC-25691 had stalled prior to impact, and this could have been precipitated by the turn that had been observed on radar. Although there was no evidence of pre-impact technical failure in the aircraft, the US Civil Aeronautics Board (CAB) concluded that the stall could also been caused by a loss of power in the starboard engine. The power loss could have been due to carburettor icing, especially considering that the meteorological conditions were conducive to the formation of ice, or could have occurred when gasoline in the right main fuel tank, to which both engines' valves were positioned, had been exhausted.

Date: 16 December 1949 (c.06:00)
Location: Near Naolinco, Veracruz, Mexico
Operator: Compañía Mexicana de Aviación SA (Mexico)
Aircraft type: Douglas DC-3C (XA-DUK)

The airliner crashed and burned on a mountainside some 50 miles (80km) north-west of the city of Veracruz, which was an en route stop during a scheduled domestic service originating at Mexico City, with an ultimate destination of Mérida, Veracruz. All seventeen persons aboard (thirteen passengers and a crew of four) were killed in the accident. Five more lives were lost when two vehicles carrying rescue workers on their way to the crash site collided later that same day.

Flying in pre-dawn darkness and cloudy weather conditions, XA-DUK was last reported at an altitude of around 10,000ft (3,000m). At the time of the subsequent accident, the DC-3 had been some 20 miles (30km) west of the normal course.

Date: 18 December 1949 (c.20:30)
Location: Aulnay-sous-Bois, Ile-de-France, Paris, France
Operator: Société Anonyme Belge d'Exploitation de la Navigation Aérienne (SABENA) (Belgium)
Aircraft type: Douglas DC-3C (OO-AUQ)

All eight persons aboard (four passengers and a crew of four) were killed when the airliner crashed and burned in a residential section of the town approximately 2.5 miles (4km) from Le Bourget Airport, serving Paris, from where it had taken off shortly before, on a scheduled international service to Brussels, Belgium. Two others on the ground, one of them a fireman, suffered injuries.

Occurring in darkness, the accident was attributed to the failure of the aircraft's starboard wing, although the cause of the break-up could not be determined.

Glossary

Aerodrome – Early name of an airport.

Airway – Designated air route, usually defined by ground-based navigational aids.

Amphibian – Aeroplane, often with boat hull, capable of landing on either water or land.

Automatic Direction Finder (ADF) – Basic navigational instrument, used in conjunction with ground-based radio beacon.

Biplane – Aeroplane with two sets of main wings (top and bottom left and right).

Ceiling – Bottom layer of partial or solid cloud coverage measured from the ground level.

Cone of Silence – Position of an aircraft directly over a navigational station, wherein the signal cannot be received.

Contact flight rules – Early equivalent of visual flight rules.

Dirigible – Powered lighter-than-air craft, usually with internal structure.

Ditching – Controlled emergency landing on water of land-based aeroplane or flying boat.

Empennage – Tail section of an aeroplane, including both the horizontal and vertical stabiliser assemblies.

Engine number – Position of a power plant on an aeroplane, from left to right when looking forward.

Feather – Adjustment of an aircraft's propeller so as to reduce drag following the stoppage of the corresponding engine.

Flight control surface – Hinged airfoil that is part of wings or stabiliser assembly that enables a pilot to steer an aircraft.

Flight analyser – Early flight recording device that can transcribe a small number of flight characteristics, such as altitude and heading.

Flying boat – Aeroplane with boat hull, normally one that can only operate from the water.

Ground-controlled approach (GCA) – Ground-based radar assistance provided to aircraft approaching to land.

Homing beacon – Ground-based facility, normally a non-directional beacon, providing navigational guidance to pilots.

Instrument flight rules – Guidelines used during a flight along an airway or specific route, usually while in contact with an air-traffic control facility.

Instrument landing system (ILS) – Standard landing aid that assists in both vertical and lateral guidance during landing approach.

Non-directional beacon – Basic ground-based radio facility, used in conjunction with airborne ADF.

Notice to Airmen (NOTAM) – An advisory made available to flight crews to provide information concerning a particular condition or hazard.

Overshoot – The abandonment of a landing approach.

Pontoon – Structure, usually attached to wings or undercarriage, capable of enabling or assisting an aircraft to float on water.

Radio range – Early navigational system, consisting of a transmitter broadcasting continuous coded signals to identify a specific airway.

SOS – Distress message that was first used by mariners but also in early aviation to indicate an emergency situation.

Spar – Internal structure that provides support to an airfoil.

Stall – Breakdown in the airflow around an airfoil, leading to a loss of lift.

Strut – Structure that assists in the support of another part of an aircraft, such as a wing.

Undercarriage – Wheels or supporting gear of an aircraft used for taxiing, take-off and landing; fixed in early aeroplanes, later became retractable in most commercial transports.

Visual flight rules – Guidelines used by pilots involving guidance of an aircraft by sight, usually independent of an air-traffic control facility.

INDEX

AIRCRAFT TYPE

Visit our website and discover thousands of other History Press books.
www.thehistorypress.co.uk